T0295804

Everyone's Business

Everyone's Business

What Companies Owe Society

AMIT RON AND
ABRAHAM A. SINGER

The University of Chicago Press
Chicago and London

The University of Chicago Press, Chicago 60637
The University of Chicago Press, Ltd., London
© 2024 by The University of Chicago
Published 2024
Printed in [printer location]

33 32 31 30 29 28 27 26 25 24   1 2 3 4 5

ISBN-13: 978-0-226-81938-9 (cloth)
ISBN-13: 978-0-226-81983-9 (paper)
ISBN-13: 978-0-226-81982-2 (e-book)
DOI: https://doi.org/10.7208/chicago/9780226819822.001.0001

Library of Congress Cataloging-in-Publication Data

Names: Ron, Amit, author. | Singer, Abraham A., author.
Title: Everyone's business : what companies owe society / Amit Ron and
    Abraham A. Singer.
Description: Chicago ; London : The University of Chicago Press, 2024. |
    Includes bibliographical references and index.
Identifiers: LCCN 2024016855 | ISBN 9780226819389 (cloth) | ISBN 9780226819839
    (paperback) | ISBN 9780226819822 (ebook)
Subjects: LCSH: Business ethics. | Social responsibility of business. | Democracy.
Classification: LCC HF5387 .R66 2024 | DDC 174/.4—dc23/eng/20240514
LC record available at https://lccn.loc.gov/2024016855

♾ This paper meets the requirements of ANSI/NISO Z39.48-1992 (Permanence of Paper).

We dedicate this book to our partners and our daughters:
Ronit, Noa, Shira, and Maya
and
Luisa and Minerva

Contents

Introduction

In 2019, the Business Roundtable—a body representing hundreds of large corporations—released its "Statement on the Purpose of the Corporation." In previous years the roundtable affirmed a view of the corporation as existing primarily for the purpose of maximizing shareholder value. In this statement, the body was now claiming that the corporation is a social institution that exists to secure the interests of all the corporation's stakeholders, including workers, customers, suppliers, the local community, and, of course, shareholders as well.

This is emblematic of a general turn in mood around commerce and its relationship to society. Where the Gordon Gekko maxim that "greed is good"[1] once dominated both the corporate discourse and the public perception, today consumers and citizens demand corporations to act in socially responsible ways. The result has been a shift in the c-suite toward things like corporate social responsibility (CSR) statements and environmental social governance (ESG) accounting. Rainbow flags color corporate logos every June, businesses release statements affirming their commitment to racial diversity, and companies scramble to demonstrate alliances with the beleaguered (at the time of writing, "Standing with Ukraine" is a particular cause célèbre). It is generally accepted that corporations are expected—both by the public at large and, increasingly, by the business community—to disavow a pure profit motive in favor of social responsibility.

Much to the dismay and confusion of this newly socially conscience business, progressive circles have been underwhelmed by this change. Many see such attempts as mere window dressing, a cynical attempt to exploit people's beliefs for profits. According to such critics, there has been no substantive change in corporate doctrine—no shift from profit to purpose. It's just that corporations have gotten better at branding themselves. Vellanki (2020) from a sympathetic perspective, for instance, asks, "Is corporate social responsibility a scam?" Larson (2022) answers affirmatively: "Corporations exist to make profits. Whatever other promises they make, from combatting racial segregation to reducing carbon emissions, that mandate always takes precedence." The corporate person is still the same profit-seeking psychopath, to use Bakan's (2003) famous and influential characterization; it has just woke-washed its hair and put on a kinder and gentler demeanor.

Critics are right that the current focus of corporations on their social responsibility leaves much to be desired. However, it's not clear that the problem with CSR is that all or most of such efforts are cynical and profit driven. The sheer volume of discussion about what businesses owe to society—not just in marketing or brand publicity, but also in influential and mainstream outlets like *Forbes* or the *Harvard Business Review*—lends some credence to the idea that people are genuinely concerned with such issues. While there's certainly money to be made by aligning one's business with popular values and causes, it also stands to reason that the popularity of those causes extends into upper management. Indeed, in some cases it is the employees who demand that businesses stand up for certain values. In other cases, it is local communities that push for this. All of which is to say, this interest in corporate social responsibility cannot be explained purely in terms of cynical profit seeking, even though there is no shortage of cynicism in business.

But there's a bigger problem with the criticism that CSR efforts are cynical. It implies that if corporations were *earnest* in these efforts, it would be better. By framing CSR efforts in terms of motivations or incentives, such criticisms assume that a more pure-hearted pursuit of social responsibility is what society needs.

We take many corporate leaders at their word that they are, indeed, trying to stick to their principles and values in the face of pressure to profit so that they may live up to Spider-Man's creed, "With great power comes great responsibility." But this mind-set misses the more fundamental problem, which is *the unequal and unjustified power that business leaders have over others in the first place.* If those at the helm of the modern corporation are pursuing only profit with no attention to anything else, this is bad for society; but if those at the helm of the modern corporation are deciding what is good for society, this may be worse! Who empowered them to make such decisions? Why should we believe them competent to do so? To encourage businesspeople to act according to their principles or beliefs is to elevate such principles and beliefs above those of others, given the social power business leaders often wield. This is at odds with democratic commitments, leaving unaddressed the fact that some are making decisions that influence others in ways that the others have no say in.

What would it look like to make the fact of potentially unjustified corporate power the central problem that efforts at corporate social responsibility or business ethics are meant to address? This book tries to answer this question.[2] Traditionally, business ethicists begin their books or their classes by covering major philosophical theories of ethics—like those of Aristotle or Kant—and then applying them to certain dilemmas of business. Or, alternatively, others start with the idea that businesses are just trying to pursue profit and then ask what the legal and customary rules are for doing this responsibly. In this book, in contrast, we take the problem of corporate power, and the threat that power poses to democracy, as the starting point for thinking about business ethics and corporate social responsibility. What obligations do businesses have given their place within societies aspiring to democratic systems of governance?

Framing the question this way, we are sorry to say, makes things considerably more complicated. In an economy such as ours, business executives have a large amount of discretionary power to interpret consumer demand and market signals when deciding on their value propositions, production techniques, and marketing strategies. Such power of course can and should be checked by legal and regulatory intervention; businesses are not (or should not be) entitled to make *any* decisions about, say, labor conditions, advertising claims, or financial record keeping, and societies constrain such power through things like labor law, consumer protection statutes, and financial regulation agencies. This discretionary power is also checked by competition in markets for capital and consumers. Yet, law and market competition are blunt instruments. Market competition is always imperfect, and legal regulations are never enforced as fully or effectively as we might like. This means that while corporate discretionary power can be checked, in an economy such as ours, for better or worse, it will not be fully eliminated.

Since corporate discretionary power cannot be fully curbed by external means, a professional ethos for business people—a conception of business ethics—is necessary. Some of the burden of curbing corporate power must fall, inevitably, on business leaders themselves! Cultivating norms and socializing people to exercise self-restraint is an indispensable tool for such purposes. This is why a power-centric approach to business ethics makes things so complicated. Corporate power is both the fundamental problem and an inescapable fact of business ethics. The existence of corporate power is why business ethics is necessary, but it is also the very thing that business ethics must try to mitigate.

Business ethicists and advocates of corporate social responsibility are hardly ignorant of corporate power. The most obvious form of power that corporations wield is their economic power in relation to other economic actors. Business ethics as a field has traditionally dealt, primarily, with this aspect of corporate power: things like conflicts of interest, honest advertising, disclosures, and so forth are about a business's disproportionate power in some specific deal or in relation to some specific set of stakeholders or clients. These are obviously crucial and important topics and have rightly been the bread and butter of both academic business ethicists and practitioners concerned with corporate compliance.

But the power corporations wield is much broader than their market power. Businesses also possess social and political power that dramatically affects how we create and establish law, how we relate to one another within society, and the degree to which communities are able to govern themselves. How should *that* power be wielded? Fundamentally, this question cannot be answered by encouraging businesspeople to do good, to have the right beliefs, or even to have the right motivations. All that does is exacerbate the problem, imposing the corporate view of what is good or right on others. Hobby Lobby, for instance, is a company famous for structuring its organization around Christian conservative values, most famously and controversially exemplified in its refusal to provide access to certain forms of contraception and birth control to its employees. Whatever the problems with this, one surely is *not* that Hobby Lobby fails to live up to a deeper conception of what is moral or socially responsible. The criticism generally levied at them, rather, is precisely that *because* they are acting according to this deeper conception of responsibility, Hobby Lobby is imposing its views of morality on its employees and customers in a way that denies the former access to some right or good to which they are entitled.

When we shift our attention from the power of businesses in markets to the power that they have in the broader social and political spheres, we notice that businesses deeply affect the way we live in both obvious and subtle ways. Such influence will not be done away with entirely in an economy such as ours. However, it can, we argue, be wielded more ethically, which entails wielding it with respect for, and in line with, democracy. This is our key thesis: whatever other ethical obligations businesses have with regard to their shareholders, stakeholders, or the economy at large, they also have an overarching responsibility to avoid corrupting and unduly influencing democratic procedures and principles.

While this sounds obvious, perhaps even trivial or tautological, what we aim to show in this book is that the effects of taking this view seriously are far reaching. Democracy is a demanding ideal, entailing a broad set of social commitments and procedures. Democracy "takes place" in formal settings like elections and legislatures, but also in more informal settings like public debates and social movements. Indeed, even day-to-day "ordinary" business decisions can have effects, both profound and subtle, on democracy. Taking democracy seriously, then, has broad implications for how businesses operate. At its most basic, taking democracy seriously requires a radical rethinking of the sorts of propriety and privileges that businesspeople are accustomed to thinking they enjoy over the operations of their business by right. If democracy is a crucial aspect of our society—and we believe it should be— and if businesses can affect the health of our democracy through their operations—as we believe they do—then their business is everyone's business.

Business Activity as a Social Subcontract

Throughout this book we refer to business ethics as being part of what we call a "social subcontract." While there is a more technical idea behind this language (which we develop in more detail in Singer and Ron 2023), the basic idea of the social subcontract evokes a certain understanding of the relationship between business, society, and democracy, where the first is empowered by the second through the third.

One of the most influential concepts in the history of political thought is the idea of the social contract. While there are many variations of it, the generic feature of traditional social contract theories is that they start with an initial condition in which society does not yet exist, a "state of nature." They then explain how, given certain features of this natural state, people establish society, a state, and political institutions, by coming to agreements about their usefulness or necessity. These hypothetical agreements are referred to as "the social contract." More contemporary social contract theories do not begin with a state of nature. Instead, they think of the "social contract" as a set of commitments implicit to our shared social practices and institutions, which we ought to appeal to when justifying our positions and views to one another (D'Agostino, Gaus, and Thrasher 2019). The question then becomes what those shared commitments are, and what sorts of justifications they allow for in political decisions.

So let's imagine that our social and political institutions—the powers of government, the types of rights we retain against the state, the criteria for legitimacy of both, and so on—are governed by a social contract. Where would business activity fit within this? One answer to this question, associated with libertarian politics, is to think of business autonomy as a protected right. According to this view, the social contract is specifically about limiting political or governmental power. Economic activity, therefore, is part of a private sphere that is generally protected from social power by the social contract (Tomasi 2012). In this tradition, private business is none of society's business, in the same way that who we choose to marry, or which religion we subscribe to, is none of society's business. The power that businesses can wield is thus not a moral concern, and it is considered freely and justly wielded when done within the constraints of law.

This is not the perspective we adopt. In our view, following other social contract theorists, the market is very much a social institution, which creates forms of power that must be justified and subject to oversight, social deliberation, contest, and revision. To make sense of the highly complex commercial system that modern businesses inhabit requires more than an appeal to natural rights. If we think of society as governed by a social contract, we must think of how business activity is structured and oriented by a competitive market as part of the terms of this contract.

Thus, we ought to think of the economy as being a "social subcontract." Just as a building contractor might subcontract the pipework on a house to a company specializing in plumbing, the social allocation of resources and talents is subcontracted to businesses in a competitive market economy. The metaphor is meant to capture two salient features of commerce required for rendering ethical judgments about it. First, commerce is a *socially constructed and structured domain of interaction*. Modern commerce isn't something that comes about naturally or spontaneously, even if we can imagine specific instances of such spontaneous organization. Rather, it is an activity that is structured by society through norms, laws, and regulation because of the economic benefits such schemes generate. In short, society enables commerce because commerce has a social function. Second, commercial institutions are marked by their *relative autonomy and the relatively uncoordinated and unplanned activity they enable*. What distinguishes markets from, say, economic planning is that businesses make various decisions based on their own judgments, evidence, and aims. Commerce, then, is a sphere of social activity established by society that operates with a relatively large amount of autonomy and discretion, so that it may contribute to social ends.

Thinking of business activity as part of a social subcontract isn't just a way of characterizing the nature of business. It also points to a large problem. If business activity is subcontracted by society in order to contribute to the fulfillment of social goods and goals, and this arrangement also gives businesses power and influence to pursue their own ends, then this scheme also puts businesses in the position to pursue their own ends in ways that don't befit their intended social purpose. Put differently, with the accumulation of political power, businesses become able to write their own terms for the social subcontract.

Democracy and Business Activity

When understood as a social subcontract, the problem of how businesses relate to democracy becomes more apparent. Democracy is a crucial means for determining what "we," as a society, seek to achieve and how we seek to achieve it. The market, in this view, is one institutional tool used to pursue socially desirable ends. Economic production and allocation are subcontracted to businesses on the theory that businesses can—when properly restrained and incentivized—do this job well. Yet, if in the process businesses acquire political power, how can we assure they are properly restrained and incentivized, and are actually contributing the goods we want them to? If business activity is a social subcontract, then protecting the democratic legitimacy of that subcontract is paramount.

There are, it should be said, many recent books about business and democracy. One of the important contributions from political theorists on the subject has been addressing how businesses ought to be governed. According to this tradition, the hierarchical structure of workplaces—where bosses are empowered to give orders to their subordinate workers—is offensive to democratic commitments. Implicit in this argument (and made explicit by some) is the insight that businesses should not be understood as merely private entities but as matters of public concern; as such, and given the modern emphasis on democratizing the powers that shape public matters, we ought to reform modern business to democratically empower workers in decision making (e.g., Malleson 2014; Anderson 2017; Herzog 2018; Ferreras 2017).

We are sympathetic to this argument (as we have argued elsewhere: Singer 2018; Singer 2019), and we touch on concerns about workplace democracy in chapter 7. However, our concern with business's effect on democracy is different. We are less interested here in the quality of democracy internal to business, and more concerned with how business affects the democratic quality of society at large. Though related, these are separate questions. A worker-managed firm may be admirably democratic in its internal governance and still theoretically engage in illicit bribery of public officials, unethical lobbying of city zoning boards, or wrongful intimidation of social movements, all of which are offensive to democracy more broadly conceived. In this book, we are mainly interested in how businesses can be more or less harmful to or respectful of democracy at this social level (though we do take on questions about the relationship of democracy at these other scales).

What does it mean to respect or harm democracy? While the book tries to offer a more detailed answer to this question, we can note here that an answer requires some understanding of what democracy is and what it requires. There is, alas, nothing like a consensus on this question, with disagreements' going back all the way to ancient Greece. However, we follow recent democratic theorists like Warren (2017), Forestal (2022), Saunders-Hastings (2022), and Bagg (2024), who locate democracy in the general commitment to ensuring the equal empowered inclusion of all in the decision-making processes that affect them. Democracy is a system in which people decide together, as equals, on how to govern themselves. This view is intentionally very broad, and it leaves open different ways of thinking about the particular meanings of deciding things together. This broad democratic commitment can manifest in different ways depending on the context and the nature of the problem being addressed. Therefore, these theories generally avoid identifying democracy narrowly with a particular method of decision making. Nonetheless, at minimum, this view of democracy implies eliminating or dismantling the entrenchment of elites' power over others. Thus, even if we can't agree on what democracy is in some ideal form, we can make note of things that are more and less conducive to democratic empowerment.

Importantly, all these views share an expansive understanding of what democracy touches. A very common way of thinking about democracy is in terms of, say, the election of legislatures, and perhaps popular participation in such political rule making. Yet, in our view, democracy isn't just about empowered inclusion when it comes to electing the legislature, or dismantling entrenched power in city hall: it is about equalizing inclusion and dismantling entrenched powers more generally. Put differently, while democracy requires resisting the autocratic wielding of state power, it is also allergic to individuals and institutions wielding outsized power through their economic influence (Winters 2011). By virtue of the influence that businesses can have in society—whether through explicit political influence or through more implicit and subtle shaping of social dynamics and their effects on the interests of citizens—businesses are often in a position to contribute to the unequal exclusion of citizens. Thus, while democracy need not require perfect economic equality, it does require that the influence of economic actors be checked.

Simply put, though businesses are special sorts of institutions, which are licensed to pursue profits in a competitive manner, this doesn't relieve them of democratic concerns. Those who make decisions in and on behalf of businesses (i.e., managers, executives, and their representatives) don't check their citizenship at the door when they enter their places of work. Nor do they get to treat their positions as another place from which to pursue pet civic projects. Rather, they take on different sorts of civic obligations by virtue of occupying a position where they have the potential to wield influence over affairs that affect others. The stakes and obligations grow in scale with the degree of influence. The bodega store owner doesn't present the same threat to democracy that a popular, long-running restaurant may in local politics; the popular restaurant doesn't pose the same threat to regional democratic empowerment that the local Major League Baseball team may when trying to extract public funding for a new stadium; and the local baseball team doesn't wield the sort of influence in national politics that, say, Meta or Amazon does. Consequently, while the sorts of democratic obligations that concern us tend to attach to the multinational corporation and not the corner store, they do attach, to different degrees and at different levels of democracy, to a wide variety of firms and organizations. At the bare minimum, business actors are obligated to be aware of the sorts of power they possess over various parties.

The Challenges of Thinking about Democracy

It is worth mentioning here that though we take for granted that the health and quality of democracy is important, this is not an uncontroversial claim. Democracy's brand has not exactly been strong everywhere (2016—with Brexit, the Colombian peace referendum, and the election of Donald Trump— is often cited as a particular low point). Its decline has been accompanied by a strand of political theory that argues that democracy is not all it's cracked up to be, with some suggesting that we entertain alternatives to it (Brennan 2016; Caplan 2007; Somin 2016; cf. Farrell, Mercier, and Schwartzberg 2023). Though we don't follow these critics, we do think their arguments deserve attention. Just as markets don't work as seamlessly as portrayed in economics textbooks, democracy often fails to work as well as portrayed in civics textbooks (Brennan and Landemore 2021). Politicians can be corrupt and cynical, citizens tribalistic and uninformed, and civic organizations opportunistic and sanctimonious. While this book argues for businesses to do better by democracy, and provides some conceptual tools for understanding how they may do so, we are not claiming that everyone else is doing right by democracy.

But while there is much scholarly work about how politicians and citizens ought to act—and therefore a language to describe how they fail to do so— there is less of an understanding of how businesses ought to act with respect to democracy. We focus on the latter, without disregarding or downplaying the urgency of the former. This focus on business cuts the other way too: there are other powerful economic actors whose influence is extremely relevant for democracy but that are not businesses. We do not discuss here the ethical obligations of superrich individuals, the foundations they set up, or the political networks they underwrite (see Saunders-Hastings 2022; Malleson 2023). These are all very important but are not part of our focus here.

As we said at the outset, taking power and democracy seriously makes business ethics very complicated. While we try to provide some practical normative guidance in this book—some concrete claims about what businesses' democratic obligations are, and what this could look like in practice—it is not our intention to provide a practical manual for deciding the ethical thing to do in each particular context. In fact, we often end up posing more questions than answers, laying bare moral and political problems that we only partially untangle.

This isn't because we are professors committed to the Socratic method, or at least it's not only because of that. A theoretical analysis of democracy does not produce a road map for how to organize the economy. While it can generate some general principled "dos and don'ts," a commitment to democracy means that the accepted practices of business in relation to democracy should themselves be subject to democratic reflection—together with others, not in a scholarly monologue. Furthermore, such democratic reflection must be informed by the insights of those working in business. While we are deeply concerned with the ways businesses can corrupt and undermine democratic practices, businesspeople often also have practical skills and knowledge that are necessary for thinking through these problems. We are not businesspeople and don't pretend to possess the experience and know-how of our readers. Putting all this together, thinking about business ethics from the perspective of democracy means being comfortable with leaving things for democracy to figure out. It also means that businesses will play a role (though not *the only* role) in such problem solving.

As a consequence, in this book we derive the ethical obligations of businesses from an analysis of their role in a democratic system of social cooperation. This is in contrast to a common way of understanding business ethics as businesses acting according to their moral convictions rather than seeking to maximize profits. We argue that businesspeople are ethically obligated to be mindful of their actions' social and political effects—both when they are pursuing profits and when pursuing what they believe to be morally good. After all, having those who are financially or commercially powerful impose their moral convictions on others is perhaps the antithesis of democracy.

Let us try to put the same point in a more general way. Often when people argue that we need to do something "because of democracy," what they mean is that we should do what they want, hopefully through a democratic process.

But living in a democracy, whatever else it requires, means that sometimes you are going to have to accept decisions with which you disagree, procedures you find annoying, and officials you despise. A commitment to democracy means that, whatever other policy or political preferences you may have (what political theorists call first-order political commitments), you must be committed to certain principles and procedures that govern how we make political decisions (which are called second-order political commitments), even when the results are deeply disappointing. Part of our claim in this book is that a business ethics informed by a democratic concern for the power of business is one such second-order commitment.

Both of the authors of this book are on the left side of the political spectrum. Yet you'll note that our claims in this book are generally not of the sort including "businesses should support a universal basic income" or "corporate executives must pursue reparations for colonial damages," even though we are sympathetic to such projects. That is, we don't counsel businesses to pursue our preferred policy initiatives or political goals. This is in part because we recognize readers and members of the business community don't generally share these views and we want to cast a wide net. But it is also for a very principled reason: we don't want to encourage businesses in the habit of using their economic and social power to determine such social and political decisions, even if these are the kinds that we strongly favor.

Philosophers and theorists, we believe, are not at their best when they are telling others what to do or how to change the world. This is nowhere more true than in business ethics. Rather, the core competency of philosophical analysis is its ability to help us better understand the social world we are already inhabiting and the possible ways it could be changed. The overall goal of the book is to help make sense of both the economic and the political practices we find ourselves enmeshed in, and the various directions such practices pull us. We are therefore primarily interested in illuminating the ways democracy and business practices are tied together, and in offering a vocabulary, an analytic tool kit, for making sense of the moral landscape this intertwining creates. While we may begin sketching out some answers, we don't aspire to do so definitively.

Outline of the Book

This book is divided into 8 chapters. The first two chapters introduce the reader to theories of business ethics, and how our political and democratic approach differs from, and contributes to, these sorts of arguments. The rest of the book considers different implications of this for business, looking at how a commitment to democracy introduces different sorts of considerations from those normally part of business deliberation and decision making.

THE THEORETICAL ARGUMENT

In chapters 1 and 2 we offer the broad theoretical argument that undergirds our book. Saunders-Hastings (2022, 6–7), in her critique of philanthropy, helpfully distinguishes between ethical, political, and democratic theory: ethical theory addresses the motivations and character of individuals, and the duties that well-motivated people should discharge; political theories "address the organization of common life and the distribution of power and authority within it"; and democratic theories are political theories that are "centrally concerned with affirming citizens' status as political equals" and are "attentive to the ways that status can be promoted or subverted" outside and within formal political institutions. This is a useful way to frame our inquiry. In chapter 1 we contend that business ethics must be understood in political terms, and not skeptically as mere opportunistic rhetoric, nor in moralized terms as simply applied ethics. We then review some of the most influential theories of business ethics—shareholder theory, stakeholder theory, integrated social contracts theory, political corporate social responsibility, and the market failures approach—and show that in their strongest terms they are best understood as political in certain respects, in that they highlight particular forms of power that businesses possess over particular groups and articulate ethical responsibilities as a way of addressing these power imbalances. While each of these theories has important uses, none of them fully reckons with the way business can affect the achievement of political equality in more general ways.

For this reason, we argue in chapter 2 that a political approach to business ethics must also be a democratic theory. While businesses may fulfill their obligations to shareholders or stakeholders to greater or lesser degrees, cultivate deliberation among stakeholders more or less fully, or abide by the overarching norms imposed on them in a diligent or an irresponsible manner, all these obligations posed by the theories of business ethics leave open the question of why we enable businesses to possess these sorts of power in the first place. Democracy entails an equalization in political access, a preference for equality in social relations, and a resistance to entrenched elite power. As a consequence, we argue, businesses are obligated to avoid using their power and influence to alter or undermine these democratic qualities of political and social decision making. If and when they do so, they affect society's ability to democratically assess the role of our commercial systems and the sorts of business conduct that are appropriate and acceptable. While the rest of the book tries to explain what this looks like, in this chapter we introduce some basic democratic goals (namely, the collective assessment of social problems and reflexive experimentation with institutional solutions), commitments (striving toward equal inclusion and undermining entrenched powerful interests), and sites where such commitments apply (in formal procedures, informal procedures, and general social relationships).

What it looks like for businesses to respect such goals and commitments at these different sites is not something that can be stated once and for all. Answering this question requires attention to the specific contexts and problems being addressed, as well as the specific ways some businesses relate to those problems and contexts. That said, at the most general level, we contend that businesses have three basic obligations toward democracy, which we call the duty toward democratic outcomes, the duty of reflection, and the duty of publicity. The rest of the book elaborates on these.

UNDERMINING FORMAL DEMOCRATIC PROCEDURES

In chapters 3 and 4 we consider the various ways business can use its privileged position to corrupt the formal institutions and procedures of democracy. This concern will seem obvious to many; checking leadership against the corrupting effect of money and self-interest is a famous and long-standing concern for democracies. What makes this difficult, however, is that in modern capitalist economies, businesses don't just have a lot of financial power at their disposal. They also have knowledge and expertise that democratic decision makers don't have, and which citizens need in order to make informed decisions. Therefore, the participation of business is necessary as a means of making sure democratic actors are properly informed.

In chapter 3 we consider more straightforward examples, instances when companies bribe politicians in illegal and illicit ways. While this sort of behavior is obviously problematic, in this chapter we explain *why* it's problematic. In particular, we argue that such activity undermines the rule of law, which is both more far reaching and more complex than is usually thought. The rule of law, at its most general, is a commitment to the idea that society ought to be governed by general and public rules, not the whims of individuals, and that the use of state power ought to be limited to enforcing these rules. But any system of laws leaves room for some interpretations and therefore can never eliminate the discretionary use of authority. Therefore, a commitment to the principles of the rule of law requires that those who hold authority must share an ethos to respect some basic underlying principles when they exercise discretion. When they interpret and apply the law, they have to do so in a way that is respectful of the equal status of all those subject to that power. Bribing and otherwise manipulating the political and legal process for corporate aims is harmful not just because it breaks the law, but also because it undermines the rule of law: it introduces partiality and inequality into a system that must strive for the impartial and equal treatment of people in the creation, execution, and administration of the law.

Taking this concern seriously helps us see not only why businesses should not engage in bribery or financial manipulation of politics, but also why they should be reticent to break the law even when motivated by values of justice or moral conscience. Even when well intentioned, a disposition to break unfavored laws allows businesses to use their power to render themselves above legal constraints in ways that are offensive to the rule of law. We illustrate this by a discussion of Martin Luther King's idea of "civil disobedience," which is one the most iconic and powerful defenses of breaking unjust laws. What we aim to show is that King's theory is actually deeply sensitive to the values of equality inherent to the rule of law, and that it establishes important criteria for when and how lawbreaking may be morally justified. According to such criteria, we contend, businesses are not generally well situated to engage in such activity. Exceptional circumstances and situations notwithstanding, businesses ought, as a rule, to follow the law and not substitute their judgment for such law following, even when ethically motivated, because of the broader political consequences at stake.

More broadly, this chapter is important in establishing a main tenet of our approach to business ethics. While in some cases businesses have to exercise judgment about substantive issues—for example, which investment plan is in the public interest, or what hiring scheme is most likely to reach marginalized groups—businesses should generally try to avoid making such decisions unilaterally, when possible; and when it's not possible, they ought to make such decisions in a way that doesn't undermine the possibility of democratic revision and contest, in all their messy imperfection. In the different chapters of the book, we describe what this judgment may entail in different spheres of business activity.

In chapter 4 we examine the practice of business lobbying, asking when lobbying the government may corrupt democracy. To do so, we pick up on the idea of corruption and try to explore it in more detail. Reviewing different theories of what democracy entails, we consider different definitions of what it means to corrupt democracy. We contend that corruption occurs when parties engage in *duplicitous exclusion*—when parties are excluded from decision making who otherwise have a democratic right to participate, sometimes without their even knowing they are being excluded. Corporate influence of government officials in ways that are unknown and unaccountable to the more general public are obvious examples. This can happen through financial contributions, patronage appointments, discreet consultations, and the failure to disclose conflicts of interest.

But such corruption can happen much more subtly, without improper quid pro quo arrangements, or briefcases full of money. Business interests can lobby the government in ways that unfairly tilt the direction of collective decision making, bending government toward business interests, and not merely offering their expertise or technical knowledge. The potential for these problems is inherent to the existence of the social subcontract and therefore can only ever be imperfectly guarded against through law and institutions. In addition to legal regulation, democracy requires the ethical self-regulation of business actors as protection against these sorts of abuses. It is not enough that businesses refrain from using their power and money to influence policy and legal decisions in the overt and illegal ways discussed in chapter 3. They must also recognize that even at their best, their views are biased toward their own interests, and that the channels of government influence are likewise biased in their favor. As a result, even legal and less overtly corrupt forms of lobbying and influence can still negatively affect democracy by the de facto exclusion or silencing of others.

UNDERMINING INFORMAL
DEMOCRATIC PROCEDURES

In chapters 5 and 6 we consider more informal, but no less vital, aspects of democracy, and the ways that businesses can affect them. Inherent to the idea of democracy is the aspiration to a certain sort of equality among parties in their relationship to government and to each other. Yet very few democracies ever achieve this sort of equality, and none in a permanent fashion. This is in part due to the pathologies of democratic politics alluded to above: legislators and political operatives are often just as opportunistic and cynical as their private-sector counterparts, and they pursue the accrual of personal power and influence in ways that are just as offensive to democratic equality if not more so. As a consequence, the formal procedures of democracy will often be imperfect, reflecting and often reproducing existing inequalities instead of institutionalizing equality.

Reconciling the fact of inequality with the democratic aspirations of equality leads us to recognize the crucial informal procedures of a democratic society. Democracy requires that people who are otherwise disempowered or marginalized by existing inequalities be able to register and signal their discontent in other ways. However, because of their place in society, businesses will often be bound up in such informal practices, either through their ability to influence these practices or as the target of their criticism.

In chapter 5 we consider how marketing campaigns can affect public opinion. To do so, we consider the significance of rational deliberation for democracy. Democracy doesn't require just formal procedures like voting for representative legislatures, but also the protected space for citizens to deliberate with one another. The goal of such deliberation is not just to increase the quality of political outcomes. The goal of reasoned debate is also to enable people to be convinced of the law's legitimacy (if not, ultimately, its wisdom) by seeing it as the outcome of an open exchange of reasons. Taking deliberation seriously as a component of democratic politics has implications for businesses, which are most obvious in their choices regarding marketing strategies. While marketing is a necessary function for business in modern economies, marketers often aim to play on people's cognitive biases in a variety of ways, which affect how citizens reason and deliberate about matters of public interest. This means there are high democratic stakes involved in how businesses opt to market their products. No less important, businesses can also affect the quality of democratic deliberation with their marketing budgets in deciding *where* they market their products. The chapter discusses the obligations that marketers may have with regard to both the types of campaigns they launch and the venues where they decide to spend their budgets.

In chapter 6, we explore instances where businesses are the target of protests, strikes, and other less deliberative forms of political activity. The social subcontract that licenses market activity grants businesses the privilege of pursuing profit in a competitive market through otherwise frowned-upon self-interested stratagems. Businesses are not charitable organizations. They thus have the propensity to respond to challengers in a similar instrumental and competitive fashion. However, what a commitment to democracy reveals to us is that such challenges are often not simply matters of dollars and cents; boycotts, protests, or strikes are not only, and in many cases not primarily, commercial or economic actions. The ability to form social movements that engage in contestatory and antagonistic behavior is crucial in democracies, which depend on such popular movements to attend to and address matters of political inequality. Put simply, such activities are political and are often the means through which democratic horizons are expanded. Social opposition to business is not the same thing as market competition and should not be responded to in similar fashion. We therefore explore the types of things that business leaders ought to keep in mind when responding to the democratic challenges and contestations of their stakeholders.

UNDERMINING DEMOCRATIC RELATIONS

Influencing government, affecting deliberation, and responding to political activity are fairly straightforward ways that business can negatively influence democratic procedures. However, business can unduly affect democracy even when not intending to engage in politics at all. This is because democracy isn't just a set of procedures and institutions, whether formal or informal. A commitment to a democratic society also makes demands with regard to how people relate to one another. Thus even in seemingly nonpolitical "ordinary business," democratic legitimacy and integrity can hang in the balance.

In chapter 7 we consider hiring and personnel decisions. Formal and informal democratic procedures are animated by a more basic underlying commitment to certain forms of background equality as a moral baseline. Put simply, the "default" position in democratic societies is that people are equal and should be treated as such. However, societies are also marked by all sorts of inequalities and hierarchies that are reinforced in a variety of ways. One crucial form of hierarchy is the employer-employee relationship. While businesses have the prerogative and need to hire the best people for the job, they must also be cognizant of how hiring, management, and organizational decisions can reinforce and amplify extant social inequalities. We discuss how inequalities in social standing, resources, and opportunity can be amplified by how businesses hire people and how they organize their operations.

Finally, in chapter 8 we consider place-specific decisions regarding investment and site locations. Just as businesses can legally, but problematically, affect the decisions and actions of elected officials, businesses can also affect the opinions and beliefs of communities. One of the ways that businesses do this is when communities come to rely on businesses' investments. As we describe it, a business's ability to "exit" a community also provides it a strong "voice" in the community's decision making and deliberation, a voice that potentially stunts the democratic quality of such procedures. Businesses are able to exert pressure, both explicitly and unwittingly, by the possibility of their decisions to relocate, invest, divest, or otherwise use their privileged position as leverage for influencing communities to alter their beliefs and decisions in business's favor. What obligations do businesses have to the communities they operate in? In answering this question we expand the discussion to explore "transnational" approaches to democracy, which contend that democratic commitments are not limited to boundaries of territorial units. Such a view helps us understand the complicated democratic obligations that businesses have toward community.

A NOTE ON AUDIENCE

As will become apparent, both authors are trained as political theorists, each with little to no business acumen or experience. There is, regrettably, a large gap between the way ethicists and political theorists talk about business and democracy, and how practitioners and citizens do. Political theorists have spent decades, centuries even, arguing about what democracy entails and requires. While these debates have not produced anything like an overwhelming agreement or consensus, they have produced a number of ideas and concepts that are helpful in understanding and analyzing democracy. Unfortunately, very little of this has seeped into the public discourse. While this is not a textbook, we have tried to write this book presuming little familiarity among our readers with the academic and theoretical debates on democracy or ethics. Without getting too bogged down in the scholarly details, we do try to provide enough of an overview to give the reader a running start in understanding the concerns and positions that have dominated philosophical discussion of business ethics and democracy. Our goal is to help those going into business to recognize both how their actions intersect with democratic processes writ large and the ethical issues that arise in these intersections.

While primarily aiming to introduce the uninitiated to concepts from democratic theory, we also try to make some scholarly contributions of interest to academics in the fields of business ethics and political theory. In the first two chapters we offer a novel political reconstruction of the field of business ethics; those familiar with the field will note that interpreting the big theories of business ethics in terms of "power," as we do, is not the standard way of doing it. We think this approach contributes to the further integration of business ethics with political theory. We also offer an account of why democracy should feature prominently in our theoretical understanding of business ethics, an argument we have made elsewhere (Singer and Ron 2020; Singer and Ron 2023), which has become increasingly interesting to business ethicists (e.g., Norman and Ancell 2018; Silver 2021; Bennett 2023), and which we expand on here. While political theorists will be familiar with the theories and ideas introduced in each chapter (and may, perhaps, find our discussion of them somewhat simplistic), we think showing how each applies to ethical decision making within business is also novel, and contributes to our moral understanding of democratic ethics and democratizing economics.

Business Ethics Is Political

What is business ethics, and how should we think about it? Should businesses be held to the same moral standards to which we hold other people? Or does the business environment imply a different set of ethical standards for behavior? In this chapter, we argue for thinking about business ethics in political terms. In light of that, we then offer a bird's-eye view of the field. This will help make clear what is innovative in the approach to questions about business's obligations toward democracy that we offer in the next chapter.

Probably the most influential and infamous answer to these questions is Milton Friedman's (1970) article in the *New York Times* entitled "The Social Responsibility of Business Is to Increase Its Profits." Polemical in nature, this article famously claimed that business managers and executives ought to resist the temptation to act in terms of social responsibility (which Friedman describes as "unadulterated socialism"), and to instead focus solely on what the corporation was empowered to do: maximize profit through all legal means. In making this argument, Friedman caused quite a bit of mischief, in at least two ways.

Most obviously, the "profit-maximization" or "shareholder-primacy" theory (as Friedman's argument is sometimes called) aided and abetted an incredible amount of bad behavior in the corporate world. Companies, armed with the belief that their only ethical duty was to their shareholders (who held the same beliefs), readily complied. As we will see, the argument is actually a bit more subtle than is usually thought. Still, the popularity of the sentiment led to a widespread belief among the managerial set that ethics and social responsibility was for others to think about, while they just focused on the bottom line. The result was an explosion in strategies that maximize shareholder value in the short term, resulting in harm to consumers, the environment, and workers.

But Friedman's argument also led to a different sort of problem in the kind of pushback it generated. Many critics looked at this corporate track record and came to the conclusion that the problem was "greed" or "selfishness." This is understandable. Friedman, after all, argued that focusing on things other than profit was an irresponsible dereliction of duty. The lack of consideration for sustainability, fair hiring practices, or consumer welfare was simply the fallout from a generation of corporate leaders taught to focus monomaniacally on profits instead of people. The fix, then, was to get businesspeople to be less greedy and adopt more social mindsets, where they balance profits with purpose, values, and the public good. Put differently, it led many to believe the problem was fundamentally an ethical problem, about the motivations and character of those in the business community. If the problem Friedman created was a generation of businesspeople without a conscience, the obvious solution was to encourage them to be conscientious, to be better, more caring people. This has meant a growing emphasis on "social" enterprise, purpose-driven companies, CSR statements, and the like. We think this is also wrongheaded.

This book is about how a commitment to democracy affects, or ought to affect, business practice. Underlying this is a different framework that we propose for what business ethics is—what it means for businesses to have ethical responsibilities, and what these ethical responsibilities entail. In our view, business ethics is fundamentally political, about the way power is distributed and wielded, and not about the quality of one's ethical disposition. In this chapter, we introduce the general contours of political approaches to business ethics, and in the next chapter we zoom in on the specific ethical problem of businesses' relationship to democratic politics. In the approach we propose, businesses have moral responsibilities far beyond a mere focus on lawful profit seeking. However, this doesn't mean we should be trying to get businesspeople to be better people or to more sincerely commit to moral values. Both such views underplay the social, economic, and political influence that businesses wield in society, and the problems that come from either a cynical or a benevolent use of such influence. Business ethics is both real and necessary for our society, but it cannot be understood in apolitical, moralistic terms. Business ethics must be understood in terms of power, and the particular power that we focus on in this book is the power to affect democratic decision making.

Executives, managers, and others in the business community sit at the helm of organizations and enterprises with vast amounts of influence. Consequently, the decisions that occupants of these roles make affect others in disproportionate ways: where they build a factory affects local communities' economic opportunities, their environmental quality, and their ability to make decisions for themselves; personnel decisions affect businesses' employees; strategic decisions affect competitors and the economy generally; attempts to lobby government or influence voters affects the broader political and social systems we all share. This power, furthermore, can only ever be tamed and constrained but never permanently eliminated. In a market economy, businesses inherently have discretion to make decisions based on their interpretation of consumer demand, the nature of the market, and so forth. Given all this, how should businesspeople wield such influence? In what ways should this power affect the way they think about their ethical responsibilities?

In this chapter we introduce this approach to business ethics. We begin by contrasting our political, power-centered approach to the approaches of those who are skeptical of business ethics as well as those who think of it in more moralized terms. We then review some of the major academic theories of business ethics. Though they are not generally thought of this way, they each can be understood as a theory of business power: what forms of power are illicit and what ethical constraints or orientations can make it more legitimate. We review these not just as an introduction to the field, but also because we think each helpfully draws our attention to some facet or aspect of corporate power and morality. Each also misses an important part of the story. We conclude with a brief explanation of why a concern with democracy is needed for business ethics, which we more fully defend in the next chapter.

Why "Doing Good" Is Not Enough

Some have characterized this social turn among businesses as an orientation toward "social justice" (e.g., Zheng 2020; Serviodo and Curry 2020). From the perspective of political theorists and philosophers like ourselves, there is a certain amount of irony to all this. The past fifty years of political theory (and arguably the past few centuries) have been marked by the dominance of a view in which the justice of our social institutions is seen as a separate question from the types of lives we, as individuals, ought to lead. When talking about "justice" or other ideas about what we owe to and are owed by society, we should not confuse them with questions regarding the sorts of people we ought to be. To put this in philosophers' lingo, we should keep "the right" (that is, what sorts of actions we are obliged or permitted to do) separate from "the good" (that is, what sorts of goals and outcomes we should value and try to achieve).

This is very counterintuitive to most who hear it for the first time: if we want the world to be a better place, shouldn't we first and foremost try to make better people? Yet, there are a number of reasons why political philosophers have generally come to emphasize the nature of institutions, laws, and social structures, over individuals' characters, virtues, and values. We review three here.

PLURALISM

One of the major reasons philosophers have deemphasized characters and values is actually fairly straightforward: we, as a society, simply can't agree on what these values are. A society in which there is relative freedom of conscience will be characterized by what the philosopher John Rawls (2005, 36) referred to as "the fact of reasonable pluralism." We will never fully agree on how we ought to live or what constitutes a good life; no amount of argument, presentation of facts, or education will undo this intractable disagreement. Trying to structure our social institutions and basic political commitments according to such values often leads to oppression and cruelty. The religious wars and conflicts that dominated the late Middle Ages in Europe, and which in some sense continue at a global scale today, are only the most obvious example of the harm that comes from one group trying to impose their vision of what is good on others. Colonialism is another example: often justifying themselves by benevolent-seeming ideas of education, "civilization," and modernization, Western nations have spent centuries inflicting an incredible amount of harm on others in the name of their particular conception of ethics and virtue.

Consequently, many philosophers have argued we should try to articulate our social duties and commitments in terms that are as neutral as possible with regards to conceptions of the good life. This is the core idea of a doctrine known as "liberal neutrality"—social and political institutions ought to govern only the interpersonal conduct of people, and only according to principles that respect individuals' abilities to decide how they want to lead their individual lives. Schouten (2019, 11) captures this well: "the neutrality constraint on liberal legitimacy holds that the legitimacy of particular intervention depends on that intervention being justifiable by way of reasons . . . that do not depend for their acceptance on any particular views about what is good for an individual or for society, apart from the views implied by values we share as free and equal citizens." To be sure, the ideal of neutrality is quite complex and in most likelihood not perfectly realizable. Nonetheless, taking pluralism seriously means that one must recognize the diversity of beliefs about what is valuable, and be anxious about attempts to impose uniformity by achieving one's ethical beliefs through the coercive power of shared social institutions.

INSTITUTIONAL DISTINCTIVENESS

Another problem with emphasizing the values and beliefs of people when talking about social justice is that it misses just how complex our societies are. In small-scale societies, and within our more local communities, everyone adopting the same or similar value orientations may be important as it allows everyone to cooperate with less reliance on formal authority. Yet in the modern world, the scope of cooperation and the division of labor is vast, encompassing the entire globe. This sort of integration is too big to be accomplished through common beliefs and values.

Instead, modern society is marked by what sociologists call "functional differentiation," spheres of interaction distinguished from other parts of society both by the function they serve in the larger system, and by how behavior is structured therein (Habermas 1975, 18–19; Habermas 1996, 342). One of the main ways social cooperation is facilitated in large societies is through markets, which encourage economic growth and efficiency by orienting people to interact in more competitive ways than they otherwise do. States are also forms of functional differentiation, where we interact with fellow citizens through norms of competitive politics (on the electoral and legislative side), bureaucracy (on the executive side), or legal procedures (on the judicial side) in order to achieve various forms of justice and order.

The key point here is that functional differentiation does away with the need for coming to thick or deep agreements on the meaning or value of things. Indeed, these institutions were developed in part because such agreements are so hard to reach. Institutions such as the market allow people to interact and reach practical agreements without agreeing on the underlying values. People don't need to agree on what, say, some electric guitar or plumbing service is truly worth, or what sorts of lives people should lead in a metaphysical or ethical sense; they just need to agree on a price (e.g., Gaus 2016, 202; Muldoon 2016, 69). The same goes for other institutions, which allow people to cooperate according to standards—for legal legitimacy, a fair bureaucratic procedure, and so on—implicit to the institutions, instead of deeper ideas about the good life (Heath 2020).

If the concern from pluralism is that a focus on values will lead to oppression, the concern from functional differentiation is that a focus on values is superfluous, and often inappropriate. While everyday morality may demand that we try to cooperate and come to agreements, such cooperation in competitive institutions like markets or sports is generally frowned on (leading to "collusion" in markets or "point fixing" in sports). If we see two adults fighting in the middle of the street, we would advise them to stop and find

a peaceful way to solve the dispute. We would not do so were the fight happening in a mixed martial arts octagon. Similarly, while we might be put off
by someone passionately defending a criminal or dispassionately following
a stodgy procedure, we will find these qualities more admirable in a defense
lawyer or an administrator, respectively. The institutional setting matters for
how we assess people's behavior. Given the specific sorts of institutions we
have developed in our societies, the roles that such institutes create, and the
specific and counterintuitive forms of behavior they require, we cannot simply apply general standards of morality to such behavior. Instead we require
norms and principles that are specific to these institutions to guide behavior
and decision making.

INEQUALITY

Related to the facts of pluralism and functional differentiation is a concern
with the fact of inequality. Inequality can refer to a number of different
things—a difference in social status, in material wealth, in decision-making
power, and so forth (e.g., Anderson 1999). We talk more about inequality in
later chapters, and the problems that arise from certain forms of inequality.
But it is important to note that affirming the importance of equality does not
imply that all forms of inequality are necessarily unjustified (Dworkin 1981).
Rather, it is common to think that certain forms of inequality *are* justified:
that experts ought to have disproportionate influence on decisions that bear
on their expertise; that people in public administration can make decisions
that apply to everyone; that parents can make certain decisions for their children; and so on. That is, while certain forms of inequality ought to be resisted,
it is not obvious that society can or should get rid of *all* forms of inequality.

Taking this fact of inequality seriously changes the moral nature of what
one is doing, in a way that an emphasis on values and character does not
easily track. While we might all agree that stealing is bad, does our analysis
change when the property is a rich man's good, and those stealing it are poor
and hungry? While we may think people are generally entitled to freedom
of speech, and therefore morally permitted to say whatever they want, we
generally also think that someone with public standing and social power has
a responsibility to use that freedom in particular ways. When we consider
that some have the disproportionate ability to affect others' lives, behaviors,
and thoughts, the ethical quality of their motives may be undermined by the
malignant political effect some courses of action can have. Consequently,
taking inequality seriously requires emphasizing a political concern about

the legitimate use of power over an ethical concern about one's values or character.

"POLITICAL, NOT METAPHYSICAL"

All of which is to say: there are a number of reasons why instilling good values, or getting people to "do good," is not the right way to think about justice. Doing so is to be insensitive to the power differentials, institutionalized division of labor, and pluralism that characterize modern society. These points combine. Because society will be marked by pluralism, institutions are developed that enable citizens to cooperate without thick agreements or shared deep values. These create particular sorts of positions and offices that come with power and influence over others. By virtue of occupying such social positions, citizens take on obligations and duties—not because such duties are part of their individual value systems, but because being relatively empowered or advantaged entails particular sorts of responsibilities.

To give a stark example: Mayor Richard Daley, the infamous machine boss of Chicago, was once criticized for nepotistically granting a city contract to his son's business. This sort of abuse of power is generally considered a grave infraction. Yet, instead of challenging the claim that he had used his office to benefit his family, Daley doubled down by answering, "It's a father's duty to help his sons" (recounted in Clark 2011, 226). What's funny about this response is that it is a totally plausible reading of a father's moral obligations, as well as an attractive way of thinking about how one ought to live more generally: fathers *do* have a duty to help their children. The problem is that moral obligations of parents are distinct from those of public office. By occupying the office of the mayor, Daley took on different responsibilities that flow not from ethical questions about how one ought to live (since Chicagoans don't and won't agree on such things), but from the fact that he was occupying an institutional role, and a position of power.

Pursuing justice, then, isn't primarily about what a good person ought to do generally. For these reasons, political theorists have tended to focus on the institutions, social structures, rules, and relationships that enable cooperation in modern societies, and ask what justice demands of them. This is why Rawls (2005, 10), famously, claimed that justice was "political, not metaphysical": it's about the nature of our institutions and social practices, not about some ethereal notion of goodness. If we are thinking of ethical duties as related to broader commitments of justice, then we ought to frame the question this way: what does some particular position—be it father, citizen, mayor, customer, or CEO—demand of the person occupying it, given the function of that position in our larger social systems?

The Need for Business Ethics

What does business ethics look like if we think of it in these terms? Given the above emphasis on institutions and political institutions, it may seem like we don't leave much room for something like "business ethics" to matter much at all. Why think about the moral obligations of business actors at all, instead of just focusing on establishing the right rules and institutions?

Political philosophers have not been terribly interested in business ethics, resulting in what von Kriegstein (2019, 103) has referred to as "business ethics denial," which rejects the possibility, desirability, or usefulness of business ethics. While we are sympathetic to the motivations of such skeptics, we think such concerns are misplaced and overstated. Still, it is worth taking the time to go over the reasons why many look askance at business ethics. Not only do they capture widely held views and important insights, but they also help us clarify what, precisely, business ethics can do and what it can't. To that end, we review some arguments against business ethics: different skeptical views that deny its possibility or necessity; structural views that see regulatory measures as rendering it pointless; and moralistic views that accept the importance of ethical obligations in commerce, but see "business ethics" as just a subset of moral theory more generally.

WHY NOT SKEPTICISM

A common perception is that given the nature of commerce, business ethics is, as the joke goes, an oxymoron. Because markets encourage people to act according to their own self-interest, people assume that businesses are inherently antisocial or amoral, making "business ethics" nothing more than cynical window dressing. Obviously, this is an understandable view: there is quite a bit of cynicism and self-interest in commerce. Furthermore, as we noted above, markets are functionally differentiated institutions, facilitating competition by encouraging buyers and sellers to pursue their narrow interests. To be successful in market activities, players have to be self-interested. Markets are set up in this way. This is why, despite the fact that their usage grows with the years, people are so confused about terms like "business ethics" or "corporate social responsibility," leading them to dismiss the whole idea. How could businesses ever be ethical when they are so focused on their own gain?

We agree that businesses often use the language of ethics and responsibility cynically. However, while there is good reason to be skeptical of any particular business in its purported aims to be ethical or socially responsible, this does not necessarily mean that the very idea of business ethics should be dismissed altogether. While the competitive and self-interested nature of commerce has to be taken seriously when thinking about the possibility and plausibility of business ethics, this does not mean ethics is pointless or unnecessary in the business world. To help see this, we will examine two versions of business ethics skepticism: one that maintains that business ethics is impossible, and another that sees it as unnecessary.[1]

"Business Ethics Is Impossible"

For skeptics who think business ethics is impossible, the main concern is that "business" and "ethics" are inherently incompatible. Business is about pursuing profit, and ethics is about being selfless, altruistic, or otherwise thinking about things other than your own gain. Business ethics is thus an oxymoron.

While understandable, this view misconstrues both "business" and "ethics." To be sure, businesses do pursue profit, and they do so in ways that make them distinct from other entities. But "pursuing profit" is a broad category. There are often multiple paths toward profit, and different ways of interpreting what "profit seeking" demands. The most intuitive is the question of whether someone should be pursuing profit in the long term or the short term, as well as the different strategies for pursuing either. The point isn't that long-term profit, which may entail spending more on workers or the community for a more sustainable business, is more ethical. The point is, rather, that businesspeople, even within a competitive and profit-oriented marketplace, have discretion (Bennett 2023) and exercise their judgment constantly. Business decisions cannot be thought of as fully determined by self-interest and profit simply by virtue of the fact that neither *can* fully determine one's choices. Business entails making judgments, and such judgments invite the question of how to assess their quality. Even if businesses were concerned only about self-interest, their discretionary power invites the question of whether they are doing so in more or less ethical ways.

More importantly, "ethics" is not just about being selfless or altruistic. While it is true that morality may demand we not do certain things that we might otherwise want to do, this does not exhaust what morality entails. Generally speaking, we might think that morality is about prohibitions, permissions, and obligations: what we can't do, what we may do, and what we must do. Perhaps morality says, generally, we are prohibited from harming others even if it benefits us, or that we are obligated to help others who are in need.

But morality also says we are permitted to, say, choose to eat salad instead of soup, or pursue some career over another. That is, ethics or morality isn't just about when our self-interest must be tempered, but also about what is an appropriate or legitimate expression of that interest. To say "business is about profit and not about morality" assumes that the pursuit of profit is permitted in the first place. Morally speaking, this permission may be right or wrong, but either way it is not an amoral claim.

Despite the joke, then, business ethics is not an oxymoron. Business judgment always invites ethical evaluation, and the claim that business need only concern itself with self-interest is itself an ethical claim. This does not mean to suggest that businesses never use the language of "ethics" or "responsibility" to cover up their self-interested intentions; they often do. But note that even criticizing businesses for being so cynical and opportunistic is itself a moral criticism of their intentions and their actions. Such a criticism presumes a moral standard that businesses are not abiding by.

"Business Ethics Is Unnecessary"

So business ethics is itself not an oxymoron; indeed, the claim that it is, upon further reflection, seems confused or incoherent. A different skeptical claim is that the long-term social benefits of allowing businesses to operate in a market freed from moral constraint are likely to be greater than the harm from the immoral actions. The fact that business ethics is possible doesn't mean we should pursue it, according to this view. The only morality that matters for business is the moral permission to engage in business!

According to such a view, the only way one can profit in a market economy is by producing a good or service that someone wants in a way that is better or cheaper than a competitor's way of doing it. Thus, markets transform self-interest into prosocial behavior because the only way to pursue one's interest is by doing or making something for someone else. This is what Adam Smith meant by the "invisible hand" of the market ([1776] 1981, 456 [WN IV.ii.9]): without intending it, everybody contributes to the public good, even though they are only each individually thinking of their own gain. To add moral constraints into the mix—to demand that people engage in commerce with their self-interest encumbered in any way—is to attach cuffs to the marketplace's invisible hand, stunting its ability to produce the social goods we want it to (Gauthier 1982).

In one sense, as we will see later, this is a plausible theory of business ethics, one advocated by, among others, Milton Friedman. However it doesn't work as a dismissal of business ethics. The problem with this way of thinking is that markets are often imperfect and don't function in this idealized way. Indeed, if we think about it, real-world markets are actually full of obligations and duties. While market competition can be a quite powerful way to organize economic activity, it also has large downsides. In particular, by cultivating and encouraging this sort of self-interest, markets make long-term trusting relationships difficult or costly, requiring much in contractual and legal enforcement (Williamson 1985). One way modern economies deal with this is by creating group-oriented institutions—firms, often taking the legal form of corporations—that enable concerted collective action in a way self-interested market behavior cannot. Firms aim to facilitate economic activity by creating environments where people can function as teams, to directly and explicitly work together. Now, to be sure, within this environment, people also jockey for their own gain: bosses try to get workers to work as hard for as little as possible; ambitious employees try to position themselves favorably in comparison to their colleagues; less ambitious employees try to get by doing as little as possible without getting in trouble. But fundamentally, they do this within an environment where they are purposefully and explicitly working together. Whereas in markets people pursue their self-interest and cooperate incidentally as if guided by Smith's invisible hand, in firms people are compelled and encouraged to work together explicitly by the very "visible hand" of management, organization, and bureaucracy (Chandler 1977).

This "working together" creates certain types of expectations, and room to deliberate, regarding what sorts of obligations a business has—both toward its stakeholders, and toward society at large. Businesses inherently introduce a space for ethics by virtue of their social and deliberative nature. Even if you think businesses should just pursue profit for shareholders, one is essentially saying that those who work for the company (from the CEO on down) have an obligation to do so (Heath 2009). Whatever one thinks of that position, it is a decidedly moral obligation that stems from the fact that businesses are collaborative enterprises where norms are at play (Singer 2018).

For this reason, if we take the "business" part seriously, we have to take "ethics" seriously as well. The problem isn't that business is inherently amoral or antisocial. The problem is the pervasive view that takes the antisocial character of businesses to be justified and thus lets businesspeople off the hook. The skeptical view of business ethics, then, is less a denial of business ethics, and more a specific view of business ethics—one that says businesses ought to just pursue profit. Ultimately, as we review below, such a view would have to be justified on moral grounds.

WHY NOT (ONLY) REGULATION?

Others concede this point—that there is morality at stake in commerce, which needs to be taken seriously—but deny that "business ethics" is a useful way of approaching the question. The thought here is that behavior within the market is so determined by the structure and forces of competition and strategic thinking that thinking in terms of "ethics" is toothless. If we want behavior to change within the market, we must change the market through regulation and legal intervention.

This is in keeping with the general thrust of political philosophy described above. If we think of justice as pertaining first and foremost to the basic structure of society, and not to individuals' character, then focusing on the ethical decision making of market actors is a distraction. Instead of trying to think about what ethical action looks like within capitalism, political theorists generally argue, we need to go about reforming (or, for some, altogether abolishing) capitalism. Instead of saying, "It is ethical to do x but not y," we ought to be trying to prohibit y and incentivizing x, using the various institutional and policy levers we have at our disposal (for an example of this sort of argument, see Rönnegard and Smith 2024).

Indeed, focusing too much on the ethics or responsibilities of businesses might keep us from this crucial process of structurally containing and regulating them. The term "corporate social responsibility" has its origin in the early twentieth century when captains of industry used it to argue that regulatory law and the welfare state were unnecessary: we could just rely on the benevolence and responsibility of corporate powers themselves to address the problems (Marens 2012). Indeed, one "business case" for social responsibility is that embracing such responsibilities can ward off regulators (Carroll and Shabana 2010, 89), enabling firms to constrain themselves on their own terms instead of those imposed on them by the state. Thus, many reject focusing on business ethics because it is a red herring, directing energies and trust toward corporate leaders, when we ought to be focused on structurally constraining them.

Such critics are surely right that business ethics is no substitute for legal and regulatory intervention in the economy. They are also right that both historically and currently, programs of CSR and business ethics are used precisely to forestall such regulation, or to make it seem redundant and unnecessary. It is worth noting here that that business ethics, as a field, is not only about managerial decision making, but also about how such decisions and behavior are institutionally constrained. The necessity and significance of regulation does not do away with the need for business ethics but points to the importance of such macro-level considerations.

However, even if we understood business ethics only in terms of managerial decision making, the necessity of regulation would not render it superfluous. Part of the problem with this sort of argument is that it drastically overstates both how effective and how encompassing regulation and law can be. While it is very important that we establish the right regulatory or industrial relations regime, we must recognize that such mechanisms will always be imperfect in their ability to compel behavior or enforce standards.

To see this, one only needs to consider the importance of ethical standards for state bureaucrats. What's telling here is that state bureaucrats are, in theory, thoroughly rule and law bound: their jobs and tasks are the result of political processes and movements resulting in precisely the sorts of laws and interventions we need to regulate an economy. And yet, what analysts have noted (e.g., Zacka 2017; Heath 2020; Monaghan 2023) is that even the most low-level of state bureaucrats have discretionary power that no feasible amount of law or oversight will fully eliminate. Consequently, developing an ethics of public administration is a crucial project in order for a society to have capacious and just state institutions.

If this is true for state bureaucrats, it is obviously true for market actors (Wangrow, Schepker, and Barker 2015), whose behavior is not prescribed by policy or regulation! Surely, limiting and regulating markets is a very live and appealing political option; the study of business ethics does not rule out adding more, even radical, regulations or interventions. But even a fully planned economy where markets and private property were abolished wouldn't do away with the need for professional ethics: it would require books about the ethics of economic planners, and how *they* should use *their* discretionary power. While economic behavior must be constrained and structured by law, it will never be fully dictated by it. A space for discretion and prerogative is unavoidable. Given this, we must ask what the acceptable ethical bounds are within which that discretion can be exercised.

Furthermore, this view—that a proper regulatory environment can regulate away unwanted business practices—falls into the framework that we try to avoid in this book: one in which there are clearly good and clearly bad actors. Those who put their faith in regulating businesses cast legislators and regulators on the side of the good, as standing for the interest of the public, reining in the diabolic firms. But, in real life, this is too simplistic. Laws and regulations do not always stand for the interests of the people or for their will. They are often biased toward those who have the power to tilt the political process toward their interests. Indeed, it is often particular businesses or industries that have such powers. As we explore in the coming chapters, a concern for democracy does not mean that we assume legislative and regulative processes always act in the interest of the public.

Though legislators are not always good guys, this of course does not mean that such regulatory levers are unimportant. Business ethics is no substitute for regulatory intervention. Our point is that it cannot be simply relegated to the sidelines with the hope that regulatory constraints will make it redundant. Instead, it is better to think of business ethics as a complement to regulation. We must ask what we want out of our commercial systems, what sorts of regulation and structural change are required to bring it about, and what sorts of ethical standards economic agents must abide by in light of both. And we must do so while recognizing that in the real world neither of them will provide us with perfect answers.

WHAT WOULD KANT DO?

Having argued that the behavior of economic agents is always subject to ethical evaluation, we ended the previous section reaffirming the need to set ethical expectations for economic agents. The question is what these expectations should be. One intuitive way to answer this question is to turn to the classics in moral theory. There are philosophical and religious traditions that grapple with the question of what the right thing to do is. Those who find one such tradition helpful for thinking about the general question of moral obligation would want to consult these same sources for thinking about the obligation of economic agents. When faced with some tough business dilemma, they might ask questions such as "what would Kant counsel," "what does Aristotle suggest," or "how should a good Christian act in such a situation?" This is sometimes referred to as a "universal approach" to business ethics because it approaches the dilemmas of business ethics as subtopics within a more general domain of moral theory (Buckley 2013, 696). Such an approach starts by formulating general criteria of right or good independent of the business context and then uses those to address the more narrow question of "is this particular set of business practices good or bad?"

One point in favor of universal approaches is that they give us a good degree of critical distance when assessing business practice. If we are drawing on more general overarching principles—be it the golden rule of the Old Testament, Kant's categorical imperative, or something else—there is little chance we will end up simply rationalizing business practices as we find them. We will be holding businesses to the higher authority of a more general moral standard. If you look through the pages of business ethics journals you will find a number of very interesting arguments that apply utilitarianism (e.g., Gustafson 2013; Jones and Felps 2013), virtue ethics (e.g., Koehn 1995; Sison 2010; Alzola 2012), or Kantian philosophy (e.g., Scharding 2015; Bowie 2017) to business ethics, which speaks to the power of such an approach.

However, the universal approach to business ethics is also limited. Many professions and roles are defined not just in terms of the service they offer others, but also in terms of the special sorts of obligations and permissions they have. Most people are not morally permitted to drill holes in people's skulls, nor do they have obligations to, say, save the lives of enemy combatants. But doctors are both so permitted and so obligated. We generally don't think people have a moral obligation to provide defenses for the indefensible, but because of the way our legal system is set up, lawyers do. The point is that often professional roles are marked by morally counterintuitive permissions and obligations.

This is also true for business. With regards to business ethics, what makes commercial activity counterintuitive is that it is characterized by precisely the sorts of behavior we tend to discourage in everyday life: it is competitive and not cooperative, and it encourages participants to be oriented toward private interests and not other-regarding. Saying one should simply "do the right thing" in the business context as one would do elsewhere is essentially to say one shouldn't participate in the market at all (similar to asking a tennis player not to serve hard because it is not friendly toward the other player). Of course, the special roles of business can be accounted for and justified by reference to various moral theories (e.g., Bowie and Duska 1990 with regards to Kantianism; Alzola 2018 with regards to virtue ethics). Yet, in many ways this sort of role for morality often works on a logic of its own, functioning much like an emergent property in science; while it is possible for physicists to explain human behavior, economics is going to be more useful for explaining, say, the effects of technological innovation on wages. Similarly, though we may be able to explain why some set of roles is justified by reference to first moral principles, the morality that attaches to the roles is often not reducible to those primitive justifications (for a more thorough discussion, see Sankaran 2021).

But perhaps even more importantly, we must recall the facts of pluralism and power discussed above. Society will always be marked by ideological disagreement over basic metaphysical questions, and people who occupy spaces in society like a corporate executive are also in positions of disproportionate power and influence. If we consider pluralism—the existence of multiple systems of beliefs—to be an important moral fact about society, frameworks for adjudicating how businesspeople ought to exert their power over others should not be drawn from belief systems or values that others will see as alien and disagreeable.

Simply put, universalist approaches have difficulty taking into account the functional differentiation of the market, and the power that market actors often have.

Theories of Business Ethics as Theories of Corporate Power

Taking stock, the skeptics are wrong: business ethics is a necessary component of a just and fair society, which no amount of legislation and regulation will do away with. And yet the most intuitive ways we have for thinking about ethical conduct—in terms of instilling the right virtues or applying the correct universal moral theory—seem inadequate. Business ethics must provide standards, criteria, or frameworks for thinking about moral decision making, but in a way that takes seriously the context within which business decisions are being made, and the sorts of roles businesspeople occupy when making such decisions. That is to say, it must offer a moral framework that is sensitive to the power that businesspeople wield. This is what we mean when we say that business ethics must be understood in political terms.

Though they don't put it this way exactly, business ethicists have, over the past fifty years, developed theories that try to articulate obligations informed by the power held by business managers. In a certain sense, then, these can be understood as political theories, articulating the responsibilities that come with occupying the social office of the manager or CEO. We go over five influential theories: profit-maximization theory, stakeholder theory, integrated social contracts theory, political corporate social responsibility, and the market failures approach. We do this for three reasons. First, for those unfamiliar with the field, this is meant to provide a quick overview of the different theories of business ethics. This is a stylized account, emphasizing the political aspects of these approaches. Consequently, and second, we aim to show that each of these theories had helped clarify different aspects of business ethics and the political nature of business. However, and third, we also want to show each misses crucial aspects of the political power that businesses wield, and their moral consequences. This sets up our focus on democracy and business ethics, which we begin to lay out in the next chapter.

PROFIT-MAXIMIZATION THEORY

One way to begin, which has been one of the dominant approaches to business ethics over the past half century, is by grounding one's theory of business ethics in the particular aspects of the corporate form, and the specific sorts of relationships and power dynamics that corporations tend to structure and establish.

Milton Friedman's "profit-maximization" theory of business ethics, mentioned above, is an example of this approach. Friedman claims that the defining feature of the modern corporation is the *principal-agent relationship* between corporate executives and shareholders. A principal-agent relationship is any situation where some party (the principal) needs another (the agent) to act on the principal's behalf or in pursuit of the principal's interests. There are many examples of this in modern society: lawyers are agents for their clients, legislative representatives are agents for their constituencies, wealth managers are agents for the people whose money they handle, and so forth.

What is significant about principal-agent relationships is they entail a problem of power—agents can manipulate their position to pursue their own self-interest as opposed to that of their principals. Again, the examples are legion: lawyers can overbill or can pursue plea deals instead of exoneration in order to cut down on their time and avoid potentially embarrassing losses; politicians can use their positions to curry favor with other powerful interests instead of pursuing the interests of their constituents. For Friedman, the fundamental problem of business ethics is that corporate managers are agents charged to pursue the interests of their principals, the shareholders (Marcoux 2003). In this view, entrepreneurs ask people to invest their own money in their business because they believe in its potential to generate profit. Using this money for any other purpose is, according to Friedman, to exploit one's power as an agent.

Thus, contrary to popular conception, Friedman's argument is not that businesspeople ought to disregard ethics in favor of profits and self-interest. It is not an amoral view. Rather the argument is that to pursue profits within the limits of the law *is* the ethical obligation and the best way to check against executives abusing their power (see Heath 2009). Corporate executives are always able to use their position to pursue their own interests because of the separation of ownership and control in corporations. This might mean using corporate wealth for their own enrichment through, say, self-dealing, wasteful spending on perks, or shirking. But it can also mean using corporate resources to pursue their own moral worldview, sacrificing shareholder wealth in order to advance some social or moral concern the executives personally have. For Friedman, business executives ought to deprioritize the ends they, as individuals, would pursue—even laudable ends, like charitable giving—in favor of the ends their principals want.

The profit-maximization view sees pursuit of profit as the best way to check the *agential power* that business managers possess for two reasons.

First, because Friedman assumes that this is in fact what shareholders want, to do otherwise is to violate the principal-agent agreement. This is of course not always or obviously true. Increasingly, shareholders want companies to mitigate their pursuit of profit in favor of some other social concern or issue. That said, whatever else shareholders want, they also tend to want a return of some kind. Thus, as principals of the corporation, and absent explicit directions otherwise, corporate agents ought to assume that shareholders want them to pursue profit or increases in share value (or both). The second reason for emphasizing profit, however, is more interesting. The problem with telling businesses to pursue something in addition to profit—to pursue profit and sustainability or profit and justice—is that it leaves it in managers' hands to decide which they prioritize when, and how to do so. Claiming profit seeking to be the core ethical responsibility of businesses has the benefit of imposing a more rigid constraint on the power of the executive.

Thus the profit-maximization theory of business ethics is not quite as cynical or skeptical as it sounds. What's more, it actually has built into it a degree of concern for the power that corporate managers wield. And yet, there are still large problems with this view. To ground a special obligation to pursue profit in an obligation to work uniquely in the interests of the shareholders assumes shareholders had the initial moral privilege to focus so myopically on profit in the first place. Why should we think shareholders are entitled to an agent who focuses on profit on their behalf, at the exclusion of other moral concerns? Profit-maximization theorists simply assume that competitive profit seeking is morally permissible in the first place and that corporations ought to be seen as the vehicle of shareholder value. But from the perspective of the ethicist, that is precisely what needs to be answered! Why should we see corporate power as being properly wielded solely in service of shareholders?

STAKEHOLDER THEORY

Stakeholder theorists attempt to fix this overemphasis on profit seeking by noting that corporations are composed of many stakeholders, and not merely shareholders. To see corporate social responsibility solely in terms of profits is to wrongly empower executives to pursue shareholders' interests at the expense of other constituencies. Or perhaps to put it differently: thinking in terms of profit focuses on only one aspect of corporate power—the power to pursue interests of shareholders. But it ignores, and perhaps exacerbates, the power corporations have over others. The twentieth century saw developments in labor law, consumer protection, antitrust law, and public safety policy precisely out of a recognition of the danger of this sort of power if left unchecked (R. E. Freeman 1994). To focus only on the agential power that executives have over shareholders is to ignore the other axes of corporate power that have so preoccupied capitalist societies.

As a consequence, while businesses have to care about their shareholders' interests, stakeholder theorists argue they also have an obligation of care toward their various constituencies who interact with and contribute to the value created by the corporation (Philips et al. 2019, 3; see also R. E. Freeman 2017, 454, 458–59). Arguably, the stakeholder paradigm has displaced profit-maximization theory as the dominant way of thinking about businesses among the corporate elite. As we mentioned in the introduction, the Business Roundtable in 2019 issued a new statement on the purpose of the corporation, superseding previous documents they had released claiming that corporations exist for the purposes of their shareholders. Instead, they now assert other purposes as well.

> While each of our individual companies serves its own corporate purpose, we share a fundamental commitment to all of our stakeholders. We commit to:
>
> - Delivering value to our customers. We will further the tradition of American companies leading the way in meeting or exceeding customer expectations.
> - Investing in our employees. This starts with compensating them fairly and providing important benefits. It also includes supporting them through training and education that help develop new skills for a rapidly changing world. We foster diversity and inclusion, dignity and respect.
> - Dealing fairly and ethically with our suppliers. We are dedicated to serving as good partners to the other companies, large and small, that help us meet our missions.
> - Supporting the communities in which we work. We respect the people in our communities and protect the environment by embracing sustainable practices across our businesses.
> - Generating long-term value for shareholders, who provide the capital that allows companies to invest, grow and innovate. We are committed to transparency and effective engagement with shareholders.
> - Each of our stakeholders is essential. We commit to deliver value to all of them, for the future success of our companies, our communities and our country.

Despite their differences, it is worth noting how similar profit-maximization theory and stakeholder theory are. Both of them are grounded in the corporation's principal-agent relationship and the potentially worrisome power that bestows on the corporate manager. Both of them therefore largely think of ethics in fiduciary terms, which means that the corporate agent has an ethical

obligation to use discretionary power in the interests of the principals it is empowered to serve. These theories differ in terms of who they think the corporate principal is. In contrast to Friedman, stakeholder theorists contend that the
corporation has numerous principals—workers, customers, suppliers, shareholders, and the surrounding community—all of whom are owed ethical concern by corporate executives.

Stakeholder theorists are right to emphasize the broader social power
that corporations exert over these disparate constituents. If Friedman was
right that executives must subordinate their own interests to those of their
principals, his suggestion that the principals are only the shareholders seems
unjustifiably myopic, especially considering the development of labor and
consumer protections, as well as investors' interest in other stakeholders. However, stakeholder theory also runs into its own problems. This is because
stakeholder interests often pull in different directions: investing in workers
can result in less profit going to shareholders; lowering the price for customers may mean imposing costs on the community; and so on. Saying "managers should act in the interests of their stakeholders" just raises the questions:
which stakeholders and when?

It is telling that the Business Roundtable's statement, before affirming
stakeholder theory, begins by noting that "each of our individual companies
serves its own corporate purpose." The competing interests of the various
stakeholders makes stakeholder theory, on its own, indeterminate, requiring other normative theories to specify how the various stakeholder interests
ought to be prioritized. Given this, each corporation serving "its own corporate purpose" becomes a rather large and significant admission since the
question of how to balance these concerns will ultimately fall on managers.[2]
That each corporation will have its "own purpose" actually implies that each
corporation will have its own ordering and prioritization of these stakeholder
interests—what stakeholder theorists refer to as the corporation's "normative
core" (e.g., R. E. Freeman 1994, 413–14).

This points to two limitations for stakeholder theory. First, stakeholder
theory appears somewhat toothless as an ethical theory, since "pursue all
your stakeholders' interests" can be interpreted in numerous ways. Indeed,
as stakeholder theorists have admitted, profit-maximization theory can be
reinterpreted as a stakeholder theory, where shareholders happen to be prioritized (e.g., R. E. Freeman et al. 2010, 12). Second, and relatedly, this in-
determinacy bolsters the power of the corporate executive, entrusting them
with the determination of how to prioritize these various ends. As Easterbrook and Fischel (1991, 38) once put it: "A manager told to serve two masters
(a little for the equity holders, a little for the community) has been freed of

both and is answerable to neither. Faced with a demand from either group, the manager can appeal to the interests of the other." This is even more so the case with stakeholders who are less organized, such as consumers and nonunionized workers, which makes it easier for management to attribute interests and demands to them opportunistically. Consequently, in trying to push back against the power of shareholder interests, stakeholder theory ends up justifying the power of managers to make weighty decisions on the basis of their own corporate values. As Orts and Strudler (2009, 610) captured it, in stakeholder theory "ethical constraints and principles are transmuted into mere considerations or interests to be 'balanced' against other considerations and interests" by management. This is no small matter, considering the stakes involved. Balancing the competing claims of different stakeholders— for example, deciding whether the business should increase wages, hire more employees, or open a new branch in a low-income community—raises substantive questions of social justice. Stakeholder theory essentially empowers business managers to make these judgments.

But what competence or legitimacy do they have in deciding these weighty moral and social questions? If profit-maximization theory unjustifiably empowers shareholder interests in its quest to tame the power of managers, stakeholder theory unjustifiably empowers managers in its quest to tame the interests of shareholders and pursue the interests of other stakeholders.

INTEGRATED SOCIAL CONTRACTS THEORY

The weakness in stakeholder theory we described in the previous section is well captured by one of its most influential advocates, Larry Fink, the CEO of BlackRock, the largest asset manager in the world, in his (2022) letter to CEOs aiming to assure them of stakeholder theory's noncontroversial nature: "Stakeholder capitalism is not about politics. . . . It is capitalism, driven by mutually beneficial relationships between you and the employees, customers, suppliers, and communities your company relies on to prosper." For many critics, the claim that stakeholder theory "is not about politics" is precisely the problem with the theory, namely that it leaves the power that corporations wield, and that managers wield as their agents, uninterrogated. What is needed isn't a theory of business that is apolitical—this is, we have been arguing, not possible. Rather, we need a conception of business ethics that renders explicit the implicit political nature of business ethics: demanding that businesses wield their power in an ethical way requires us to think beyond the power that they have vis-à-vis stakeholders.

One of the crucial developments in academic business ethics of the past thirty years, borne out of this recognition, is the theoretical framework known as "integrated social contract theory" (ISCT). Originated by Donaldson and Dunfee, ISCT aims to articulate a theory of business ethics that is grounded in broader principles than merely those implicit to the corporate principal-agent relationship. While stakeholder and shareholder theories are surely right that fiduciary duties are crucial, ISCT aims to draw attention to the broader contexts in which businesses are located, and the justificatory and normative burdens such contexts bring. If there is an origin point for explicitly political understandings of business ethics, ISCT is a strong candidate because of its focus on managerial power more broadly understood in social and political context.

Where the fiduciary approaches like profit-maximization and stakeholder theories take the corporation and its offices as a given, the main goal of ISCT is to situate such institutions within the diversity of cultural contexts in which modern business takes place. Put simply, to claim that managers have the fiduciary obligation to pursue the interests of their shareholders or that of their stakeholders is to beg the question as to whether such fiduciary obligations are morally justified in the first place. Answering this question is more complicated because the world is such a diverse place, with different communities and cultures affirming different moral values and principles.

Integrated social contract theory seeks to answer this question by drawing on the social contract tradition, which grounds political and social obligation in the hypothetical or implicit consent of those participating in the relevant communities. The main innovation of ISCT is to distinguish macro-level from micro-level social contracts. The macro contract reflects the overarching principles that would be hypothetically agreed to by all (given the optimal conditions). Microcontracts are the agreements implied by each of the actually existing communities we find ourselves involved in (Donaldson and Dunfee 1999, 19). These are related, according to ISCT, because the macrocontract would entail the right and ability to enter into these more specific and microcontractual agreements because of the social need for "contextually appropriate rules" that facilitate cooperation (Donaldson and Dunfee 1999, 37). The norms of microcontracts (which involve everything from nation-states, to industrial sectors, to specific corporations, to small towns, to trade associations [40]) gain moral force because they are justified by (and to the extent they are consistent with) the broader principles of the macrocontract. Business ethics, in this view, is derived from abiding by the various actually existing microcontracts that one's business entails and operates within, insofar as such contracts are consistent with the larger macrocontract.

The ISCT model of business ethics can be likened to a set of Russian dolls. The outside doll is the macrocontract's "hypernorms"—universal ethical precepts that all hold—which houses the "moral free space"—the freedom of individuals to establish authoritative communities—within which lower-order microcontracts are established. Acting ethically in business requires being cognizant of which dolls one is housed in, and what each level demands. The crucial development here is the insight that businesses cannot simply help themselves to the sorts of power that fiduciary arguments assume (whether of shareholders or of stakeholder-inspired managers). The power of businesses generally is derived from, and accountable to, the larger norms of the communities of which they are a part and the moral hypernorms to which all communities are subject. Integrated social contract theory is thus deflationary in a provocative and powerful way, rendering business as simply a part of a larger moral order, and not apart from it or at the center of it. Furthermore, in its emphasis on microcontracts, ISCT draws attention to the vast diversity of moral orders throughout the globe and demands that businesses humble themselves by following the norms of the local communities they find themselves in.

This was a major step in situating business ethics within political theory, one to which we owe much. Yet, in its emphasis on attending to the pluralism of local norms and the universality of hypernorms that contextualize business operations, ISCT misses the significance of power in shaping what they call microcontracts, and the contest over how to justify what they call macrocontracts. Though there is a concern with things like "exit" and "voice" in the justification of microcontracts, ISCT takes a very voluntaristic approach to communal norms: extant communities' norms are authoritative to the extent that they are implicitly consented to by virtue of a majority of members following them. But of course the fact that norms or rules are being followed does not mean they have been agreed to or are valid. Norms can develop and be adhered to not because individuals all agree or consent to them, but because each believes everyone else agrees with them or because they are intimidated into doing so. Similarly, even when they are agreed to, often these are not agreed to in a comparison with other alternatives, leading to modes of operation that are to the benefit of those in the position to dictate terms (Knight 1992). That is, the trouble is not simply that individuals are often not choosing or consenting to the norms of the community; rather, because communities are shaped by internal power dynamics and external institutional influence, the idea of "moral free space" is troubling on its face. All of which is to say, viewing communities as actually existing social contracts borne of a moral free space that individuals have offers a far too simplistic understanding of how social orders come about, obscuring the messy (and often unjust) politics that go into establishing these orders.

Hypernorms are meant to provide ballast against this possibility; existing communities that fail to abide by the hypernorms of the macrocontract are not to be seen as legitimate. However, like the politics that are obscured in the creation of microcontracts, ISCT undersells the degree of contest over what they take to be the thin universal substantive norms of the macrocontract. These two problems compound each other. It is not simply that community norms are the product of contest and power struggle and that there is great disagreement over the nature and content of hypernorms: it is that often the nature of the former impacts and affects the way the latter is conceived of. This is especially true with business interests that reflect a certain type of micro-contract but also may have influence in determining the nature of higher-order microcontracts, or the way hypernorms surrounding, say, property rights or contracts are understood.

Simply put, whereas ISCT rightly draws attention to the way in which business must be understood in context of, and relation to, broader norms (and the pluralism of such norms), it has less to say about the political nature of that context: the unequal and unjust ways such norms often come to be accepted, and the contestatory means by which these norms are changed.

POLITICAL CORPORATE SOCIAL RESPONSIBILITY

A different way of putting all the above is that in trying to capture business ethics in terms of fiduciary obligation, both stakeholder and profit-maximization theories fail to capture the political dimensions of corporate power. Thinking in terms of the power and responsibilities that agents have with regards to their principals is to assume that businesses' moral responsibilities are (1) inward oriented, toward the parties that relevantly constitute the company in some way (see Singer 2023), and (2) contractual, grounded in what one party owes to another by virtue of an explicit or implicit, but real, agreement. In trying to situate business ethics within a scheme of social contracts, ISCT challenges this inward orientation but doubles down on the voluntaristic conception of ethics as grounded in agreement and therefore fails to take seriously the political processes by which such norms come about.

An approach to business ethics sensitive to political processes must be focused not only (or even mainly) on the outcomes—say, the incorporation of a shareholder-oriented corporation with an agent obliged to his or her principals, or the existence of community and its attendant rules. A political approach must be deeply concerned with the processes by which such norms and institutions are established, and their legitimacy.

Animated by precisely this concern, a school of thought known as "political corporate social responsibility" (PCSR) contends that the modern corporation has come to occupy state-like power in various parts of the globe (Scherer and Palazzo 2007). Modern global problems like climate change are not easily captured by extant jurisdictional lines, and businesses often operate in parts of the world where state capacity is at best fleeting or sporadic if not nonexistent. As a consequence, there are various instances where corporations operate in what we might think of as legal and political vacuums, where there is no centralized authority to establish or enforce the rules by which commerce and social interaction happen.

In such instances, PCSR theorists claim, the corporation essentially occupies the role of the state: corporate policy and decisions become something like the law of the land. Yet though they fill this statutory and legal vacuum, they do not correct what we might think of as the legitimacy vacuum: corporations often act like states but without the various mechanisms and procedures that we rely on to legitimate state power. Theorists of PCSR thus challenge ISCT on the grounds that the norms they counsel following are not obviously justifiable (Gilbert and Behnam 2009). To render such norms justifiable, PCSR theorists argue that corporate social responsibility requires corporations to take on these procedures in order to be legitimate. Namely, they contend that corporations must enable, and be receptive to, deliberative input from those affected by their decisions.

This is, in some sense, an attempt to correct the deficits of both stakeholder theory and ISCT, politicizing the former and proceduralizing the latter. Corporations are also seen as having responsibilities to their various stakeholders, but with two crucial distinctions. First, corporate power is understood in PCSR to be something imposed on these stakeholders, not agreed to by them. Second, and crucially, managers are not understood to be capable or trustworthy to determine stakeholder interests, community norms, or hypernorms on their own. Stakeholders and community members must actually have the ability to deliberate on, and have influence in, corporate decisions. Thus corporations shore up their legitimacy deficit and the justifiability of the norms they follow by adopting democratic procedures.

Political corporate social responsibility theorists rightly capture the political power that modern businesses wield. Indeed, they somewhat undersell the extent of this: by framing this corporate power in terms of the withering of state power, they miss the political power that corporations wield even in places with strong, capacious states. But in asserting democratic deliberation as a solution to this problem, PCSR theorists also overstate their case, not fully recognizing the distinctive orientations that markets and states establish among their subjects. While corporations often do in fact wield state-like power, they are also constituted to have, and respond to market incentives that cultivate, an instrumental, profit orientation. Given this, it's not clear "how the instrumental logic of the marketplace would be a suitable social site for the stakeholder discourse needed to uncover standards of socially responsible corporate conduct" (J. Smith 2019, 133). In locating some corporate actors as occupying a state-like role, PCSR theorists overlook the functionally differentiated nature of the market and the subsequent distinction between the business corporation and the state.

In doing so, PCSR does not fully recognize the inability of democratic deliberation to combat the strategic and instrumental orientation of the corporation, such that the former easily becomes a way to whitewash and rubberstamp the latter (Hussain and Moriarty 2018). Put differently: addressing the corporation's political power without taking seriously how it is the result of the corporation's economic power and economic positioning can fail to deal with either. Corporations, economically constituted and oriented as they are, are not suitable institutions for filling the juridical space they often occupy. Asking them to do so only serves to exacerbate the problem.

THE MARKET FAILURES APPROACH

If, instead of asking how to legitimize the state-like power of corporations, we ask whether and how the corporation's economic power is coherent with social justice, we get a different sort of story. This is what the "market failures approach" (MFA) attempts to do. Instead of beginning with the corporation and its relationships, understood in either principal-agent or state-like terms, the MFA begins with the broader social context within which businesses operate. Yet instead of seeing the corporation as nested within various communal norms that are the outgrowth of moral free space, the corporation here is understood to be determined (not merely constrained) by the larger market system in which it operates. The ethical obligations of businesses do not come from the fact that businesses are a collaborative venture, freely entered into by consenting individuals, but from the fact that society as a whole is a collaborative venture in which businesses are an institutionalized part (Heath 2014). Functional differentiation must be centered in a way that fiduciary, ISCT, and PCSR theorists tend not to do.

According to this view, we as a society have created a thing called the market where we encourage businesses to compete with one another. Fair enough so far, but this raises the big question: *why* does society have an institution that encourages businesses to act in such a competitive and antisocial manner? The answer, simply put, is that the competitive nature of the market system incentivizes businesses to anticipate what people want in order to make profit. When the price for something is high, it signals scarcity, thus prompting entrepreneurs to enter the market or existing businesses to increase supply; similarly, if businesses are able to predict such things successfully, and they produce goods or services that people want, there is demand for it, and they can charge higher prices. When they are not successful, they must charge less. Thus, prices (or changes in price) are responsive to what people need or want. Put more generally, by letting businesses compete, the market tends to generate prices that reflect how relatively scarce (relative to demand) some goods or services are. These prices then enable firms, and by extension society at large, to make decisions regarding production, employment, and distribution. Prices that are shaped by market competition help direct society in making decisions about production and allocation but without the need of an all-knowing central planner.

Thus, according to the MFA, businesses compete and pursue profit not because the market is some lawless state of nature or because firms have some natural right to pursue profit. It is because this sort of apparently antisocial behavior, when properly contained and structured, happens to create benefits for everybody. This is why corporate shareholders and their executive agents are entitled to pursue profit: because within the system, doing so benefits society by increasing efficiency.

However, while profit seeking in properly contextualized ways can contribute to efficiency, these contexts often don't exist in the real world. In our nonideal economies, there are many ways to make profit that don't produce social efficiencies. These are "market failures," instances where the market does not produce the efficient results it promises. Businesses that profit off of market failure exploit their economic power to gain profits in unjustified ways. The MFA thus contends that while businesses are morally permitted to pursue profits generally, they are not morally permitted to do so in ways that exploit or exacerbate market failures. The morally permissible strategies are limited to those regarding decisions over what to produce, how to price what is produced, and implementing innovations in production and personnel (Heath 2023, 94–95), and they exclude things like taking advantage of information asymmetries, imposing negative externalities on others, and short-circuiting market competition (99–101).

As a result, a whole slew of common business practices—using misleading marketing techniques, cheaply disposing of one's waste, setting up barriers to entry, seeking favorable government regulation, and manipulating price, to name just a few—are unethical according to the MFA, constituting the wrongful use of economic power for unjustified ends. If I am running a business and making a profit, but my profit is in part due to not spending the money needed to avoid polluting my neighbors' water, or to misleading my customers regarding the material used in manufacturing and production, I am exploiting my position by profiting in ways that are contrary to the purpose of competitive profit seeking in the first place. I am undermining the efficiency that commercial activity is meant to promote by misusing the economic power gained by the imperfections of the market.

Taking efficiency as the critical standard by which to judge commercial activity helps us identify wrongful uses of economic power. But it also assumes that we can isolate values and institutions: that we can talk about markets and the efficiencies they produce without talking about, say, states and democracy. The MFA assumes that we can think of markets as functionally differentiated to achieve efficiency through competitive interactions, while other institutions handle other concerns through other means: the welfare state handles inequality through bureaucracy and state power; the courts handle certain aspects of justice through legal adjudication; elections and representative institutions handle legitimacy through democratic procedures; schools provide education; and so on.

But our world is not so neat and tidy. The problem with the MFA is that it doesn't just assume that our world is functionally differentiated. It assumes our world is *perfectly* differentiated, that each set of interactions works separately from the others—where social and political institutions operate independent of market influence and vice versa. As the PCSR theorists rightly note, the economic position of businesses often translates into political and social influence, which are not appropriately assessed and evaluated in terms of efficiency.

Given the plurality of values our society seeks to balance, and the variety of institutions we use to pursue these values, we must recognize that the power of business cannot be constrained or legitimated solely according to efficiency. To effectively tame corporate power, we should not be seeking the morality implicit to the competitive market alone but the various values that are implicit to our social and political systems more broadly, which always interpenetrate one another.[3]

Conclusion

We've gone over five of the more influential accounts of business ethics on offer, looking at them in terms of the problem of corporate power. This over-

TABLE 1. Theories of business ethics understood in terms of power

	Face of power focused on	Ethical prescription	Face of power underexplored
Profit maximization	Managerial power over corporate parties	Corporate behavior should be oriented toward shareholder value and constrained by law	The power of shareholder interests that affect other parties
Stakeholder theory	Shareholder power	Corporate behavior should be oriented toward and constrained by the interests of all stakeholders	The power of managers to determine, at their discretion, the correct balance of stakeholder interests
Integrated social contract theory	Managerial power in social context	Managerial decision making should be subject to the authentic and legitimate norms of the communities of which they are a part	The processes by which norms come to be authentic, and the means by which they are challenged
Political corporate social responsibility	Political power	Corporate decisions must be made legitimate through democratic processes of deliberation among stakeholders	The economic power that corporations wield and are beholden to, which deliberation is not capable of subduing
Market failures approach	Economic power	Corporations must avoid profiting off of market failures	The political power that corporations wield when their actions affect, incapacitate, or exploit the weaknesses of social institutions

view is not intended to point to one "right" answer. Theories are generally generated to make something clearer or to highlight the relevance of some phenomenon that is otherwise hard to capture; in doing so, theories inevitably obscure or downplay other things. The point here was to show how each of these different theories brings some aspect of corporate power to bear while leaving others unaddressed. We summarize this in table 1.

Part of the problem is that each of these theories tries to capture businesses assuming they are one particular thing and thus beholden to one particular value, principle, or procedure: fiduciary obligations, agreed-on norms, corporate deliberation, or market efficiency. As we argue in the next chapter, what businesses are meant to do, the norms they must abide by, and how the power they wield ought to be constituted, are themselves political questions affected by political processes. Democracy, at the societal level, is the process by which such questions ought to be answered and, therefore, is essential to determining business's social responsibilities. What the legitimate means of pursuing profit are, which stakeholders are owed particular regard, what local norms are legitimate, what sort of corporate authority is acceptable, and what counts as a market failure: determining of all these is dependent on a functioning democratic society that can decide such things effectively, fairly, and competently.

If business ethics is fundamentally about constraining the power that businesses possess, and democracy is an essential background process for determining what aspects of that power need to be constrained and how, then businesses' ability to affect and undermine democratic processes is a crucial topic for business ethics to consider, which the theories on offer, despite their many strengths, don't quite address. Therefore, while ethical obligations of business cannot be derived straightforwardly from a general theory of morality, neither can they be exhaustively derived from the more proximate extant institutions and norms of commerce. Businesses, crucially, have an obligation not to use their power to undermine the more general democratic processes by which such norms and institutions are legitimated and justified.

At its most simple, business ethics is about discharging the duties associated with the role of business manager or executive. These are not always the same as one's day-to-day obligations: one has special privileges but also special responsibilities by virtue of occupying any social role. The privileges associated with business are the competitive pursuit of profit in a way that is often distasteful in everyday settings. Yet, the responsibilities that come with this are also important. While divergent in focus and political orientation, the various theories of business ethics covered in this chapter all agree that (1) managers' actions are constrained by fiduciary obligation, but that (2) the permissible discharging of these obligations is itself constrained by broader rules and principles. Business ethics, then, is fundamentally about treating people and their interests as they are entitled to be treated while acting in a rule-bound way. All the theories reviewed here draw attention to important ways in which certain dimensions of corporate power might hamper fulfilling this basic premise. What the rest of this book tries to show is that democracy is a crucial background assumption for determining what people are owed in which contexts, and what sorts of rules are justified in constraining this activity. Thus, an ethics crucial for business is the general political obligation to avoid undermining democratic processes.

2

Democracy and Business Ethics

In the previous chapter we argued that business ethics is best understood in political terms: as fundamentally concerned with the power that businesses wield. We then reviewed a few of the major theories of business ethics to show two things. First, even if they do not put it this way exactly, all the major theoretical approaches to business ethics are political in the sense we mean it. Second, while they each have strengths in terms of the problem of power they aim to address, all these theories also have blind spots with regard to some other aspect of corporate power they cannot so easily account for. In this chapter we begin to offer our own contribution, which foregrounds the power that businesses wield, and its effects on democracy. We do this without diminishing the insights gleaned from other approaches. Concerns about fiduciary obligations, the moral imperatives of community life, the empowerment of corporate stakeholders, or the obligations imposed by the market system itself are all real and significant sources of moral constraint that help us address crucial social problems that modern commerce presents. Our contention, however, is that the wisdom and legitimacy of these various institutions—the firm's principal-agent relationships, the communities in which firms operate, or the market system that orients their behavior—presumes some set of procedures and criteria according to which we can deem them wise, legitimate, or effective in the first place.

Democracy is a crucial means by which societies handle disagreement when deciding on the sorts of problems they aim to address, as well as the institutions, policies, and rules needed to address them. It is common to think of democracy in purely procedural terms—a society is democratic if there are competitive and fair elections to select political officers who are meant to act as representatives of the people that select them. In this chapter we seek to show that although democracy includes such institutions, it is not

limited to them, but also includes broader social commitments to equalizing sources of social power. Consequently, while democracy entails certain
procedures and processes when it comes to the government, it also generates
ethical obligations among citizens more generally. Being people who occupy
particular roles that come with power, businesspeople have an obligation to
discharge this power in a way that respects, and avoids undermining, democratic norms and processes.

The Social Subcontract

In the introduction we described business activity as part of a "social subcontract," and it is useful to recall this idea. As we noted, this social subcontract is meant to capture two salient features of commerce, namely that it
is at once socially constructed and, yet, relatively autonomous. It is socially
constructed in the sense that, though small-scale trades and production may
come about spontaneously, in modern economic and political systems, commerce is enabled by, facilitated by, oriented through, and emanates from formal institutions—for example, enforcement of contracts, legal regulation,
and politically created infrastructure—as well as informal social norms and
expectations (Malleson 2023). Despite this social construction, commerce is
relatively autonomous in the sense that businesses make various decisions
based on their own judgments, evidence, and aims. Firms are free to select
the sorts of ends they strive for, and the means by which they strive for them,
constrained by the law and market competition. By thinking in terms of a
social subcontract, we understand business activity as something established
and licensed by society, and established to have a relatively large amount of
practical autonomy and discretion.

Just as the builder of a computer system might subcontract a technical
piece of coding to a competent business, societies subcontract the achieve-
ment of certain important social goals to this domain of activity we call the
market. The market is allowed and structured to function in its own peculiar
ways because of the outcomes such functioning is expected to produce. Yet,
just as subcontractors of a computer system are given autonomy to design
their code in their own particular way only so long as they meets certain conditions (the product is delivered by a specific date, the specs are compatible
with the larger system, etc.), the autonomy and free-form of market competition is conditional on two important premises:

- First, the commercial system must effectively achieve the ends that it
  is enabled to achieve. As we saw in the last chapter, the market failures

approach makes a compelling argument that the efficient allocation of re-sources is the best justification for the existence of markets. Consequently, society reserves the right to intervene in and reorganize market activity in order to correct or stem the tide of market failures—instances when markets produce inefficient allocations of resources.

- Second, the market must do this in a manner compatible with, and not disruptive of, other important social ends. That is, the commercial system must not compromise or contaminate other features of the more general social contract. As a result, society reserves the right to intervene in and reorganize market activity in order to keep it from disrupting the achieve-ment of justice—social, procedural, political, or otherwise.

Of course, these premises mean, first and foremost, that market activity can and ought to be legally regulated to assure both its efficiency (through, for example, consumer protection laws or environmental regulation) and its compliance with other social concerns (through, for example, laws that limit corporate campaign finance). However, as we noted in the last chapter, so-cial intervention and government regulation are always imprecise, faulty, and difficult to enforce, even when well intended (and, in the real world, such intentions cannot be assumed). Consequently, achieving such ends must also involve businesses adopting ethical restraint, following the spirit of the laws and regulations, even when they could practically get away with not doing so.

This means, on the one hand, following the market failures approach in counseling businesses to avoid strategies that run counter to the implicit mo-rality of the market—efficiency. However, this ethical duty extends beyond efficiency. Businesses must avoid engaging in strategies that will tend to un-dermine significant features of social justice (see Singer 2019). Whatever else this includes, this must also include avoiding activity that will tend to under-mine the democratic processes through which the meaning of social justice is articulated.

Two Types of Obligations

In the previous section, we argued that businesses have to conduct them-selves in a manner compatible with, and not disruptive of, important social ends including but limited to efficiency. One of the crucial social ends that is overlooked by most theories of business ethics is the prerogative of society to decide what these social ends are and how to pursue them. While we might be able to stipulate at a very abstract level that markets ought to contribute to efficiency and generate wealth, as the market failure approach does, what such stipulation entails and requires will not have one single or constant answer. Indeed, if you look at contemporary politics and debates over the carbon tax, the minimum wage, and the like, we see there is massive disagreement about the very question of what the social role of businesses is! The structure and function of commerce in a society is not etched in stone, but written provisionally in pencil, and it is subject to change, debate, and revision. The ends of market regulation (whether through legal constraint or ethical restraint) can not be figured out by philosophers, except at high levels of abstraction. Instead, the "why" and "how" of market regulation is for society to decide through broader political processes. Businesses, as subcontractors, have an obligation to respect these broader social processes.

Because of this, and following democratic theorists like Knight and Johnson (2011) and Chambers (1996), it is helpful to think of businesses as possessing two different sorts of ethical obligations flowing from the social subcontract, which are referred to as "first-order" and "second-order" norms. Businesses' first-order obligations are those that specify how to act in particular situations—the "rules of the game" by which society regulates business activity. In saying this, we do not mean that such obligations lead to a blind abiding by laws. These first-order obligations are complex social-political determinations about the sorts of constraints businesses ought to respect, given what society expects economic systems to accomplish; this requires interpretation and judgment. First-order obligations for businesses include what are normally thought of as moral rules: not lying to consumers, not manipulating stock prices, ensuring worker safety, and so forth. Parsing out these obligations is the stuff of the theories of business ethics we reviewed in the last chapter. As we have seen, each theory argues for some understanding of what business's legitimate place in society is and then offers an ethical understanding of how business should wield its power given such an understanding.

But there is a second sort of ethical obligation that businesses have. If first-order obligations depend on the results of political processes, then second-order obligations are those pertaining to the processes themselves. First-order obligations pertain to the rules that must be followed; second-order obligations pertain to how the rules are made. Businesses must respect not only the outcomes of political processes but also the second-order rules that govern these political processes. This is a crucial distinction between the approach we adopt in this book and those reviewed in the last chapter. Viewing business activity as part of a social subcontract implies not only that businesses must abide by the obligations that attach to their social position, but also that they must abide by the obligations that attach to the political processes that determine their social position (see Singer and Ron 2020; Singer and Ron 2023).

Why Democratic Obligations?

Why does this second-order obligation toward political processes lead to a particular respect for *democratic processes*? There is a fairly simple answer to this. In most developed market economies, the political process is (or aspires to be) democratic. Therefore: businesses have ethical obligations toward democracy because democracy is, in fact, the process by which many societies use to determine other obligations. As such, it must be respected, creating second-order obligations of businesses toward the democratic quality of politics and government.

This argument is good as far as it goes, but it is limited. Many societies in which businesses operate aren't democratic. The logic of the argument above would suggest that when businesses operate in a society governed by a dictator, whose coterie determines the rules of commerce, or in a captured economy where corporations end up making the rules, then businesses have an ethical obligation to respect *those* systems. But this does not seem right. There may be prudential reasons why businesses should go along to get along in a certain social context, or why they might be excused for doing so. But we surely don't think businesses have a moral obligation to uphold dictatorships or oligarchies.

We therefore want to make a further argument: businesses have an obligation toward democracy, not only because or when they happen to operate in a democratic society; they have such obligations also because democracy has a moral priority on its own as a second-order procedure, one that transcends a particular context. This does not necessarily mean that businesses ought to fight for democracy or become the vanguards in the quest to remove the yoke of dictatorship—businesses are not generally well suited to be the vehicles of such democratic reform. But, rather, more simply, a concern for democracy must inform businesspeople's ethical judgments, even when the societies they operate in are themselves not democratic or have significant democratic deficits. Put differently, we argue that businesses have obligations to underlying democratic principles that go beyond any obligations they might have to the particular laws and regulations that govern their conduct in some specific place or context.

But what is the value of democracy? Why follow democratic procedures, whatever they may be, rather than allowing, say, experts or benevolent rulers to make decisions? One of the conventional answers to this question is based on the moral value of participation: when decisions are made for a community, they ought to be made by the community (e.g., Pateman 1970; discussed in Forestal 2022). Therefore, everyone in the community ought to be able to participate in some way in making those decisions. It is worth noting that this claim—that all citizens ought to participate in creating the rules that govern them—is hardly uncontroversial. An influential group of philosophers and social scientists (e.g., Brennan 2016; Somin 2016; Achen and Bartels 2016; Caplan 2007) have made a strong case against the capacity of ordinary citizens to participate in democratic decision making. This literature contends that citizens are predictably underinformed about relevant issues, and thus incompetent to select proper representatives; politicians, on the other hand, have incentives to exploit and pander to these cognitive shortcomings of the citizenry when campaigning or governing, thus exacerbating the problem. Consequently, according to this line of argument, what democracy actually ends up doing is empowering the systematically uninformed to select the systematically corrupt to engage in bad governance. The ascendance of demagogues and authoritarians throughout the world, who rise to power by democratic means, has only provided grist for these skeptics' mill. They therefore suggest that we replace democratic participation with, or at least deprioritize it in relation to, markets or the rule of experts.

However, the case we present for democracy is not entirely based on the categorical value of participation. Rather, what we want to emphasize is the capacity of democratic processes to allow reflexivity (the ability to revisit and revise previous decisions and commitments) and social learning (the ability for societies to discover, and adapt to, new facts and ways of doing things). In the understanding of democracy that we present here, democracy does not simply mean everyone gets to participate always in everything. Participation is an important and sometimes necessary venue for collecting information about the beliefs, preferences, and needs of the people and is therefore essential. Popular participation may also be important for curbing the power of elites. But it is not the be-all and end-all of democracy. Democracy, in our view, is a system of governance that takes as a social fact the institutional pluralism necessary to solve various problems in a modern and complex world. Decisions are made in different sorts of institutions, each designed to tackle a particular problem of social cooperation: markets, administrative bodies, corporations, courts, community-based organizations, and others, all of which allow participation in limited forms that are particular to that institution (sometimes for reasons not dissimilar to those offered by democratic skeptics). This is what we called the fact of institutional distinctiveness in the last chapter—institutional contexts demand specific modes of conduct that must be assessed, at least partially, on their own terms. Given the differences in these various institutions and their importance for democratic problem solving, we cannot expect the same degree and type of participation to occur in all institutions (nor should we demand as much).

But this institutional pluralism doesn't relegate democracy to the bench! One of the problems with the social contract language is that it provides a false sense of concreteness to political affairs: as if there are fixed, transcendent, and knowable principles and goals that a society has and might simply consult when trying to decide what to do. This is, of course, not the case. Rather, this institutional pluralism invites the question of how a society marked by disagreement and diversity ought to judge which institutions should be used to address which problems, as well as to assess whether these institutions are doing so effectively or ought to be altered. In the absence of perfect knowledge of how to achieve the ends we wish to achieve, we will have differences of opinions regarding what course of action to pursue in any given instance. We need a means for drawing from these differences in opinion to make the best decisions we can. Democratic norms and procedures are necessary because they provide ground rules and a framework for how to do this.

But even more fundamental than finding institutional solutions to social problems is determining what counts as a "problem" or a "solution" in the first place. General social goals or values are subject to wide disagreement. For instance, should we structure our economy to maximize wealth in the aggregate, to benefit the least advantaged to the greatest degree possible, or to equalize people's income and opportunities? Even if we could solve that disagreement, oftentimes the various goals of a society conflict with one another or are vague and indeterminate. How should we balance economic growth with environmental protection? And how is economic growth understood? Do we strive for long-term, but slow growth, or a strategy of fast economic development that will nevertheless eventually plateau? Democracy entails adopting procedures and norms that address these important disagreements in a manner that reflects and ensures people's social and political equality.

This last point about equality is crucial. Taking institutional pluralism and context seriously will mean that the actual procedures needed for democratic inclusion are not going to be fixed once and for all, but will be responsive to the sort of social problem under consideration and the sorts of contexts most conducive to consider them. Put most generally, what democracy requires is ultimately something for democracy itself to figure out. Democracy cannot be reduced to a single social process (e.g., election or parliamentary debate) that determines the "right" answer.

However, the fact that democracy is a complex system with no central "command and control" process leads to indeterminate guidance for those who want to strengthen or implement democracy. Given this, recent democratic theory (e.g., Saunders-Hastings 2022; Bagg 2024; Klein 2022) has made the compelling claim that what democracy is most concerned with isn't elections or participation per se, but rather with equalizing the balance of power, and undermining sources of entrenched power (both in the state and in the economy). The procedures familiar to democratic societies (competitive elections, broad-based parties, representative legislatures, participatory government, etc.) are important because they tend to disrupt power imbalances in a way that enables the reflexivity and social learning that we want democracy to achieve. Of course, the degree to which such power and influence must be equalized is a weighty debate, which we don't pretend to answer here. Even without a final agreement on the nature of equality, we can say that (1) equalization of power and influence tends to be more democratic, and most importantly, that (2) grave inequalities in power and influence across citizens are offensive to democracy.

Democracy is therefore not a uniform demand that all decisions in society be made according to one procedure. Rather, democracy is marked by the commitment to make sure that however a society decides to solve problems, it strives to do so in a way that equalizes sources of power, and combats extant sources of entrenched influence. Striving for this requires a bundle of procedural and social commitments (more on which below). What we want to draw attention to here is that it also requires ethical commitments in the form of second-order democratic obligations. There are general second-order civic obligations that apply to all who occupy the "office" of citizens (Elliott 2023, 17). But there are also more specific second-order obligations that apply to those who occupy positions created by the institutional pluralism of society, such as those who make or execute business decisions. By occupying the particular office of businessperson, people occupy positions that command power (politically, economically, and socially), while also being in an economic and organizational context not necessarily well suited for democratic participation and reason giving (given its privileging of means-ends, business-oriented reasoning). For this reason, businesspeople have obligations to mitigate the negative effect their office can have on the way societies make decisions of social concern.

A Recap: Democracy Is Necessary in a Nonideal World

By way of a restatement on why democracy is important for business ethics, we offer a somewhat stylized thought experiment that may help drive the point home (those less interested in thought experiments may feel free to skip to the next section). Imagine an ideal world,[1] which works exactly the way we want it to without imperfections. One might think that if some very wise people, who are experts in designing a political system, could identify perfect terms for a social contract, with enough specificity and concreteness, then we could have solved all potential political problems. In such a world we have no need for democracy, since the social contract already specifies the basic principles from which to deduce the right laws. Therefore, this first-best world could be ruled by a benevolent dictator who would be chosen purely for his or her ability to deduce the correct course of action based on a correct reading of the facts, and perfect understanding of the principles embedded in the social contract.

If we start making things more realistic, we see that things get more complicated. First, let's start with the economy. Let's say limited information and scarcity leads the benevolent dictator to institute a market economy. Furthermore, let's assume that this market economy works much like ours, which is to say, imperfectly. So, the dictator hires a benevolent economist, whose job it is to identify market failures and fix them. If a market for a certain product incentivizes manufacturers to use a process that may be hazardous to the environment and to society at large, the economist would recommend the right regulatory schemes to disincentivize it.

In this world, like ours, the market would involve regulation, government intervention, state-granted monopolies, and public provision of services. The addition of these elements would necessitate a social subcontract to specify how businesses should operate given the strictures laid out by the benevolent economist (similarly to what the market failures approach is asking businesses to do). But following the ethical guidelines of the social subcontract in this idealized world would be easy enough, since the benevolent economist has clearly identified the inefficiencies and prescribed clear and effective rules to correct for the market failures.

Now let's make this world more realistic and remove this assumption that the benevolent economist is omnipotent or fully effective. The economist is now not able to recognize or predict all market failures, and the interventions for solving the ones he or she does recognize are blunt instruments; they fix an aspect of the problem, but imperfectly, and create other problems in the process. Thus, despite the "fixes," market failures persist, interventions are clunky, and the social subcontract is therefore underspecified; there are things that the benevolent economist just did not know or never got around to adding. The best we can hope for is a decently efficient economy that is cobbled together with a mix of markets, firms, and government action, none of which function perfectly, and not all of which are put into place appropriately. Instead of the deductive process depicted above, the economy is structured by a series of trials and errors and muddling through, informed by improving-but-ever-imperfect theories and understandings of how the economy works.

As a consequence, there will be *disagreement* about what economic intervention ought to look like. The result will be a number of different benevolent economists, all with different opinions about what to do in any given instance of economic policy. How will the dictator decide whom to follow in some particular instance? One thing the dictator may try is to institute some procedure for experimenting with the various possibilities. Recall that we assumed a benevolent dictator would be workable only because we started with the assumption that there was no conflict about our social values and how to achieve them. But, now, when there are conflicting views for how to fix market failures, there is a reason to opt for something less dictatorial, perhaps electing candidates for benevolent dictator and benevolent economist based on their visions of how to fix the economy (Pamuk 2021).

This helps us understand an important role for democracy: to provide ground rules for navigating the unavoidable differences of opinions regarding what course of action society ought to pursue in any given instance, and frameworks for processes of social experimentations that are needed to test and evaluate potential courses of action. Experts are still important. But because of the limits on expert knowledge, we need some sort of procedure that chooses from or arbitrates among the various views that these experts bring to the table (Bennett 2024). This also means that the terms of the social subcontract will depend on the outcomes of the democratic procedures instituted: such procedures will determine which benevolent economist's views will shape the market and determine which forms of behavior businesses can engage in. We thus begin to see the importance of second-order obligations for the social subcontract of business.

However, this is still a highly ideal and idealized world. As we've been describing it, while there are disagreements about the facts and theories of economics, there is broad agreement about what it is we want the economy to accomplish. But of course in real-world politics we actually often disagree on ends as well as means. We disagree not just on how to regulate the economy, but on what the economy is and on what we want it to do.

So now, instead of assuming that the social contract yields perfect and perfectly agreeable social objectives, let's assume there is disagreement over what the social contract suggests we ought to be aiming for in any particular situation. We know there is something we agree on by virtue of our ability to live according to a shared set of social practices and institutions. The problem is that our overarching social values and principles are often too vague or conflicting to settle disagreement. Even more importantly, *we often don't even agree on the overarching values in the first place.* Here we see just how much of an idealization the idea of a "social contract" is. At best, a hypothetical social contract can capture a family of ideas that we embrace, a "trajectory" that we share (Muldoon 2016), but even then, the ideas won't cohere or fit perfectly with one another, and so disagreement is unavoidable.

Thus, we need democracy not just because we disagree on the facts of the matter: we disagree on what matters. In our far-from-ideal world we disagree about the sorts of institutions and policies we should choose in order to achieve the ends that we also disagree on. We therefore require some shared set of procedures and norms that we can appeal to when confronted with necessary-to-solve yet potentially insolvable social problems. Democracy entails adopting egalitarian procedures and norms that address these important disagreements in a manner that enables the reflexivity and social learning needed to solve complex social problems. While there are independent moral reasons for a commitment to equality at the core of democracy, these commitments also serve the important pragmatic purpose of encouraging the broad collaboration and inclusion of diverse perspectives (Anderson 2012) necessary to ensure that decisions and goals are open to ongoing revision and experimentation. We close this chapter by reviewing some of these broad democratic commitments, and the broad obligations that businesses have in light of them; the rest of the book explores both in more detail.

Democratic Commitments

We will have more to say throughout the book regarding different sorts of democratic procedures and how they work. Each chapter introduces some concept important for understanding democracy and how it affects business. For now, we can identify three core democratic commitments that flow from the commitment to sociopolitical equality.

First, *democracy requires formal features like competitive elections, inclusive enfranchisement, and accountable representatives.* These formal commitments enable decisions to be made in spite of disagreements, and to be made in a manner reflective of citizens' basic equality. We will see later that this last statement is something of a sore point for democratic theorists, since there is a long-standing debate over just how equally citizens must be treated and positioned in order for democracy to be legitimate. We note here that what distinguishes democracy from aristocracy or competitive authoritarianism is that some conception of equality is treated as a moral default. While there are many reasons for this (which we touch on in more detail in chapter 7), for our purposes now, this egalitarian default is necessary because we lack knowledge or agreed-on reasons to diverge from it.

Second, *democracy requires the open expression and exchange of ideas.* This is secured through a variety of familiar practices: the effective enforcement of basic liberties (the freedom of speech, press, and association); a functioning and effective set of media that contribute to the flow of information and ideas; access to education; and so forth. Again, there are many justifications for these basic liberties, many of which focus on their importance for a commitment to basic human dignity, or inalienable natural rights. From the perspective of democracy, these are all important because they contribute to a society's ability to make decisions in a reflexive way, allowing individuals to reflect on their own beliefs and preferences through conversations with fellow citizens, and potentially change their minds.

Third, *democracy sometimes requires the ability to register social concerns in nondeliberative fashion* through actions like protests, boycotts, strikes, and other familiar mechanisms for signaling discontent. This is important from our perspective for similar reasons as above: collective decisions require open and accessible communication of information and ideas. This includes the communication of discontent and concern. We list this as a different category, however, because of its different character and its different purpose. In a more ideal situation, the mere communication of opinion and information would be sufficient. However—given that different parties have different degrees of power, disproportionate access to communicative media, and disparity in material resources—the communication of discontent, disapproval, and unpopular ideas must sometimes come in the form of more adversarial actions. This means not only that contestatory action is vital for democracy, but also that the institutional and organizational resources for engaging in this sort of action is vital.

In sum, democracy is a means of making decisions, given our inability to know the things we need to know, and agree on the things we need to agree on, which consists of three important commitments: a commitment to accessible and competitive elections, votes, and representative government; a commitment to the free flow of information, ideas, and opinions; and a commitment to the freedom to signal discontent through nondeliberative demonstrations. We note here that a commitment to democracy so conceived does not require that "the people" decide everything in all instances—or that the democratic procedures we adopt, say, to decide who will be our elected officials should also be adopted to determine how workplaces should function. It does not foreclose such possibilities either. Democracy is a way we choose how to order things borne of a commitment to social equality, which importantly may very well involve ordering things through markets, hierarchies, lotteries, bargaining procedures, and so forth.

This raises a question, then, with regards to our core claim: if democracy is about selecting institutions and practices, which themselves need not be democratically organized, then why should we believe that democracy has anything at all to do with business or business ethics? Wouldn't the very idea of a "social subcontract" suggest that businesses and markets are precisely the sort of institutions that societies have chosen because they work better than governments and their democratic procedures? Why saddle our subcontractor with the sorts of inefficiencies that led to the subcontract in the first place?

Business must abide by and respect democratic norms and procedures *not* because any particular democratic decision is of such great value. Democracy works, when it does, only in the long run by virtue of its capacity to change course and correct itself. Business needs to be concerned with democracy because it is situated in such a way as to stunt the role that democratic procedures are meant to perform. Specifically, democratic procedures are meant to decide on and shape things like commercial activity, the terms of the social subcontract of business; but the social subcontract necessarily will empower business in all sorts of ways—by granting them autonomy in impactful decision making, allowing them to accrue wealth, and rendering them most knowledgeable about various aspects of the economy and society. This means that business will be in a position to influence and shape the democratic procedures that determine the social subcontract in various ways: using their wealth to influence elections, their economic influence to affect others' preferences and positions, their expertise to shape people's perceptions of the issues at stake, and their relative autonomy to subvert the decisions that democratic procedures have rendered.

Three Principles for Democratic Business Ethics

What are businesses' obligations with respect to democratic commitments? What duties does a subcontractor have to democracy? However else we answer these questions, one part of the answer must entail being aware of how one's business activity can affect formal democratic procedures. This will include familiar issues relating to firms' participation in electoral politics (e.g., questions of campaign finance), in legislation (e.g., questions of lobbying), and in the execution of policies (e.g., questions of regulatory capture), which we discuss in more detail in chapter 4. But democracy is not limited to these more institutional and formal sets of practices. The way in which we assess our social institutions and understand what it is we as a society value will also be shaped through informal interactions and processes of deliberation (as we discuss, for instance, in chapter 5). This means that business's ethical obligations vis-à-vis democracy apply beyond formal or institutional political actions.

What makes this difficult is that interpreting and acting on these ethical responsibilities is a form of discretionary power itself, potentially elevating the judgment of the incorporated few over that of the many regarding the meaning and demands of democracy. A commitment to democracy (replete with its procedures and its principled commitments to equality) should lead to a profound discomfort with businesses having this sort of disproportionate influence in the interpretation of such things. At a very broad level, we can identify three duties that businesses have toward democracy.

The duty to democratic outcomes. The first ethical demand that businesses must satisfy is to respect the outcomes of established democratic processes: to abide by the laws, regulations, and directives produced by those duly elected. This would mean respecting not merely the letter of democratically established law but the spirit of such laws: avoiding taking advantage of lax enforcement, underspecification, and loopholes, and recognizing the expectation embodied in such directives as a moral constraint (Norman 2011; Silver 2021). As citizens, businesspeople might disagree with these constraints and find them misguided. This is part of the fact of pluralism. But they have to respect that such constraints are for democracy to decide.

The duty of reflection. This second duty of businesses to democracy is to be aware of how they may be affecting democracy, in both direct and indirect ways. This requires a business to treat its effect on democracy as a crucial part of intracorporate deliberation, in the way that profit, growth, strategy, human resource management, legal compliance, and "corporate social responsibility" are. This demands not just a personal ethos of being conscientious. The ability of citizens to properly discharge their civic obligations requires creating the right contexts that are most conducive to reason giving, reflexivity, and information gathering (Forestal 2022; Farrell, Mercier, and Schwartzberg 2023). The quality and extent of our ability to reflect and act on things is affected by the physical and social environments we inhabit at any given moment. We affect our environments all the time—whether its the seating arrangements in classrooms, the lighting for a dinner party, or the air temperature in a comedy club—not just for the sake of comfort, but because doing so in different ways tends to induce different results. The more power an entity has, the more it can affect its environment in both intended and unintended ways. Given the particular priorities and expectations that attach to corporate decision making, realizing the duty of reflection requires significant organizational resources to allow the time and autonomy needed to be properly reflective about such things.

The duty of publicity. This third duty of democracy demands that businesses make public the relevant details of such democracy-affecting behavior, and to offer reasons that are scrutable to the public for what they are doing, so that the reasons can be properly deliberated on and assessed. Now, what counts as "public" is going to be context specific. Sometimes this will mean opening the process to the broader public; sometimes this means addressing a narrower body that is duly representative of the public (Anderson 2017). Furthermore, we have a fairly broad conception of what counts as reasons in such contexts: the key feature is that businesses must make transparent and accessible that which is necessary for public scrutiny and democratic deliberation, which means not defaulting to claims of proprietary privilege. It also means giving an account of such practices and actions, by offering justifications and allowing for public critique and contestation of such proffered reasons.

These duties are stated at a high level of generality to be sure. We consider more specifically what they mean practically in the coming chapters, when they are refracted through specific aspects of democracy and specific business practices.

3

The Rule of Law and Ethical Obligation

In the previous chapter, we distinguished two different obligations that businesses have: first-order obligations to abide by the relevant laws, regulations, and norms; and second-order obligations to respect the processes by which these laws and regulations are determined. In this chapter, we begin exploring the potential tensions between the two obligations by elaborating on the ideal of the rule of law—the principle that society ought to be governed by known laws rather than the arbitrary whims of those who hold power. While certainly not without its detractors, the rule of law is a widely held principle, forming a baseline both for many political theories and for global discourses on political and economic development. We thus use it as a fairly uncontroversial starting point; while reasonable parties disagree about various aspects of what justice demands, they might still all agree that at a minimum, state power ought to be rule bound and nonarbitrary (Heath 2020, 255). That said, the rule of law's relationship to democracy is not straightforward, with many believing that they are separate, if not opposite goals. We contend that regardless of whether the rule of law *requires* a commitment to democracy, it is still an important aspect of the democratic project. Instrumentally, the rule of law often enables the sort of stable political order necessary for democracy to function well and over longer periods of time. At a deeper level, the rule of law and democracy are linked by a shared commitment to equality, as we shall see. Thus, generally speaking, a business ethics concerned with democracy ought also to be concerned with the rule of law.

We tackle this topic from two directions. In the first section, we look at cases where businesses go low, so to speak, and break the law for the purpose of enriching themselves. Bribery of public officials is a straightforward example of this, which we use to illustrate the significance of the rule of law and its relationship to democracy. That businesses ought not to bribe legislators and regulators is, admittedly, a fairly uncontroversial point. However, in the second section, we examine cases where business lawbreaking appears much more high-minded, done out of a conviction that the laws are wrong and unjust. Can businesses disobey laws they believe to be bad, given commitments to the rule of law and democracy? After reviewing some ideas about "civil disobedience"—for example, when principled lawbreaking may be just and consistent with an underlying commitment to the principles of the rule of law and democracy—we argue that, generally speaking, businesses ought not to engage in such actions. Businesses are not the sort of actors who can justly engage in civil disobedience, and they should therefore generally default to the position that they must follow laws, even ones they think are unjust.

At a more general level this chapter is a bridge between the more theoretical argument of the previous chapters and the application of this perspective to specific topics we discuss in the rest of the book.

The Rule of Law

In July 2020 Larry Householder, the Speaker of the Ohio House of Representatives, was arrested for what has been referred to as "likely the largest bribery, money laundering scheme ever perpetrated against the people of the state of Ohio" (Armus 2020). In 2023, Householder was found guilty and sentenced to twenty years in prison (US Attorney's Office 2023). The basic charge was that Householder accepted $60 million worth of donations from FirstEnergy, an investor-owned nuclear power company, in return for a bill that would give $1 billion in taxpayer funds to bail out FirstEnergy plants. Within a year Householder was forced to resign, and FirstEnergy agreed to pay a fine of $230 million, one the largest fines in history, for its role in bribing a public official (Levenson 2021).

It is helpful to start a difficult topic with something less controversial, and it seems fairly uncontroversial to say that this is egregious behavior, on the part of both FirstEnergy, who paid the bribe, and officials like Representative Householder, who accepted the bribe. But *why* is this wrong? Why shouldn't public officials accept such payments? More importantly, for our purposes, why shouldn't businesses try to bribe such officials? The easy answer, of course, is that these activities are illegal. However, our purpose here is to inquire into the reason these activities are illegal. What are the justifications for forbidding businesses from paying politicians for doing their bidding?

Most theories of business ethics agree that businesses have a general obligation to obey the law. Indeed, sometimes business ethics is described as being concerned with "beyond-compliance norms" (Norman 2011). The basic thought is that complying with the law is the uncontroversial baseline, with the question being what else, if anything, businesses are ethically obligated to do. Yet there is an underlying question about *why* businesses should respect the law. For some, abiding by the law is important for business because to do otherwise is costly. There is the penalty for breaking the law, which can involve high fines or even jail time, both of which are bad for the business's bottom line. There is also the reputational penalty, which can be equally damaging. We can think of this as the instrumental view of the law: businesses should obey the law because it is in their interests to do so.

Yet there are problems with this view. Most notably, oftentimes businesses are rich enough that they can absorb the penalty without much problem. From a cost-benefit perspective, it may be worth it for businesses to break the law and risk the penalty, either because the benefit for doing so is great, or because they have the legal resources to beat the case even if they are caught. This was put most starkly and infamously by legal theorists Easterbrook and Fischel (1982, 1177): "Managers do not have an ethical duty to obey economic regulatory laws just because the laws exist. They must determine the importance of these laws. The penalties Congress names for disobedience are a measure of how much it wants firms to sacrifice in order to adhere to the rules; the idea of optimal sanctions is based on the supposition that managers not only may but also should violate the rules when it is profitable to do so." If the law is worth following only because of the price of punishment, and if there is great profit to be had in breaking the law, then sometimes corporate crime does pay.

Williams (1998, 1265) famously referred to this as the "law-as-price" theory, and many have criticized it, contending that businesses ought to obey the law for noninstrumental reasons. Rather, businesses should obey the law as a matter of principle. They should follow the law simply because it is the law.

Of course, the claim that businesses have a principled obligation to obey the law just raises the question of *why* the law should command such respect. One simple answer is surely that businesses are composed of people, and people don't discard their law-following obligations upon entering the c-suite. This is not entirely true: businesses are composed of not just individuals, but also legal privileges, bureaucratic procedures, and stipulated goals (see Singer 2018), which actually makes them different in important respects from their individual owners or members. Thus, as we shall see, we actually think businesses have additional obligations to function in a law-bound manner that ordinary individuals don't have. Still, it is worth taking seriously the question of why following the law ought to be seen as a moral matter in the first place: why, generally, ought people to follow the law?

There are many possible answers to this, and we need not get mired in deep questions about the philosophy of law. For our purposes it is worth noting that the purported obligation to obey the law is also bound up with questions about democracy. After all, one of the more basic qualities of democratic government is that it provides a means—namely through popular elections, representative legislatures, and constitution-bound procedures—for establishing legitimate laws that people must follow. Indeed in the last chapter, we contended that with regard to politics, businesses had two general categories of obligation: first-order obligations to follow the legitimate rules established by the political process and the ethical duties implied by those rules; and second-order obligations toward the rules that govern that rule-making process. In both instances, if democracy matters, so do the legitimate rules.

A basic reason why people should obey the laws was given by John Locke. Locke was concerned with how to establish a political society that simultaneously secured order without infringing on people's rights. Though his answer was not what we'd call democratic today, Locke thought a crucial part of ensuring people's rights and their security was through the construction of a legislature: "In well-ordered commonwealths, where the good of the whole is so considered, as it ought, the legislative power is put into the hands of diverse persons, who duly assembled, have by themselves, or jointly with others, a power to make laws, which when they have done, being separated again, they are themselves subject to the laws they have made; which is a new and near tie upon them, to take care, that they make them for the public good" (Locke [1689] 1980, chap. 12, sec. 143). The goal, according to Locke, was to ensure that laws were always and only for "the public good." Ensuring this required, first of all, that lawmaking be done by a diverse body of people who were duly assembled. Today, we interpret this differently than Locke did, viewing it as crucial that this legislature be democratically elected.

But however the lawmakers were selected, the crucial part of Locke's passage above is that the laws must also apply to the lawmakers. In contrast to kings, who made the law but were above it, the lawmakers had themselves to be subject to the laws they made. This would ensure that the laws were to the benefit of those they constrained, since ultimately those who made them would also be constrained by them. This is the basic idea of what we now know as "the rule of law"—that the law is to govern everyone, including and especially those who make the law.

As we will see, "the rule of law" is an important principle not just for lawmakers, but for businesses as well. In terms of businesses' second-order obligations, the rule of law helps explain why it is wrong to assist lawmakers in breaking the law—particularly in forms of illegal bribery or corruption—since doing so undermines the rule-bound quality of society, which enables democracies to govern themselves. But it also helps clarify their first-order obligations with respect to abiding by the laws themselves. Even though the laws that the democratic process creates are often imperfect, and sometimes deeply flawed, businesses must recognize that they are generally not in the position to make these judgments themselves. Respecting the rule of law means that businesses have an obligation not to undermine the rule-bound nature of lawmaking, and to avoid using their economic power to escape the constraints of the law, even laws with which they disagree.

WHAT IS THE RULE OF LAW?

In 1975, the famous Marxist historian E. P. Thompson caused a stir among historians and philosophers in a book he wrote about eighteenth-century English legal history. In the conclusion of the book, Thompson made what his colleagues found to be a startling claim: "the rule of law . . . it seems to me to be an unqualified human good." This came at the end of a book that showed in excruciating detail how the English elite pushed oppressive laws through Parliament; furthermore, Marxists generally don't affirm the existence of unqualified human goods, much less identify something like the rule of law as such a good. Yet Thompson was making the subtle point that even when laws are made and pursued in deeply cynical and self-serving ways, by being articulated as "laws" they tend to take on an influence that restrains even the powerful. Where Locke saw the importance of a certain type of legislature, Thompson was drawing attention to the idea that, even when laws reflect and perpetuate injustice, "there is a very large difference . . . between arbitrary extra-legal power and the rule of law" (1975, 264–65) since the latter invites legitimate contest in a way that the former doesn't.

What exactly is the rule of law, and why would it be so important? One way of getting a handle on the concept is to think about what the rule of law is meant to be contrasted with: the rule of man (or woman, though this distinction was introduced by the ancient Greeks who thought about politics in gendered terms). When a society is ruled by a person, there may be laws, but laws in such societies are the tools of authorities to get others to do as they will. The rulers are not beholden to the law; the law is beholden to them. They rule through law; they are not ruled by law. As a consequence, those subject to such laws can have no confidence in their consistency, since they are administered at the ruler's whim. One can not be sure that the law will be adjudicated with any sort of fairness, since those responsible for administering it are not, themselves, bound by such constraints.

The "rule of law" is said to exist when the above state of affairs is kept sufficiently in check. As the British jurist Tom Bingham (2007, 69) put it, the rule of law holds "that all persons and authorities within the state, whether public or private, should be bound by and entitled to the benefit of laws publicly and prospectively promulgated and publicly administered in the courts." Or put similarly, "it is a vision of society as governed by a set of general rules, with the legitimate use of force restricted to the enforcement of these rules" (Heath 2020, 285). Thus the rule of law requires that those in power be subject to the same set of laws as those they govern; that those subject to laws have clear expectations and understandings of what it demands of them; and that the law be administered in a similarly clear, predictable, and rule-bound manner. This is the most basic formalistic definition of the rule of law. It says that the rule of law exists when the law's application, execution, and adjudication are as independent of human discretion and volition as possible. Furthermore on this view, even when the laws are unjust, there is a value in such laws "ruling" (that is, being the governing force of a society), since in doing so they bring a standard by which the powerful can be checked and held to account.

This may seem straightforward enough. What makes this difficult is that all societies of sufficient size or complexity will always put people in positions where they have *discretionary* or *prerogative* power to make decisions not covered by the rules, and where others are obliged to obey such decisions (Shane 2013; Zacka 2017). If the rule of law demands that the law be as separate as possible from human discretion, then the rule of law is always under threat given the fact of powerful people in society. For this reason, legal theorists have further contended that the rule of law requires not merely formal characteristics of law and lawmaking, but also the proliferation of an ethics informed by the rule of law, a "rule of law culture," which enjoins powerful actors to make decisions in light of shared interests as embodied in the law (Shane 2013, 24) or a shared commitment to equal citizenship (Heath 2020, 257). Put simply, while the rule of law has important formal components, it also entails a set of norms and informal practices that tame ineliminable discretionary power.

Generally this idea is used in reference to how public officials ought to wield their discretionary power. According to this view, the rule of law is undermined when discretionary power is wielded in a way that makes the law subservient to the will of individual people. In the FirstEnergy case, this is straightforwardly the case in a number of ways. Most obviously, FirstEnergy allegedly induced someone who occupied a public position of power—one where the law is harder to apply—to abuse his position in favor of private economic interest. But perhaps even more insidiously, these actions erode the public's trust in the impersonal and impartial nature of the law. This points to a broader way of thinking about a rule-of-law culture. The law's efficacy requires not just that it be created, administered, and adjudicated in a rule-bound manner, but that it be perceived as such by those who are expected to obey it. Such perceptions are necessary for enabling citizens to have clear expectations about what the law demands. The rule of law, then, requires general *social respect* for the law, demanding that those in power not undermine this respect, in a way that extends beyond those occupying public office.

The rule of law, then, has formal, procedural, and social and ethical dimensions. Formally, the rule of law requires that laws be universal and general in their scope. Procedurally, the rule of law requires that the creation, execution, and administration of law be done in a way that is rule bound, accessible to all, predictable, and transparent. Socially, the rule of law depends on a culture of people recognizing and believing these things, and powerful actors using their inevitable discretion in such a spirit, so that they respect and follow the laws as governing norms. By introducing partiality into the law, encouraging those who create the law to do it in a way that is not bound by rules, and by sowing mistrust and suspicion among citizens, bribery scandals like that of FirstEnergy undermine these crucial bases for the rule of law.

WHAT DOES THE RULE OF LAW HAVE TO DO WITH DEMOCRACY?

You may have noticed that nowhere in the above discussion of the rule of law was the term "democracy" mentioned. Indeed, many have argued that the rule of law is fundamentally antithetical to democracy. The etymology of democracy comes from the combination of the Greek words "demos" (meaning "the many" or "the people") and "kratos" (meaning "rule" or "power"), giving us a term that refers to the "rule of the many" or "the rule of the people." But if "the people" are ruling, then can "the law" be properly understood as ultimately in charge? Wouldn't democracy seem to require that law be understood mainly as an instrument of the empowered masses? Similarly, insofar as a society is ruled by law, it would seem to imply that the rule of the masses is constrained and not fully empowered. Can democracy's empowerment of the people be seen as compatible with the formal, procedural, and social demands of the rule of law? Or is the rule of law an inherently antidemocratic ideal?

One prominent answer to this question, offered by the German philosopher Jürgen Habermas, is that these ideals are not just compatible but mutually reinforcing, despite appearances otherwise. This is because each strives to secure a different aspect of the same social good: autonomy. We will talk more about autonomy in chapter 5. For now, we can note that the rule of law fundamentally seeks to protect *individual* autonomy, by ensuring that persons are only ever subject to coercive rules that are legal, nonarbitrary, and predictable. Democracy, on the other hand, fundamentally seeks to protect *collective* autonomy, by ensuring that a community of people is governing itself according to rules and officers that it itself has, in some sense, chosen or authorized. But these dimensions of autonomy require each other: a people cannot effectively govern itself if the individuals within it are not protected from arbitrary forms of power, since that will stunt their ability to participate in such civic efforts. Similarly, the formal and procedural elements of the rule of law cannot be put into effect if they aren't seen as legitimate, and legitimacy depends on people seeing such rules as not being imposed on them, but as democratically authorized.

Thus the rule of law and democracy are, to borrow Habermas's term, "co-original" (Habermas 1995). Democracy requires the rule of law to ensure that individuals are sufficiently protected from the arbitrary use of social power. But the rule of law requires democracy to ensure that the laws are not imposed illegitimately on a people. When we talk about the rule of law being undermined or corrupted, then, we are not only talking about the subversion of the law's impartiality and generality. We are also talking about undermining a people's ability to govern itself.

DOES THE RULE OF LAW HAVE A SUBSTANTIVE DIMENSION?

Given this relationship between the rule of law and democracy, some scholars have argued that the rule of law also has an important substantive dimension in addition to its formal, procedural, and social dimensions. That is to say, the rule of law demands that certain kinds of law, protecting certain kinds of interests, be enacted and enforced.

In an influential book on the rule of law, Bingham (2011) famously described the protection of human rights as a necessary dimension of the rule of law. Many others, including the UN Development Program, have similarly seen the rule of law in terms of not just the "how" of the law's formulation and implementation, but also the "what" of the substance of the law's protection, requiring things like freedom of speech and religion, access to shelter and education, and protections from state and domestic violence. If democracy requires the rule of law in order to ensure that social power is wielded in a nonarbitrary way, then the rule of law must—in this view—include the protection of individual rights from the most egregious and foundational forms of harm. A general, procedurally transparent, and impartially adjudicated body of laws that do not protect such basic rights cannot be said to constitute a legal system governed by the rule of law.

Paul Gowder (2013) has captured this in a particularly elegant way, which bears directly on the relationship between the rule of law and democracy. For Gowder, the rule of law is first and foremost about securing social and political *equality*. In its commitment to general, accessible, and predictable rules, the rule of law aims to ensure that all members of society are treated as equals before the law, that all have equal access to its protections, and that all share equally in its burdens. Normally this is thought of in vertical terms: that those holding offices and positions of power not be given special treatment or affordances, but be equally subject to the law. Yet, it also implies a certain type of horizontal equality: that individuals within society not be treated differently by the law or the institutions charged with its applications. In this view, the rule of law demands that people's standing before the law—in its creation, application, or adjudication—be equal and not distorted by facts of wealth, social status, or demographics.

It should be noted that this is not a universally held view; many important theorists of the rule of law deny this thicker, more substantive conception of law. Friedrich Hayek contended that the equality of citizenship intrinsic to the rule of law was fulfilled by how law was administered (not its content). Lon Fuller, adopting a far more minimal conception of equality, contended that equality before the law could be ensured simply by virtue of law being explicit, public, clear, coherent, consistent, and capable of being followed. Heath, for this reason, notes that there is no principled "correct" way to answer the extent and nature of equality that ought to inform the rule of law (2020, 289), though he contends that the rule of law should generally be less demanding than what we think justice or democracy demands. Still, even if not universally held, the substantive views offered by Gowder, Bingham, and the United Nations, are widely held and, more importantly, help illuminate the crucial ways that the rule of law is bound up with a commitment to equality, in a manner consonant with democratic principles.

The rule of law thus demands the law take on certain forms (e.g., generality), that it be applied according to certain procedural specifications (e.g., rule boundness, predictability, and transparency), that it resist the effects of social hierarchies on its creation and interpretation (and be perceived, and internalized as such, by society generally), and arguably that it meet a minimal substantive threshold (e.g., protecting basic rights and interests). All of this contributes to the functioning and legitimacy of democracy by securing individuals' ability to participate in, share the burdens and benefits of, and be recognized by civic life as equals.

If the allegations are true, in bribing a legislator, FirstEnergy didn't just break a law, induce others to do so, and corrode society's trust and confidence in the law, all of which are bad enough. In doing this it corrupted the rule of law and democracy at a deeper level by undermining the social equality that both ideals rest on, in at least three ways. First, it wrongly induced a legislator to participate in the lawmaking process by reference to his individual interests. Second, it elevated the standing of some (namely FirstEnergy and its stakeholders) above others in terms of their standing before the law. Third, it introduced reasons unbefitting a democratic and rule-bound society into lawmaking, in the sense that the bribe was meant to induce the legislator to make law according to partial reasons that not all could recognize as relevant.

In the last chapter we introduced the three basic duties of democratic business ethics—the duty to democratic outcomes, the duty to reflection, and the duty to publicity. What the above helps us understand is just how demanding the duty to democratic outcomes is. It is not just about following the rules; it is about doing so in a manner that maintains the integrity of a rule-bound order. This is especially demanding for powerful actors. As we will see in the rest of the book, taking these concerns seriously has implications for business beyond straightforward cases of bribery. Businesses can induce government officials to act according to partial interests in ways that are perfectly legal, but that are ethically problematic (as we will discuss in the next chapter); businesses are able to negatively affect the reasons used to debate political decisions (as we will discuss in the chapters on marketing and investment); and businesses can elevate the sociopolitical standing of some over others, or take advantage of existing unequal standing (as we will see in the chapters on social movements and HR). Thus, because the rule of law is not just a formal or procedural demand, but one that entails social and political commitments, it implies a number of "beyond-compliance" ethical considerations for businesses as well.

Is There an Obligation to Follow Bad Laws?

Bribery is a straightforward example of an activity that is both illegal and intuitively wrong; the discussion above was meant to explain why it is both wrong and illegal by reference to the principle of the rule of law. While helpful for clarifying certain things, the FirstEnergy case perhaps stacks the deck too much in favor of the law. Many laws are not obviously as justified as the antibribery laws that FirstEnergy and Householder broke. In fact, many laws may seem patently absurd and unjustified. In the United States, historical events like the Boston Tea Party or the civil rights movement are just the most well-known examples of a tradition of resisting or breaking laws when they are unjustified. So far we have discussed why respecting the rule of law is consistent with and, in fact, required by the idea of democracy. We now turn to discuss the question of whether, in general, there are sometimes justifications for disobeying laws, and whether businesses in particular may be justified in doing so.

Consider Uber.[1] The recently unearthed Uber files disclosed many corporate actions including allegedly illegal problematic practices of political influence and deeply cynical approaches including the violent behavior of protesters. They also showed something that observers had been claiming for some time, namely that Uber had an explicit strategy of trying to operate in cities where their services were illegal. At its outset, Uber services were illegal in many of its target markets because of existing laws that protected traditional taxicab services, requiring things like medallions or special licenses, which were highly regulated and controlled. Many saw such lawbreaking as obviously unethical. Yet, Uber's response was often to point back to the problem with those laws. Why should taxis be so protected? Aren't these laws an unfair form of protectionism that inflates the value of taxicab drivers who happen to be fortunate enough to possess these artificially scarce medallions? That is, maybe Uber broke those laws, but what if those laws deserved to be broken in order to open the market and better serve consumers?

Can businesses like Uber break the law when it is a bad law? While we may grant that businesses ought generally to respect the rule of law and the various considerations that implies, it's less obvious that any particular rule or law should command such respect, especially when we may have reason to think it's an absurd or unjust law. In the process of crafting technical regulations, the weaknesses of the democratic process can allow powerful interests to steer the process toward outcomes that are in *their* interests, thus tilting the playing field in their favor. These flaws can lead toward the undermining of the rule of law more generally.

If built-in weaknesses of the democratic process produce regulations that are written to favor their competitors and not the interest of the public, why should businesses always respect these laws? If the process is vulnerable to manipulation by some, why shouldn't businesses recognize that some laws are going to be bad and therefore worthy of being broken? Indeed, some might even argue that this latter orientation is good for democracy: because democracy will often produce bad laws, a business community willing to break such laws is an important counterbalance for democracy, helping return the system to a sort of equilibrium.

In the remainder of this chapter, we want to argue against this view. It is true that democracy neither always produces good outcomes, nor does it create an unconditional duty to obey unjust laws. There are certainly instances of unjust laws that ought to be resisted. Still, we argue that because of the way they are organized, businesses are generally not in a position to form judgment about what is in the public interest. Businesses generally ought to defer to the law, and at the very least be skeptical of their own judgment regarding what laws deserve to be broken.

Civil Disobedience

In political and legal theorizing about the rule of law, there is a strong tradition of arguments regarding whether lawbreaking is ever justified. These are generally known as theories of civil disobedience. While the ideal of law is perhaps a worthy one, in reality all recognize that the particular laws that the democratic process generates are often used by the powerful to oppress the marginalized. Championed and practiced by people like Martin Luther King Jr., Mahatma Ghandi, and Henry Thoreau, the idea of civil disobedience contends that people are justified, and sometimes obligated, to resist such laws. This is a powerful tradition in America and elsewhere and has been widely influential. Indeed, cofounder and then-CEO of Uber Travis Kalanick, would sometimes refer to the tradition of civil disobedience to justify Uber's flouting of local laws (Dale 2017; Davis, Noack, and MacMillan 2022). If we are entitled or required to break unjust laws, then might this justify companies like Uber breaking the law as an act of civil disobedience? We examine these theories in some detail to explain why, in most cases, they do not apply to profit-seeking entities. While exceptional circumstances exist, generally speaking, businesses are not entitled to engage in civil disobedience.

THE RULE OF LAW AND CIVIL DISOBEDIENCE

Political philosophers who are committed to the rule of law have incorporated this idea of legitimate civil disobedience into their theories of constitutionalism. John Rawls is one of the most famous examples of this. Taking his cue from the example of King, Rawls defines civil disobedience as "a public, nonviolent, conscientious yet political act contrary to law usually done with the aim of bringing about a change in the law or policies of the government"

([1971] 1999, 320). Breaking this down, we can note that civil disobedience involves breaking the law, but in a political and public manner: one breaks the law but in service of the principles that underlie our political order and in a manner that is addressed to the public in order to induce political change. Such acts, though illegal, are actually important for a society governed by the rule of law: "By resisting injustice within the limits of fidelity to law, it serves to inhibit departures from justice and to correct them when they occur. A general disposition to engage in justified civil disobedience introduces stability into a well-ordered society, or one that is nearly just" (336).

It is worth noting here that there is a large scholarly debate on the idea of civil disobedience, with many taking issue with Rawls's articulation of it: on some accounts, which Scheuerman (2015) has referred to as "anti-legal" views of civil disobedience, this rule-of-law-friendly conception of civil disobedience forecloses the possibility of radical political action since resisting injustice may involve violating this fidelity to "law" precisely with the aim of destabilizing an unjust order (Morreall 1976; Celikates 2016a; Celikates 2016b; Pineda 2021). The debate is too large to get into here. We focus on the Rawlsian interpretation because it is the view of civil disobedience most applicable to businesses. More radical approaches to the rule of law may permit a wider range of lawbreaking activities, for a wider range of reasons, but generally won't look kindly on corporations doing this, since it is often their power and position in society they envision civil disobedience targeting. We focus on this more legalistic understanding of civil disobedience not because it is necessarily the right view (though we think it has much to recommend it), but because it is the best candidate for offering a principled justification of principled corporate lawbreaking.

Indeed, on first read, the Rawlsian view may seem to provide a pretty sound argument in favor of corporate civil disobedience; if a disposition to break unjust laws helps to stop or correct injustices, then why not sign up businesses (who have the resources and standing to do so) to do their part? Yet one will notice that the above quotation from Rawls is full of qualifications like "within the limits of fidelity to law" or "to engage in *justified* civil disobedience." What makes civil disobedience difficult is knowing when such rule breaking is actually justified or done with fidelity to the law. The fact that you or I might think some law is unjust does not mean that we are correct in our view; we may be using civil disobedience to help rationalize breaking a law not for political reasons but for personal reasons.

The point of having law in the first place is that we don't always agree on such things, and so we need some settled publicly available set of guidelines that all can recognize and follow, in spite of disagreement. One might then criticize the doctrine of civil disobedience, as Rawls later notes, because "it invites anarchy by encouraging everyone to decide for himself, and to abandon the public rendering of political principles" ([1971] 1999, 341). While civil disobedience is an important part of a lawful and just society, we need some way to make sure that people are sufficiently constrained in appealing to it, so as not to undermine the rule of law completely.

KING'S THEORY OF CIVIL DISOBEDIENCE

This was a very live concern for Martin Luther King Jr., arguably the most famous modern practitioner of civil disobedience in the United States. In his famous 1963 "Letter from Birmingham City Jail," King notes the tension inherent to his practice of civil disobedience in Birmingham, where he was arrested: "Since we so diligently urge people to obey the Supreme Court's decision of 1954 outlawing segregation in the public schools, it is rather strange and paradoxical to find us consciously breaking laws. One may well ask, 'How can you advocate breaking some laws and obeying others?'" ([1963] 1986, 293). When claiming that justice demands breaking some laws, how do we avoid introducing too much disregard for the law? At a more practical level, we might ask: how do we know when we should break the law and when we should observe it?

King offers a both substantive and procedural means for doing this.[2] Substantively, King contends that we ought to break "unjust" laws, which are essentially those that don't live up to basic standards of the rule of law—"an unjust law is a code that a majority inflicts on a minority that is not binding on itself. This is difference made legal"—or democratic legitimacy—"an unjust law is a code inflicted upon a minority which that minority had no part in enacting or creating because they did not have the unhampered right to vote" ([1963] 1986, 294). For King, in order for a law to be worthy of being followed it must be universally applied and made in accordance with democratic equality.

Yet, in order to ensure that these criteria are followed and laws are not broken capriciously, King also lists steps that one must undertake prior to engaging in civil disobedience. First, one must make a concerted effort to research the case and learn whether in fact such an injustice is occurring. Second, one must try to deal with the unjust law through all legal means of negotiation and contestation. Only when these fail is civil disobedience to be pursued, though even here there are important constraints. First, prior to such direct action King, following Ghandi, contends that activists must go through "self-purification," a disciplining regimen to make sure that when one breaks the law one does it in the right manner and spirit. This is important because, second, the point of civil disobedience is to bring about a change in the law, and it therefore must be done in a public manner and under public scrutiny, since the target of the action is the public more generally. Finally, and relatedly, King contends that "one who breaks an unjust law must do so openly, lovingly . . . and with a willingness to accept the penalty" ([1963] 1986, 294).

Importantly, these standards are enforced through social means. When King discusses civil disobedience it is not of isolated individuals. The civil disobedience that King discusses is the lawbreaking actions of those who are part of a *movement*: people are actively researching and planning the actions with one another, and also helping to discipline one another, with the goal of collectively affecting public opinion to bring about political change.

Put differently, King offers criteria for deciding both which laws are deserving of being broken, and which parties can legitimately break them. Crucially, on both ends is a desire for impartiality and multilateralism. It is not merely that one's disagreement with a law that makes it worthy of being broken: the law must violate the basic precepts of the rule of law and democracy, since the absence of those undermines its status as law in the first place. Even such an unjust law must be properly approached when one breaks it: one must break it for the right reasons and in the right manner. Breaking a law because one is likely to benefit from breaking it or because one is angry, doing so in a nonpublic manner, and not publicly accepting the punishment for it, saps civil disobedience of its political effect and turns principled lawbreaking into undisciplined, individual acts of rebellion. Thus civil disobedience must be done with, and oriented toward, others.

SHOULD BUSINESSES ENGAGE IN CIVIL DISOBEDIENCE?

What the above shows is that while it is true that laws can be less than great, and that some laws merit being broken as a consequence, this does not mean just anyone is entitled to do so at any time. Figuring out which laws are unjust, and deserving of disobedience, demands certain things of the would-be lawbreaker. The question is whether businesses are generally positioned to make such judgments. Of course there are certain laws—one can think of laws made under Hitler or governing slavery and Jim Crow—that it would seem anybody would be licensed to break. Yet, when considering King's criteria above, it seems that businesses generally should not think of themselves as legitimate vehicles for civil disobedience, that such lawbreaking should be aberrational and exceptional. This is because of (1) the way businesses are constituted, (2) the incentives to which businesses are predisposed to respond, and (3) the power that businesses wield.

Constitution. It is sometimes said by critics of corporate capitalism that businesses, and especially corporate businesses, are psychopaths—recklessly and dispassionately pursuing profit without concern for its toll on others (e.g., Bakan 2003). This is drastically overstated. Contrary to popular conception, there is not actually a general legal requirement for corporations to be pure profit-maximizing machines (Stout 2008). Even in the standard business corporation, managers actually have wide latitude and discretion in determining corporate strategy and balancing the various corporate ends that come with such determinations.

That said, it is perhaps more fair to say that businesses generally, and corporations especially, are constituted to be *instrumental* sorts of institutions. Generally speaking, businesses are not created with the intention of figuring out what sorts of things they are trying to achieve. Whether at the business planning stage, during the pitch meeting, in talking to potential investors, while advertising to customers, or in selling to shareholders, the aims of the business are presented as a given, with people accepting the terms or passing on them, based on whether they want to be part of the scheme. The degree to which stakeholders actually have any influence in determining and deliberating on such ends is very low, notwithstanding the lip service often paid to such things. Businesses are designed to figure out what means will get toward the end that brought stakeholders to the table, not to reflect on the ends themselves.

This sort of instrumental orientation means that businesses are generally ill equipped to engender the sort of "purification" that King talks about. Legitimate civil disobedience requires a type of reflection regarding the basic principles of legal and democratic legitimacy, and whether one is breaking unjust laws for the right reasons and with the right disposition. The business environment, because of its instrumental orientation, is not ideal for bringing people together in such a spirit and is more likely to produce instrumental justifications and rationalizations for breaking the law (Heath 2008).

Incentives. Related to the instrumental orientation of businesses are the incentives they are structurally oriented to respond to. Again, businesses don't necessarily psychopathically pursue profit. Still, by virtue of operating within a competitive marketplace, businesses are forced to consider the bottom line at least insofar they are able to keep their business viable (whether minimally in terms of keeping on the lights and servicing debts, or in terms of making enough profit to satisfy or entice investors). Whatever other goals or ends a business pursues, doing so efficiently and in a way that enables the business to continue is unavoidable.

There should always, then, be skepticism regarding businesses engaging in civil disobedience. To protect against opportunistic lawbreaking, King notes it is important that people engage in civil disobedience not because it is in their individual interest to do so but because the law is unjust. Insofar as businesses are likely to profit or benefit directly or indirectly from breaking rules, we should see this as an unjustified form of civil disobedience. This becomes especially true when one thinks about the importance of publicly and willingly enduring the penalty for breaking the law. If businesses try to dodge such penalties or spend legal fees to fight them, they are not showing fidelity or respect to the law generally but instead are trying to disregard the law for their own parochial reasons. If a business is breaking the law and benefitting materially from doing so, we should be deeply skeptical.

Power. Even when businesses are not benefitting from breaking the law—that is, even when going against their material incentives to be disobedient—there is another reason why businesses are generally poor subjects for civil disobedience. This relates to the political quality of civil disobedience. The goal of civil disobedience is, in tandem with others, to draw attention to the injustice of some law or government direction with the hopes of impelling others to force a change in the law. What is important about this is that it is fundamentally multilateral: the goal is to act in concert with some in order to spur larger collective action toward political change.

The problem however is that businesses are often acting unilaterally. When they break laws they are generally doing so on their own, based on their own internal determinations, and not in concert with others. Furthermore, the goal is generally not to galvanize others to action. It is rather to break the law because it is still in their interest to do so, or to evade the consequences because they have the resources to do so, or to force the change of a law by dint of their own economic influence. Put differently, civil disobedience is primarily justified as a tool that enables the collective empowerment of those who are otherwise relatively disempowered, and generally subject to unjust laws, to challenge and correct such injustices. Yet businesses are generally not so disempowered. Their structure enables the gathering of resources and a type of collective action that individuals do not have, and their financial and social power gives them the ability to push for change through more legal means.

Conclusion

We reiterate here that this doesn't mean that under no circumstances should businesses ever break the law. Nobody would blame businesses for disobeying the Fugitive Slave Act, for instance, or not obeying directives to engage in genocidal violence. Still, these are best understood as exceptions rather than the rule for business. A commitment to the rule of law means that justifiably breaking the law requires meeting extremely high standards for fulfilling the duty to reflection and the duty of publicity (as embodied in King's account of "purification" and public acceptance of punishment), which businesses are rarely in the position to fulfill. Given the high levels of so-called white-collar corporate crime, abiding by the law is a more important ethical imperative and should function as a north star for businesses; civil disobedience will always be a temptation to rationalize interested and bad behavior, which undermines the rule of law.

As we've tried to show, this is a serious harm since the rule of law is an important democratic good, if not an "unqualified human good." The rule of law helps generate stability and stable expectations, which are crucial for securing the autonomy of individuals. Such autonomy is a prerequisite for participating in democratic government. Furthermore, the rule of law also aims to establish the equality of individuals with respect to the law's scope, application, and administration. In doing this, the rule of law helps secure the relative equal standing of individuals in society. As we will see in the next chapter, this sort of equality is a vital aspect of what it means for a society to be democratic.

4

Lobbying and Democratic Corruption

In the last chapter we considered a straightforward example of corporations exerting unethical influence on government, in the form of bribery. What we saw was that the ethical problems of such activity are actually broader than they might first appear. It is not just that such activity is generally illegal, and therefore constitutes an unethical breach of law. The reason why that activity is problematic—the reason why it is illegal for a company to bribe an official in the first place—is because it harms the democratic and rule-bound character of a society. As we saw, bribery does this in three ways: it prompts officeholders to abuse their discretionary power, and to craft law according to their own private interests; it gives the bribers and their interests unequal standing before the law; and it undermines social trust in the rule of law, political procedures, and their integrity.

The simpler way of saying all this is that such activity *corrupts* democracy, by undermining people's equal standing in the creation, application, and adherence to law. But once stated this way, we begin to see that bribery is only one particular, and particularly objectionable, way for businesses to try to influence government. Businesses can influence government in a number of ways that are not necessarily illegal. Can other forms of influence be considered corrupting of democracy? The case of bribery should prompt us to worry that businesses may undermine the integrity of democracy and law unintentionally, even when they are careful to abide by the rules.

In this chapter[1] we consider another case of businesses directly affecting government, but in a way that is legally sanctioned: lobbying. As many are aware, an extremely large amount of money and professional resources go into lobbying activities. In contrast to bribery, which is illegal in essentially every jurisdiction, lobbying is often legally sanctioned and heavily regulated.

Indeed, in some instances, lobbying is encouraged. For example, the United States' Administrative Procedures Act does not merely allow for lobbying but actively invites interest groups to provide comments on administrative rule making in order to provide important input for government officials. Indeed, though most think of lobbyists as targeting legislators when they are creating laws, or contributing to campaigns of candidates when they are running for office, a very large percentage of lobbying efforts (and a larger percentage of effective lobbying efforts) target this "notice-and-comment" phase of rule making (Dwidar 2022; see also Yackee 2020; Yackee 2019; Yackee 2015).

Yet, even when businesses are lobbying governments in this legal fashion, they may still be affecting politics in problematic ways. If their influence undermines the degree to which other citizens are included and considered in the rule-making process, businesses can corrupt democratic governance. As a consequence, even when not breaking the law, businesses must exercise ethical judgment and restraint when attempting to sway government officials. In this chapter, we explore the contours of these ethical judgments.

Lobbying is of course a controversial activity, and so there are already standards that ethicists have introduced to explain why and how lobbyists should act when they ply their trade. After reviewing some of these, we argue that such standards only get so much of the story right and presume a functioning democracy operating in the background. We therefore argue that lobbyists should adopt an "anticorruption" standard. To get at what this means, we review three different models of democracy—the "classical," the "realist," and the "problem-solving" models—to look at what corruption means according to each view. While each has its merits, which help us understand a different aspect of how businesses can corrupt democratic governance, we think the problem-solving model is most useful. We conclude by considering the different sorts of corrupting behavior lobbyists can contribute to, in this problem-solving model, and the sorts of ethical concerns such activity should prompt.

Truth and Public Interest

Drawing on the US Lobbying Disclosure Act, we define lobbying as engaging in written or oral communication with public officials (of any branch) in order to affect the formulation, modification, adoption, or execution of a governmental law, rule, or program, or the appointment of people to public office, excluding such communication that is part of people's role as journalists, politicians, or other professions who make such communication to the general public. We begin by reviewing two ethical standards that people have advanced when discussing such activities: the "truth" standard and the "public interest" standard. Both are plausible and intuitive ways of thinking about lobbying: lobbyists should avoid being deceitful and should avoid undermining the public interest. Their merits notwithstanding, these standards don't track the problem that lobbying can present for democracy, which is how to determine whether such standards are met. We then argue that the harm of lobbying to democracy is in its corruptive effects, and therefore that *avoiding corruption* should be the main standard that guides the ethics of lobbying.

"TRUTH" AND LOBBYING

The "truth standard" claims that the main ethical lapse of lobbyists is the misrepresentation of facts; consequently, the main ethical principle that ought to inform lobbyists' judgment is the obligation to be truthful and faithful to the facts when engaging public officials. If we are going to have people trying to persuade and influence politicians, asking them to be honest when doing so seems crucial. Indeed, such a view ties into a plausible justification for the existence of lobbying in the first place, namely that businesses have access to knowledge and information that others do not, and that sharing such information is beneficial for the policy-making process.

President Kennedy captured this well when he described lobbyists as "expert technicians [who are] capable of explaining complex and difficult subjects in a clear, understandable fashion" (quoted in Ostas 2007, 34). Hall and Deardorff (2006, 69) describe lobbying as a "legislative subsidy—a matching grant of policy information, political intelligence, and legislative labor to the enterprises of strategically selected legislators. The proximate political objective of this strategy is not to change legislators' minds but to assist natural allies in achieving their own, coincident objectives." According to this view, the justification for lobbying is tied intimately to the lobbyist's particular information advantages. Truthfulness seems to be a moral standard implicit to lobbying.

Lobbyists are important for democracy, in this view, because they have expertise on particular areas of social and economic life that policy makers otherwise lack, and are capable of rendering such expertise in intelligible fashion. Without ennobling their status too much, in this view, lobbyists are like scientists in that both are given a degree of autonomy to engage in a process that is opaque to the rest of society, in order to generate information that benefits society at large. As such, their ethical obligations are similar to those of scientists. They need to speak truth to power, even when the powerful aren't interested in hearing it. They also have an obligation, when presenting these more complex ideas in simpler forms, not to oversimplify or distort the message. Lobbyists' obligations are to the facts and ideas that they have privileged access to and not to their more narrow interests.

THE INADEQUACY OF "TRUTH" AS A STANDARD

The problem with the truth standard can be seen by looking at the problem with the analogy between lobbyists and scientists. Even if we assume that scientists have access to truth claims that are uncontroversial, the question of *which truths* are being emphasized is important. The very nature of the legislative or policy-making process is that it requires balancing different kinds of considerations. It requires not only considering true information but also placing this information in the relevant context. Thus, it is not a question of merely "are legislators being exposed to true facts" but "which truths are the legislators being exposed to and how?" One can present a completely factual account of, say, the positive effects of energy production, and this can still be distorting if it is not matched with other facts about harms, costs, or tradeoffs.

Furthermore, such an analogy is based on a misguided view of what *scientists* do, let alone lobbyists. Scientists don't distill conclusions from the ether; rather, they are attached to institutions like universities and laboratories, and they partake in research programs, from which they derive the material resources and conceptual theories that ground their research endeavors. These research programs and theories direct them in what they choose to study: what questions are important, what sorts of causal factors are worth focusing on, what observations count as good data or evidence, and so forth. The validity of any particular statement that scientists are making depends on this entire network in which it is situated. Our confidence in various scientific claims rests on that scientific community being in some kind of agreement about the overarching model or paradigm that gives evidence its meaning.

When we compare this to the lobbying context, we see the problem immediately: an overarching and shared paradigm or model is *exactly* what political societies don't have! Whereas climate scientists might be able to agree on some metric or model for determining whether or not climate change is happening, democratic politics doesn't have an agreed-on consensus for what counts as a metric for determining a policy response to this problem, or even in recognizing if this is a pressing problem at all. The norms and procedures associated with democracy are needed precisely because of this absence.

However, insofar as we allow lobbying to continue, we don't expect lobbyists to wait until such a democratic consensus arises before pushing their line. Such consensuses are not long lasting in democracies if they are ever reached

at all. A commitment to truth, then, is a necessary but insufficient standard
for holding lobbyists accountable. The main problem for democracy isn't that
lobbyists are always actively disseminating information that they know to be
false. Rather, the problem is more insidious: even when presenting facts, they
promote one particular set of facts informed by one particular way of looking
at a problem, which can still mislead.

The truth standard, accordingly, is all too easily met.

THE "PUBLIC INTEREST" AND LOBBYING

The most common criticism of lobbying is that it undermines the public interest: by allowing moneyed groups to try to influence politicians, we invite
these private interests to alter legislation that is supposed to be in everyone's
interests. Consequently, the most common proposed ethical standard for lobbyists is that they refrain from doing this by putting the public interest ahead
of the particular causes that they are advocating.

Just like the case of the truth standard, the reasoning for the public interest standard is intuitive. Lobbyists are also, primarily, citizens. As such they
experience the consequences of the policies that they advocate for. If they
lobby for causes that will bring about less clean air, their lungs will suffer
as everyone else's, even if their pockets are better lined for doing so (Barley
2007). Because they don't check their citizenship at the door, lobbyists have
an ethical obligation not to let their private interests override or undermine
pursuits that benefit the public more generally (Ostas 2007).

This implies a different way of understanding the justification for lobbying. Instead of thinking of lobbyists as communicating privileged information they have about particular industries or policies, the "public interest" standard implies that lobbyists are important because they convey the
attitudes and interests of constituents to their representatives. This is associated with what is sometimes called a "pluralist" or "polyarchal" approach
to democracy, where different interest groups compete to influence the political process (Dahl 1971; Cohen and Sabel 1997). This has been justified in
a number of ways, one of which is that this competitive lobbying process
creates an environment where many interests are brought to the table, none
of them powerful enough to win the day on its own; thus all participants
are encouraged to provide reasons that can be accepted by others (Gutmann
and Thompson 1996). When legislators or citizens propose a law, they cannot
simply justify it by claiming that it is good for themselves—they are forced to
explain why it is good for everyone. Lobbying, in this view, is an important
mechanism for bringing the reasons and perspectives of those affected by a

policy to bear on its formulation. Lobbyists must bring these perspectives to bear in a way that doesn't undermine the public interest.

THE INADEQUACY OF "PUBLIC INTEREST" AS A STANDARD

Whatever the merits of a pluralist approach to democracy, in the specific case of business lobbying, the public interest criterion runs into a large tension. This is because, as we argued in previous chapters, businesses are particular sorts of institutions that we have subcontracted precisely *to pursue their parochial interests* because it contributes to various social goods (in particular an efficient allocation of resources). However society decides to regulate or ethically constrain them, in market societies businesses are constituted so as to engage in competition with other businesses in the pursuit of their own particular ends.

How should these peculiar institutional creatures approach the practice of lobbying? Advocates of the public interest standards expect businesses to stop being themselves, so to speak, when they engage in lobbying. To simply say "pursue the public interest" misses the complexity of the situation in at least two ways. First, it ignores that businesses are simply not inclined to do that by constitution and because of the incentives they face. Second, and more subtly, it misses that commercial institutions are designed to contribute to the public interest by allowing individual parties to pursue their own private interests.

The public interest standard, then, while capturing an important intuition about civic-mindedness and its relationship to democracy, runs afoul of certain facts about the business world that we can't assume away. In so doing, it gives businesses the opportunity and motive to dissemble and disguise their parochial interests in the language of the public good. The public interest standard therefore seems both implausible and inappropriate. It is implausible because businesses are, in some sense, defined by their being freed from the normal social and civic obligations that constrain us in most of our lives. We don't *really* expect businesses to be model citizens tirelessly pursuing the public interest. It is inappropriate because it asks businesses to make judgments about the public good that they are not positioned or constituted to do well.

Where the truth standard is too easily met, we have reason to doubt the capacity or inclination of business to meet the public interest standard given the organizational imperatives we reviewed in the last chapter. Indeed, even if businesses try to meet this public interest standard, we'd be rightly skeptical of their efforts.

Corruption and Democracy

The same problem afflicts the "truth" and the "public interest" standards: both of them underplay just how *political* these sorts of constraints are. "Just the facts" is not much of a constraint at all for lobbyists, given that they are often not in the business of flat-out lying, but of spinning and skewing. The question isn't whether lobbyists ought to tell the truth, but which side of the truth they present to whom. Similarly, to claim that lobbyists must pursue the public interest is just to raise the question "the public interest according to whom?" The answer, inevitably, is "according to businesses that are constituted to be neither inclined nor capable to make such a judgment." Ultimately deciding which framework the truth should be cast in, or how best to measure the public interest, is a political judgment.

Lobbying inherently raises difficult questions; there are important reasons why lobbying ought to be allowed (e.g., because it provides important information for decision making), and other important reasons to think it can raise serious problems. It is not possible to deduce the right balance between these the pros and cons of lobbying from pure theory or first principles. What sorts of lobbying will count as "good" lobbying is contingent on various contextual and institutional facts, as well as social and cultural preferences, which are local and particular to a given jurisdiction at a particular time. As we saw in chapter 2, it is the job of democratic processes to weigh these different considerations and to establish and modify what we described as the "first-order rules" of lobbying—that is, the laws and regulations that govern businesses' lawful and legitimate engagement with politicians and public officials. Of course, as we saw in chapter 1, regulations are never perfectly created or fully enforced, and thus ethical constraints are necessary. Business lobbying needs to be constrained, then, not according to first-order political judgments about what truths are relevant or what the public interest is, but by second-order concern for the democratic processes by which regulations are established. Businesses must avoid lobbying practices that contribute to the corruption of democratic rule making.

What is corruption, and how does one contribute to it? In the last chapter we discussed a fairly straightforward case of corruption in the form of illegal bribery. Yet what we saw is that the bribe wasn't unethical just because it was illegal. It was unethical because it undermined democracy and the rule of law. What other legal sorts of things qualify as corrupting in that view? To address this question, we introduce three general models of democracy, which we call the "classical" view, the "realist" view, and the "problem-solving" view.

Each of these understands democracy in different ways, and as demanding different things. For our purposes here, what is interesting is that they each highlight a different potential problem of corruption for democracy. To better understand these models of democracy, and the harms of corruption, we go into each into further detail and explain the dimension of corruption to which each draws our attention.

Corruption and the Classical Model of Democracy

According to the classical view, democracy is a decision-making procedure that is designed to speak on behalf of the public. To understand this view, it is useful to recall the original meaning of the term democracy. Ancient Athens offered a new model of regime. Unlike regimes that were ruled by one individual (monarchies or tyrannies, depending on whether the ruler was virtuous), or regimes that were ruled by a small cabal of people (aristocracies or oligarchies), ancient Athens claimed to be a democracy: a regime where the people (demos) hold the power (kratos). But what does that look like? It is easy to understand what it means for a king to rule. The king gives orders, and everyone else follows.

But what does it mean for "the people" to rule? In Athens, the claim that Athenian political institutions allow the people to rule was based on the institution of the Assembly. All eligible (adult male) citizens met at the Assembly to debate certain policy issues and to vote on them. The conventional idea of democracy follows the Greek experience: democracy is achieved through institutions that allow a large number of people to make decisions together through processes that involve a combination of debate and voting.

THE GOOD OF DEMOCRACY ACCORDING
TO THE CLASSICAL VIEW

In this classical understanding, democratic institutions and processes are designed to turn individual wills into a collective will—to allow the people to speak (and issue orders) in a way that is analogous to having the king speak. Of course, this then raises questions about what the best procedure is for forming and expressing such a collective will. Does democracy require wide participation of everyone or only occasional election of representatives? If there are elections, are there electoral systems that reflect a common will better than others (like, say proportional representation versus first-past-the-post systems)? How do we ensure that issues are discussed in a thorough and informed way? These are only some of the many questions raised by such institutions. Nonetheless, the belief is that the goal of these procedures is to get an outcome that can be rightly described as the voice of the people.

Implicit to this is the idea that pursuing the interests of "the people" requires either the participation or the effective representation of the population in the political process, hence the importance of general elections and political liberties in democratic politics. But this, in theory, need not be the case. What is wrong with hoping that a benign and informed autocrat will make decisions that are in the best interests of the people? In other words, why do we need to care about the voice and participation of the people, when we can just track their interests with leaders who are properly benevolent or expert (or both) in such matters? As we suggested in chapter 2, democratic theorists provide two kinds of answers to the question.

First, we generally don't really know what our interests are before we have had a chance to think about them and weigh alternatives. Similarly, we don't know what others' interests are until they've had the opportunity to debate and consider things themselves. Democracy allows decisions that are more informed in the sense that they allow us to reflect better on what we want, and they allow us to take into account what other people want, in a way that a benevolent and intelligent autocrat cannot. In that way democracy is uniquely able to approximate the general will, according to this classical view, which reflects our considered individual and collective interests.

Second, we evaluate processes of decision making based not only on the outcomes they produce, but also on the values that they embody. Democratic procedures, for the classicist, capture a fundamental commitment to the equality of everyone in a way that a benevolent autocrat inherently cannot. By positioning citizens equally relative to each other, democracy uniquely allows a common interest to emerge and hold sway.

CORRUPTION ACCORDING TO THE CLASSICAL VIEW

This classical view of democracy implies a fairly straightforward understanding of what corruption entails: to bring about a political outcome that is not in the public interest. The various procedures associated with democracy and the rules that govern the lawmaking process are designed to bring the common will to bear in government by making the people's voice and interests manifest. If democracy is viewed as a machine that is designed to produce a certain good, corruption is wrong and harmful because it makes the machine produce a defective good.

To return to the FirstEnergy scandal from last chapter: When House-holder allegedly accepted money from FirstEnergy, and thus was influenced to spend public funds on their project instead of another, he subverted this process by using the power entrusted to him for his own personal interests, thus not allowing the public interest to be made manifest. When FirstEnergy allegedly offered these bribes, they attempted to get decisions made about public funds to be made with their interest having disproportionate influence, disrupting the equality of standing and participation that democratic procedures are meant to secure. But such illegal and straightforward bribes are not the primary or only form of corruption in the classical view of democracy. When businesses or other actors engage in actions, even legal actions, that keep citizens from participating effectively in the process, or that disrupt the equal positioning of citizens in that process, this would qualify as corrupting actions.

Corruption and the Realist Model of Democracy

The second model, often described as a realist theory of democracy, contends that it is not useful to think about democracy through the concept of public interest, either rejecting the concept of "public interest" completely, or at least denying that democratic procedures have any connection to it. Instead, for realists there is nothing necessarily right or fair or just about the outcome of the democratic process and certainly nothing about it that has anything to do with a "public interest" or "common will." Instead, democracy is endorsed for much thinner procedural reasons.

THE GOOD OF DEMOCRACY ACCORDING TO THE REALIST VIEW

If it is not about articulating the public interest or the voice of the people, what is the value of democratic institutions and processes? In the realist view, democracy is desirable because it is a preferred system for managing conflict. Politics, being the domain of seeking and exercising power, is inherently a domain of conflict, with different factions, classes, and personalities vying to hold influence. As human history has demonstrated, such conflict can easily lead to extremely brutal forms of violence and suffering. Democracy, according to the realist, allows peaceful resolution of conflicts because it builds competition into the system—competition is baked into the cake of democracy, as it were. By internalizing competition, democratic politics are able to tame it and make it less destructive. As E. H. Carr (1941, 55) suggested, democracy "substitutes the counting of heads for the breaking of heads."

Competition, as institutionalized in democratic elections and party systems, has two advantages. First, because they know they may possibly prevail in the next election, and because they can be reasonably assured not to be subject to persecution by the ruling party when opposing them, those out of power are less prone to resort to violence. Second, competition encourages dynamic adaptation to new conditions. In economics, the opposite of competition is monopoly; in politics, we call this autocracy. The problem of political monopoly is not, according to the realist, that autocrats are necessarily evil and malign, or incapable of pursuing the public interest. The problem is that without the need to compete and without others having a hope to replace them, such regimes are unlikely to be stable, and more likely to abuse their power.

According to the realist, candidates compete for office by trying to win the majority of votes. This is desirable not because the majority is more right, or it is more fair to follow the majority, but because votes are the "currency" of political competition. The advantage of competition for votes over other forms of competition is that it tends to be more effective in ensuring stability. Whereas the classical view emphasizes political outcomes that are representative, the realist approach emphasizes political *order*. Classical democrats want democracy to produce moral outcomes; realists strive for stable outcomes.

The realist approach is by its very nature elitist. It rejects the idea that democracy is government by the people, where ultimate power resides in citizens and is articulated by representatives. Instead, as Schumpeter ([1943] 2003, 269) writes, realists strive to "make the deciding of issues by the electorate secondary to the election of the men who are to do the deciding. To put it differently . . . the role of the people is to produce a government, or else an intermediate body, which in turn will produce a national executive or government. And we define: The democratic method is that institutional arrangement for arriving at political decisions in which individuals acquire the power to decide by means of a competitive struggle for the people's vote." The thought here isn't that the competition between elites over voters guarantees that politicians will pursue policies that people want. For realists, part of the point is that often ordinary people don't understand or care enough about politics to know what they want (Caplan 2007). Instead, parties and politicians act like corporations that try to sell their brand. People "shop" for politicians often in the same way as they shop for a car—based on the "image" it projects, based on the celebrity who endorses it, or based on the brand their neighbors or family tends to be loyal toward. Without necessarily endorsing or celebrating this form of decision making, realists think this model of democracy both captures the reality of democratic processes and is realistic in what it expects from people.

CORRUPTION ACCORDING TO THE REALIST VIEW

For the classical view of democracy, the harm of corruption is straightforward: because democracy is meant to capture the general interest, corruption occurs when (and is harmful because) this process of discovering and articulating the general interest is stunted. In the realist model, the very distinction between clean and dirty politics, between legitimate and corrupt practices is far murkier. This is because realists don't think that there is a "right" outcome or that democracy produces it. Rather, democratic procedures are a device of coordination. There is nothing inherently better or more right in choosing one procedure over the other. Democratic processes are preferred because, but only insofar as, they more reliably produce stability in both the short and the long term.

By way of analogy, consider chess. In "touch move" versions of the game, a player must move a piece if he of she touches it, while in others that is not required—the player can touch a pawn then opt to move a rook. Now, imagine that while one player is not looking, the other player has touched a piece but regretted the move and pulled his or her hand back. That is cheating according to the touch-move rule. Maybe if the player were forced to move the piece touched, he or she would lose the game. But are people who can win under one rule better chess players than people who win under the other rule? Probably not. This rule is simply an agreement about one element of the rules of the game that could have been otherwise. The cheater might not be a good person, but violating the rule does not make this person a bad chess player. A realist says something similar about politics. If under some voting rules company A would get a government contract and under different voting rules company B would get the contract, neither outcome is more or less democratic because one set of voting rules is not inherently more right than the other. There might be good reasons for why we need to adhere to the rules of the game, but these reasons have nothing to do with the quality of democratic decision making.

In this perspective, corruption isn't about undermining the people's ability to rule or speak for themselves. Corruption, rather, is simply the limiting of political competition, and its harm is that it tends to produce political monopolies. Corruption of democracy is wrong not because it leads to immoral, unjust, or unrepresentative results, but because it tends to destabilize the political order. FirstEnergy and Householder, according to the realist view, weren't engaged in corruption because what they did distorted the public character of political outcomes or the egalitarian character of political processes. Rather it corrupted democracy because it threatened the stability of our political order in at least two ways. First, by encouraging public officials to break the law, it lessened citizens' trust in the rule-bound nature of political processes, decreasing confidence that democratic procedures are operating fairly. Second, by giving illegal and unfair monetary support to a legislator, FirstEnergy stunted the competitive nature of policy, giving Householder an undue leg up in a way that can lead to political monopoly.

Corruption and the Problem-Solving Model of Democracy

For the classicist, democracy is a mechanism for identifying the general interest, and for the realist, democracy is a method for managing conflict in a peaceful way. For what we call the problem-solving model, democracy is a dynamic method for solving problems that inevitably arise when diverse people cooperate with one another. To be sure, all models of democracy are dynamic, in the sense that they acknowledge a continuous need to adapt and change by passing laws and making policies to adjust to new circumstances. Those who believe that the right laws can be eternal are usually not supporters of democracy. Still, the classical model in particular, but also the realist model, sees the challenge for democratic theory as establishing the procedures that govern the process by which people decide on the actual rules. The basic premise of democracy in these views is that even if people don't agree about a particular piece of legislation—the first-order rules—they do agree on a set of procedures for how to adjudicate their disagreement—the second-order rules. This more basic agreement on the rules of the rule-making game allows for the dynamism of the process of making first-order decisions about laws and policies.

THE GOOD OF DEMOCRACY ACCORDING TO THE PROBLEM-SOLVING VIEW

For the problem-solving model, what is unique to democracy is that it allows for, and even emphasizes, the ability to modify second-order rules (Knight and Johnson 2011). Democracy is not about specifying *the* rules that would turn the messiness of public opinion into a proper public decision. Instead, democracy is fundamentally oriented toward answering questions regarding how society should be organized, and how best to facilitate cooperation. Democracy is a way to specify the basic parameters of how to go about answering these questions, or what would count as an answer to these questions, but it doesn't seek to provide a full picture of it.

Mark Warren (2017, 39) describes this problem-solving model of democracy in this relatively simple fashion: "If a political system empowers inclusion, forms collective agendas and wills, and organizes collective decision capacity, it will count as 'democratic.'" We can discern three criteria here.

> *Empowered inclusion.* First, democracy requires that people affected be empowered to be included in the process of decision making. The "empowered" part is important, because it means democracy isn't just about being formally enfranchised, but having the requisite abilities and resources to participate in an effective manner.
>
> *Agenda setting.* Second, this empowered inclusion must then be structured into something we can discern to be a "collective agenda." We don't assume that a "collective will" exists prior to the democratic process, nor that there is one correct way of ascertaining what it is. Rather such a collective agenda is understood as something that is created as a result of democratic processes, and is necessary for democracy to be effective at solving problems.
>
> *Decision making.* And third, these processes must produce a way of making decisions in light of these collective agendas. That is, democracy requires not just empowered inclusion and the formation of agendas, but also some means for finally deciding on some course of action.

Note that this approach does not specify what is needed for people to be inclusively empowered, what processes are best for constructing a general agenda, or what decision-making procedures are most appropriate for effecting democratic decisions. In contrast to the other two models of democracy, the problem-solving approach starts with the assumption that there is no one right way to solve problems democratically. The best way to instantiate and institutionalize these three criteria will be different in different environments. Democracy is not a one-size-fits-all proposition, and so we cannot derive the right way to manage social cooperation from theory. Rather, democracy requires experimentation with these second-order rules, but within a commitment to empowered inclusion, and recognition that there will always be disagreement about what "democracy" implies in particular contexts.

CORRUPTION ACCORDING TO THE
PROBLEM-SOLVING VIEW

To understand corruption in the problem-solving model, let us review why realists do not see corruption as such a fundamental problem. For the realist, it is impossible, or rather meaningless, to specify a set of procedures that will capture the true, or right, or legitimate will of the people. There is no "there" there to capture. There are multiple procedures that would meet the minimal democratic requirement of allowing organized competition between elites, and the choice between them is rather arbitrary. Corruption, therefore, does not bring about wrong decisions, for the simple reason that there is no yardstick to determine which decisions are right. This is the stuff of politics.

For the problem-solving model, the yardstick for democracy is not the ability to get answers right but a society's ability to learn from experience and to adjust second-order procedures accordingly in light of the commitment to empowered inclusion. One does not need to know what the public interest is (or even assume that such an interest is stable and knowable) to know that some policies or pieces of legislation do not work well and need to be changed. The harm of corruption to democracy in this view is therefore not that it leads to wrong answers or stunts the general will. The harm of corruption is that it undermines this reflexive ability.

Mark Warren, on this score, characterizes corruption helpfully as "duplicitous exclusion." He suggests (2006b, 804) that corruption involves three elements: (1) an unjustifiable exclusion, (2) duplicity with regard to the norm of inclusion—that is, the excluded have a claim to inclusion that is both recognized and violated by the corrupt in an opaque manner—and (3) that the exclusion normally harms at least some of those excluded to the benefit of others. Put simply, a democracy is corrupted when people who ought to be included are deceptively or cynically excluded to their detriment. There are obviously a number of practices that result in such harms. However, such practices are particularly corrupting because they undermine the trust that a system of democracy and law requires (as we saw in the previous chapter).

Trust is, itself, a multifaceted idea, with different meanings. Citizens in a representative system must trust that their representatives will follow their interests. That is, they must trust their agents to hold up their end of the principal-agent relationship. But at a more general level, citizens must trust in the integrity of their representatives' speech, that they are abiding by the norms and standards of their office. The ability to trust that representatives are pursuing constituents' interests requires this more general feeling of trust, as it is the latter that allows citizens to assess the former. Corruption as duplicitous exclusion means that people are made to believe that they are included in the decision-making process but are in fact excluded. The duplicity makes citizens lose the second-order trust in their ability to judge whether their representatives are trustworthy. More generally, such duplicity makes citizens distrust the entire project of democracy as an approach for addressing the problems of cooperation.

The Ethics of Lobbying Revisited

When it comes to lobbying, classical views of democracy see such activity as inherently dangerous, aimed at undermining democracy's ability to track the public interest. Insofar as they think lobbying should be allowed at all, classical theorists of democracy think lobbyists must avoid seeking their particular interests through the political process, and limit their influence to matters of public interest. Realists are far less concerned with the practice of lobbying and mainly worry about the way lobbying can be used to create monopolies and disrupt the political order that structured competition engenders. We follow the pragmatist, problem-solving approach in part because it captures the strengths of both views. The classicist is right that we should be concerned about the degree to which people are represented, but the realist is right that this is not because doing so captures the interest of "the people." It is because having different interests and views represented in decision making is the most helpful way to address social problems. The question of whether lobbying should be allowed and how it should be regulated is one component of the problem-solving "exercise" that democracy requires. The ethics of lobbying, according to this model, will be mainly concerned with not undermining democracy's second-order competence through practices of duplicitous exclusion. We now turn to some of the practical implications of adopting this standard.

DUPLICITOUS EXCLUSION AS A STANDARD
FOR EVALUATING CORRUPTION

It is important to emphasize that, for this standard, exclusion and duplicity are not in themselves necessarily a problem. Given that democratic decision making is complex and takes place across multiple sites, some exclusions are built into the democratic process. Not everyone can participate in making every decision: municipal elections are limited to residents of particular cities, certain regulatory decisions are trusted to experts, and so forth. Furthermore, insofar as we allow people to be strategic with their voting, legislative ambitions, or efforts in persuasion, we cannot expect people to be completely sincere when engaging in politics. Therefore we cannot rule out duplicity tout court.

On a first glance, then, duplicitous exclusion might appear to be a very narrow standard. However, we argue that the application of this standard is actually quite broad, and neatly captures many of the harms intuitively associated with corruption. Business lobbying helpfully illustrates this, as a practice that can unethically corrupt democracy by duplicitously excluding others. One might object to this, claiming that businesses *cannot* exclude others through lobbying because they engage in a terrain that is regulated by the political system (Jaworski 2014). Insofar as other citizens are excluded from democratic processes in favor of businesses, this might be wrong and undemocratic, but it is not clear that *businesses* are engaging in the exclusion or in corrupting behavior. In such an instance businesses may have a responsibility to alter this framework, but it's not clear that they themselves are corrupting the process.

We disagree. Businesses are not passive participants in a regulatory terrain that is set up by the political process; businesses are part of the political process, and often active participants in shaping this terrain. They therefore have the capacity to affect it in negative, corrupting ways. Here we sketch three ways businesses can exclude in a duplicitous way through lobbying, and thereby contribute to the corruption of democracy: (1) what we call "epistemic corruption," whereby businesses exclude others from access to relevant knowledge, (2) "representational corruption," whereby businesses exclude others from the ability to represent themselves, and (3) "access corruption," whereby businesses crowd others out from the political process, limiting their access.

EPISTEMIC CORRUPTION

Business lobbying can duplicitously exclude when it involves businesses withholding information to which they have exclusive or advantageous access. There are obvious cases when an industry lobbies for policies that they and only they know will have harmful effects. For example, in 2012, GlaxoSmithKline pleaded guilty to a series of charges that included failure to report certain safety data on drugs it manufactured in its reporting to the FDA (US Department of Justice 2012). In failing to report such data, they excluded others from access to this knowledge in a deceptive manner. Government regulators believed that they had all the relevant safety information from the company, but in fact they did not. This is a straightforward example of epistemic corruption.

However, there are grayer areas. Technology companies, for example, have access to massive amounts of information that is not available to others, both in terms of how their own platforms are working (in case of social media) and in terms of how users or consumers behave. This distinction is a helpful way of thinking about corrupt and noncorrupt ways of withholding information. Meta, for instance, defends not making public its algorithms that determine users' newsfeeds on the grounds that such information is proprietary (BBC 2018). To be sure, it would be quite helpful for a democratic polity to know how this influential product works, and it may have reasons for wanting to make them share it. Again, this is for democracies to decide through normal channels of lawmaking. But insofar as Meta refuses to do so voluntarily it's not clear they are *corrupting* democratic mechanisms: society knows what they are not sharing, and why they are not sharing it (namely, because of a reasonable claim to privacy and patented technology). The exclusion of the public from such information, in and of itself, is not duplicitous. While it may be bad, it is not obviously corrupt.

The data such a company collects on its users, however, is another story precisely because the degree to which that information is collected, what it contains, and how it is used are all opaque. If a hypothetical social media company were to distribute information about its users for others' use in political campaigns—a fact pattern that is similar to what is alleged in the case of Cambridge Analytica (Federal Trade Commission 2019)—it would have a corrupting effect. They have information—information specifically about the demos, in this instance—that they are not only not making public but actively concealing that they have it and how they are using it. When this sort of information is actively or implicitly used to influence politics, it corrupts the empowered inclusion of democratic procedures and thus corrodes its problem-solving abilities.

REPRESENTATIONAL CORRUPTION

Representational corruption takes place when a business contributes to the misrepresentation of the interest of another group. These are cases where businesses do not lobby directly but through ordinary, apparently unaffiliated citizens who serve as allies (or mouthpieces, depending on how one looks at it). To simplify things, we can think of this process as involving three steps. First, a business has some political agenda, which involves, second, mobilizing people to give it credence and support; that support is then used to, third, leverage some legislative or policy change. At any of these points, there is the possibility for the business to use its influence as a way of obscuring whose interests are being represented, or who is actually responsible for the political initiative, resulting in duplicitous representational exclusion.

The most obvious example, sometimes called astroturfing, is when what appears to be a grassroots campaign is actually a campaign sponsored by a business or a business interest (Lyon and Maxwell 2004, 563; Durkee 2017). For instance, in their attempts to gain favorable regulatory environments in various cities, rideshare companies like Uber and Lyft were reported to have set up or funded numerous political committees claiming to represent citizens of different ethnic and racial backgrounds for "independent work" in Chicago, New York, and other cities. These groups, in addition to lobbying local politicians in ways that were favorable to the rideshare apps, also published op-eds (often the same op-eds, even in different languages) for local community newspapers, advocating for the new regulations (Kerr and Varner 2021). In these cases, those who claim to be speaking for ordinary people—for instance, Chicago Latinos or African Americans—are de facto excluding the actual people who belong to this group from asserting their interests. This has a clear impact on such people, since their interests have now been misrepresented in the public discussion. But this also affects other quarters of democratic decision making: onlookers who might alter their opinions or decisions based on their impressions of what some affected group's interests are, will also act based on a misinformed understanding of the stakes and consequences of some issue.

This kind of exclusion does not have to be based on a full misrepresentation (as happens when paid actors, with no relationship to the issue, claim to be authentically concerned and affected; Monteverde and Dudley 2018). The more complicated case is when actual citizens are genuinely participating in some business-backed political initiative. For example, pharmaceutical businesses can "assist" real people who might be potential patients in, say, sending postcards about issues that they feel passionate about, or calling the FDA with a well-crafted and informed script about their opinion. This is not astroturfing, because the citizens and their understanding of their interests are real. But this does not mean such initiatives are not corrupting. If businesses mobilize citizens by actively or intentionally misleading or misinforming, they are engaging in duplicitous exclusion by obscuring citizens' ability to conceive of their own interests. A case in point would be businesses who indirectly sponsor ballot initiatives with misleading titles (Whyte 2014). In such instances, citizens think they are supporting some particular political cause, while unwittingly supporting a corporate agenda.

Such instances of democratic corruption are often not black-and-white situations: almost all successful political movements involve mobilizing citizens through rhetoric, incomplete or one-sided narratives, and other "duplicitous" tactics. This is why, we argued, the "truth" is an ineffective ethical standard for lobbying. The question is the extent to which the parochial interest of the businesses that support the initiative are disclosed. Indeed, insofar as business participation is concealed, how upset would the citizen participants be when it was unveiled? Perhaps they would feel manipulated, hoodwinked into acting as puppets for a corporate agenda. But it is also possible that they would not care much, given their genuine interest or concern in the cause. The surest way to avoid having citizens feel the way they do in the former scenario is, of course, for businesses to just not engage in such mobilization efforts in the first place. Yet, if and when they do, they must be as transparent with their interests and their involvement as possible, so that people can be empowered to assess things properly and on their own merits.

ACCESS CORRUPTION

By focusing on the above instances of corruption, it may seem like we are burying the lede. Isn't the most obvious and worrisome form of corruption the straightforward example of businesses using their large bank accounts to buy legislative and political access that regular citizens don't have (Stark 2009; Dworkin 2010)? Allowing businesses to use their large financial power to lobby the government has the effect of excluding from decision making those who don't have such resources.

Recall a key idea behind the problem-solving model of democracy: that there are multiple forms and manifestations of democracy and that it is the job of citizens to choose and modify the particular institutions and procedures most fitting for them. There are some very good arguments for why excessive economic inequality inherently corrupts democracy (Saunders-Hastings 2022, 63). As a consequence, many think that democracies should actively try to undo or prevent such stark divisions in financial and economic power. We are very sympathetic to this view. But the regulation of economic inequalities and the role of money in politics are primarily issues that should be decided on through the democratic process. The question we are asking here is what ethical limitations do *businesses* have in flexing their financial weight when lobbying. The duplicity of such activity is important, notwithstanding the importance of leveling background inequalities.

To illustrate this point, note that on some occasions politicians do publicize the price tag for access. This is most obvious with lavish fundraisers where the cost of attending is listed on the invitation. Now, many have strong moral issues with these practices. But at least citizens know about them. To the extent lobbyists gain access to politicians through participating in events for which the event and the price tag is public, the exclusive character of these channels for influence is public and therefore less duplicitous. This is important because the lack of duplicity means that such exclusive practices can be the subject of critique and contestation. The guest list at the expensive fundraising gala can be scrutinized, and politicians can, in principle, be held accountable for the company they keep.

Of course, this influence is almost never fully transparent or out in the open. In order for this kind of moneyed influence to be fully noncorrupting, it would have to be totally transparent, with no citizens unaware or confused about the nature of these relationships and their effect on how policies are crafted. We could imagine a world where people know the corporate sponsors behind legislation the same way they know the corporate sponsors behind their favorite television shows or soccer teams. Even if it doesn't solve the problem of financial influence on politics, citizens would at least be fully aware of such influence and therefore capable of registering problems or concerns with regards to it.

But this is not the world in which we live. In reality, lobbyists try to limit the degree to which their legislative influence is known or detected. Because of the competitive nature of the business environment, businesses are under pressure to create a regulatory environment that fits their needs. In this environment, there are laws that regulate the manner by which they can use their money or influence to achieve this outcome. The first ethical obligation businesses have is, as always, to follow these rules. Our own personal view is that these rules should be as restrictive as possible with respect to how money can be used to affect politics. But this is for democracy to decide. Businesses generally ought to avoid using their outsized influence to tilt these rules in their favor, but the line between legitimate communication of interests and corrupting influence can be gray.

Given this grayness, what our discussion of democratic corruption highlights is a different sort of extralegal obligation, which is the obligation of transparency. Businesses have an ethical obligation to make their influence in politics as transparent as possible. This is extralegal because even if laws allow for opaque influence, dark money, or whatever, businesses should avoid using these legal shrouds. Even if some individual contribution or influence is legal, the general practice of opaque influence undermines democratic processes and citizens' faith in them.

Conclusion

This opacity of business lobbying influence, in our account, is why such practices are corrupting. What makes the practice corruptive for democracy is not necessarily that a particular decision is made in the interest of the business who lobbied, whether or not the decision itself is right or in the public interest however defined. Rather, the corruption to democracy is in that the public does not have the opportunity to consider the legitimacy of the process itself. They are excluded from it by virtue of being left in the dark.

We have tried to articulate this without asking businesses to become "public minded." We don't think it is realistic or even desirable for businesses to cease thinking about their parochial interests and try to think about the public good. Instead, we have argued that when engaging in political processes, businesses have an obligation to pursue their own interests while being cognizant of how their actions can affect democratic procedures, and the trust necessary for such procedures to be effective, and to constrain themselves accordingly.

5

Marketing and Democratic Deliberation

In the previous chapters we have dealt with explicit political activities of business, when they deliberately wield influence over the formal political process: illegally bribing public officials, or legally lobbying them. Yet, as we will see in the remainder of the book, businesses' political effects are more pervasive than the overtly political influence they wield deliberately. Businesses don't just affect democracy when they explicitly target the formal political processes of elections and lawmaking. They affect democracy in more subtle ways, sometimes without meaning or wanting to. As a consequence, the ethical obligation for businesses to respect democracy permeates ordinary business functions, ones in which there are no paid lobbyists, no lawyers, and no representatives of government agencies on the other side of the table. To understand this political influence we must delve into the more informal, but no less important, dimensions of democracy, so we can see how they are affected by business practices.

To start this exploration, in this chapter we consider marketing and the significance of deliberation for democracy. There are no modern markets without marketing, the practices by which goods are brought to the market. If we start with the assumption that under certain conditions markets may be valuable and therefore society should subcontract these activities to businesses (as we do in this book), then practices of marketing must follow. When businesses produce goods for the purpose of selling them, they have to consider how these goods will be brought to the attention of relevant potential buyers. If you are a publisher of children's books, you want to get them to children in the target age group or their parents; if you are a publisher of academic books, you want to get the books to academics in the relevant disciplines. This is why the former try to reach children and parents and the latter advertise in academic journals. They need to know what potential consumers want and how best to convince them to buy their wares.

This is all uncontroversial. Yet questions arise regarding the methods and strategies that marketers can use when trying to do this. It is understood that deceiving consumers is a wrongful marketing strategy, so much so that "false advertising" is a common idiom in modern English. In a similar fashion, others have contended that marketers ought to avoid exploiting consumers' vulnerabilities, or advertising unsafe and harmful products (Brinkmann 2002; Brenkert 1998). On such views, marketing ethics is primarily focused on abiding by principles that protect consumers from undue harm. While these are important aspects of marketing, they are not the only things marketers ought to concern themselves with. As we illustrate in this chapter, we think much hangs in the balance for democracy regarding not just what marketers say when selling products but how and when they say it.

To explain the concern, our focus in this chapter is on the importance of deliberation for democracy and the various sites in which democratic deliberations can take place. While it is common to think of democracy and politics in terms of formal processes and institutions—elections, legislation, executive agencies, and so on—democratic legitimacy also rests on more informal processes and relationships. Over the last forty years, one of the main areas of interest to political theorists who study democracy has been how people within a democratic society converse and engage with one another (e.g., Habermas 1996; Chambers 1996; Gutmann and Thompson 1996; Bohman 1996). According to such theories of "deliberative democracy," competitive elections and civil rights need to be complemented by a general practice of citizens deliberating with one another, and using specific sorts of reasons and methods of persuasion when doing so—and such deliberations should have genuine influence on more formal democratic procedures and institutions.

The marketing profession—because of the information it has about human psychology and demographic preferences, the manner by which it attempts to influence such psychologies and preferences, and the spotlight its messages garner owing to the money behind them—has a huge influence over the type of information we receive and we consider and process. When the thing being marketed is a candidate or a policy issue—that is, in the case of "political advertising"—the political stakes are obvious. The deceptive way in which many politicians market themselves, and the negative and toxic strategies they use to smear their opponents, are well known and much bemoaned.

However, and more subtly, even when the thing being marketed has seemingly nothing to do with politics, marketing campaigns can affect how ordinary citizens reason about politics. To take simple examples, which we will discuss further later, when advertisers try to generate news stories that are de facto advertisements for their product, they undermine the public's ability to trust the media. When marketers reproduce or bolster stereotypes of certain groups, they can affect the standings of members of these groups and how their claims are perceived. Marketing, then, can have significant consequences for how a polity deliberates and the democratic quality of that deliberation, not by virtue of what they try to sell, but how they do it.

It is, of course, important to not overstate how much control marketers have over consumers. One of the great marketing triumphs of the twentieth century was the marketing profession's claim to be masters of consumers' wants and desires, a view that many critics of marketing have internalized. In reality, marketing is much messier and inexact than all of that. John Wanamaker, the nineteenth-century Philadelphian businessman and civic leader, is often credited with saying that "half the money I spend on advertising is wasted; the trouble is I don't know which half" (Bradt 2016). Marketers are generally dealing with uncertainties regarding how and if their efforts will affect consumers in the way they hope. On that score, it may seem unfair to claim that marketers should also be responsible for their even-harder-to-predict political side effects. Our goal here, as in the rest of the book, is not to heap scorn on business practices (in this case marketing) on behalf of democracy. Rather, the goal is to explore different dimensions of democracy (in this chapter, civic deliberation) in order to identify the ways business practices intersect with democracy and the sorts of concerns these intersections raise. When marketers do their work, what they do and how they do it affect democracy in complex and nontrivial ways. We believe it is important for those who engage in marketing to understand and consider these ways.

Individual Preferences and Public Choices

In the last chapter we discussed business lobbying, and how such activity can corrupt democratic politics. Moving to the more ephemeral domain of citizen deliberation and the more mundane practice of marketing may seem like a pretty abrupt transition. However, as we wish to show, lobbying and marketing are actually more similar than one may think, especially with regard to how such activities affect democracy. This becomes more apparent when we understand the relationship between how we reason as individuals and how we reason as a community of citizens.

MARKETING AND LOBBYING

By attempting to influence public officials, lobbyists are invited (or invite themselves) to participate in the collective deliberation about the official rules that structure society. Similarly, advertisers are invited, or invite themselves, to "lobby" our individual, private deliberations. When a legislature is debating a bill, or executive agencies are weighing the benefits of some regulatory rule, lobbyists attempt to affect the sorts of reasons that are being offered, and how these reasons are assessed. Similarly, when we as consumers are trying to make judgments about, say, whether to buy a smartphone and which brand and model, marketers attempt to affect the sorts of considerations and reasons we use to reach those judgments. While targeting different sorts of deliberations, both lobbyists and marketers are in the business of trying to make certain reasons and justifications more salient when decision makers think about how to make decisions.

But there are two differences between lobbying and advertising that are noteworthy. The first difference is in the way they work. Both try to change minds and affect behaviors. But lobbyists engage a limited number of decision makers, with whom they cultivate personal relationships that are interactive and conversational. Generally, it is a process based on persuasion by reasons (as we discussed, the reasons themselves are both holy and unholy). In general, marketing and advertising differ in that they target a large number of people in an impersonal way. Even though they sometimes try to individualize the communication and present it as personal, marketing does not generally aim to cultivate personal relationships with those whom they target. In most cases, they send their message and track how it is received only indirectly. Furthermore, marketers try to get the targets to change their minds or behavior not only by providing reasons but also by finding ways to bypass cognitive processes and push semiconscious or unconscious means (Krishna 2012; Heath 2014). Ads attempt to persuade not only by the content of what they say but also by the images they convey, the color and shape of the font, or the ambiance of the music in the background. To put it bluntly, while lobbyists persuade their targets (sometimes by arguments and sometimes by monetary carrots or sticks), marketers and advertisers often manipulate or trick their targets (in ways ranging from benign to nefarious).

The second difference, which is obvious but important for our discussion on their effect on democracy, is in whom they target. Lobbyists target places where important decisions are being made, what we will call later in this chapter "strong publics." They target legislators and administrators who work on issues that can affect the business or the industry. Advertisers, as a profession, "lobby" everyone in regard to their everyday and often mundane decisions, even if specific marketing is meant only to target specific demographics.

Thus, while it is obvious why lobbying may be a problem for democracy, it is less obvious why marketing would be. If advertisers "lobby" our private deliberations, getting us to prefer one brand of peanut butter over another, is this really of any concern for democracy? Why would advertisers need to think about how they affect the terms of social cooperation when their efforts at persuasion focus on new shoes or vacation destinations?

INDIVIDUAL AND COLLECTIVE AUTONOMY

To understand the effect of marketing on democracy, it is useful to distinguish individual autonomy from collective autonomy. Autonomy means self-legislation. It presumes some notion of authenticity; autonomous people have some capacity to make decisions that are their own. Individuals are autonomous when they live by rules that they impose on themselves rather than ones given to them by others. Similarly, collective autonomy refers to a group of people who together live by rules that they impose on themselves. People who live under imperial rule do not have collective autonomy. They live by rules that are given to them by someone else. Similarly, if an individual makes decisions not based on their own reasons, but based on being manipulated, they live by rules that were given to them from the outside.

Those who worry about the influence of advertisers on democracy connect the two notions of autonomy. If people can be manipulated as individuals then their choices are not their own. If communities and polities are collections of such manipulated individuals, then we have reason to worry that the choices that they make together will not be collectively autonomous either. If this is the case, the mere fact of the power to manipulate—and especially, the fact of a profession dedicated to using such powers for instrumental and parochial ends—raises democratic worries.

Marketers then, by virtue of being able to manipulate how people choose, wield tools that are potentially toxic to democracy. Of course, they are hardly alone in this. As we noted earlier, politicians and their campaign managers often wield such tools in deeply toxic and offensive ways, which are often explicitly aimed at depressing voter turnout or triggering prejudicial mindsets. But whereas the corrosive nature of these tactics are clear, the dangers to democracy posed by marketing tools are more subtle; for this reason, marketers must take care that they ply their trade in a way that is sensitive to the democratic stakes involved. What are the ethical obligations of care that marketers have, given this potential danger? One possible answer to the challenge is to throw one's hands in the air and give up on the idea of democracy. If people are so easily manipulated, too bad for the prospects of democracy.[1] However, democratic theories do offer possible ways to address the challenge and to help avoid such pessimism, all of which center on enabling citizens to communicate with one another freely and openly. In this chapter, we look at such approaches and consider the ethical obligations that each response places on marketers.

Deliberative Democracy

One of the most central ideas in democratic theory in recent decades is the idea of deliberative democracy. For deliberative democrats, the key test for the legitimacy of public power isn't the presence of competitive elections or representative legislature but the extent to which such things are influenced by inclusive and reason-driven public debate and communication. Understanding why democratic theorists have come to emphasize deliberation will help us understand some of the political stakes of marketing practices.

THE MARKET VERSUS THE FORUM

The ideas of deliberative democracy emerged in part as a response to a certain way of thinking about democracy that is influenced by economic theory. The philosopher Jon Elster (1997) explains the difference by contrasting two competing frameworks for thinking about democracy: the market model and the forum model. Market equilibria occur when prices respond to changing preferences; they are indifferent to the quality of these preferences. If there is increased demand for beer, the price of beer will go up, until new supply will restore a new equilibrium. The question of whether drinking more beer is a good idea does not affect the reasoning of the different agents involved when they are acting as market agents responding to market signals. According to the "market" model of democracy, politics is approached in a similar manner: we each come to politics with preformed preferences, and democracy is fundamentally about allowing citizens to choose the product (e.g., the political party) that they think will help them advance their preferences. Politicians and parties, like firms, adjust their products in order to attract these citizen-consumers, all of whom agree to abide by the results.

In contrast, consider the forum. Forums are occasions of intensive discussion about a certain topic (say, a group of people debating gun control). In the forum, people do not simply accept each other's preferences. Instead, they try

TABLE 2. THE MARKET VERSUS THE FORUM

	Market model	Forum model
Nature of preferences	Pregiven and private	Responsive to reasons and public facing
Democratic response to preferences	Aggregation	Reflexivity
Primary democratic mechanism	Voting	Discourse and dialogue

to convince others to change their preferences. How can they do it within a forum? Ideally, they do not coerce people into changing their opinion ("favor gun control or else . . ."), nor do they buy people's preferences ("I will pay you $1,000 for voting my way"). Instead, one presents opinions and reasons in order to prompt others to reflect on their own preferences and to respond to the arguments offered.

At the same time, the forum is different from another situation where persuasion takes place—which we might label "the pulpit." When a preacher tries to convince the listeners, the process is unidirectional; the preacher gives a view, and while parishioners may respond approvingly with "amens" or coldly with silence and groans, they do not counter the preacher with opposing reasons and arguments. In a forum, by contrast, all the participants can put their preferences and beliefs on the table, so to speak. They are trying to convince others, but they also open themselves to being convinced. Thus, when we engage in a forum, we ask others to be reflective and to be willing to reconsider their beliefs and preferences. But at the same time, we commit ourselves to the possibility that our arguments will not be convincing and that we will end up changing our minds. According to the "forum" model of democracy, politics is fundamentally about how our preferences are shaped, and democracy is about making this process of preference shaping as inclusive, equal, and free of coercion as possible. The differences between the "market" and the "forum" approaches to democracy are shown in table 2.

DEMOCRATIC AUTONOMY

How should we think about democracy? Is it more similar to the model of the market or the model of the forum? If we focus only on voting, then democracy follows the logic of the market. Voting is a mechanism for aggregating the preferences of individuals into a social choice. It is a counting or aggregation mechanism for preferences. To be sure, having decisions that are responsive to the aggregated preferences of the people is important (for a sophisticated defense on the importance of voting and elections, see Chapman 2022). But, if we think of democracy purely in terms of voting, then we reduce democracy to a method for people to "shop" for their favorite party.

Deliberative democrats argue that democracy demands more than the mere aggregation of preferences, and its legitimacy rests on more than its ability to solve social conflicts by giving everybody a vote. What is important in a democracy is that it allows for *the exchange of reasons*, which is best captured by the forum model. In this view, the legitimacy of democratic decision making depends not just on the ability of a majority to decide through voting but "on the means by which the majority comes to be the majority" (Scudder 2020, 82). The health and vitality of democracy, then, rest on the degree and extent to which it allows for reasoned discussion and debate.

Democratic reason giving creates a link between the ideas of individual autonomy and those of collective autonomy. If people prefer some policy position or candidate because they were coerced or bribed to do so, their preferences cannot be viewed as autonomous since they are acting by rules that are not their own. According to the market model of democracy, we don't inquire into why people prefer what they prefer or vote how they vote, nor do we concern ourselves with what happens to those who lose a democratic contest, even though both may reveal trespasses on autonomy. In a deliberative forum, in contrast, the only method for changing people's preferences is by providing reasons. Merely stating a preference or opinion is not enough. One must explain *why* he or she thinks others are wrong and need to change their views. I don't just say, "I am against gun control." I give reasons for my position and why you should change your mind. In response, my opponents might challenge the strength of my reasons and provide counterarguments of their own. They might change their mind, I might change mine, we might find a basis for compromise, or we might all agree that we need to think about the problem in a different way. Either way, if I change my mind or they change theirs, it is because we were convinced by the reasons—the "unforced force of the better argument" as famously put by Jürgen Habermas (1996, 306)—and so we can understand ourselves as autonomous. We agree with the outcome of the democratic process not because the majority voted for it but because we were convinced that it is the right decision.

Deliberative democrats, then, see reason giving and deliberation as key means of assuring both individual *and* collective autonomy. Imagine a group of friends who want to take a vacation together and need to decide on a destination. They can make this decision in three different ways: (1) one member of the group simply makes the decision, and everyone else does what they say; (2) every member of the group votes, with the majority opinion prevailing;

or (3) everybody votes but only after having an open discussion about their expectations and how different destinations meet them. In all scenarios, the group has collective autonomy. No one from the outside is telling them where to go. It is their decision to make. But each process gives members of the group a different degree of individual autonomy. In the first, they have to follow a dictate. In the second, those who are outvoted may have agreed to the process and understand why it is fair, but they may feel the decision itself is wrong. Finally, when they have a chance to deliberate about the decisions, group members can feel that the decision is their own even if it is not their initial preferred outcome. For example, they may learn that other members strongly prefer one destination and their own preference is only a weak one, or that other members previously had bad vacation experiences in their originally preferred destination. An open and fair process of deliberation in which everyone's voice is heard can give individuals the ability to view collective decisions as related to their own individual reasons.

STRONG AND WEAK PUBLICS

Thus, in contrast to more formal and procedural conceptions of democracy, deliberative theorists put great emphasis on openness and equality when citizens engage in reason giving. This of course raises questions regarding the practical dimensions of such deliberations. Where does this equal and inclusive reason giving take place? Societies are too large to fit into a town hall meeting, let alone to organize and coordinate such in-depth sorts of deliberation among so many people, each with his or her own time constraints. Furthermore, as we discuss in the next chapter, there is no foolproof way to seal any actual deliberation from existing power inequalities such that only the power of "good" reasons can prevail (for an overview of such concerns, see Gilbert, Rasche, et al. 2023). Thus, even if we think the deliberative ideal sounds good—we vote only after long deliberations where everyone tries in earnest to give reasons, hear reasons, and reconsider their initial positions—it seems impossible to put into practice. How does a deliberative approach to democracy apply to our actual politics and society?

In trying to think through the totality of the social interactions that may involve the mutual exchange of reasons, the philosopher Nancy Fraser (1990) has offered a useful distinction between weak and strong publics. Strong publics are forums where the exchange of reasons is directly tied to decision-making capacity. Legislative bodies are the main example of such strong publics. What's important to note is not just that such forums are more empowered with authoritative decision making, but also how that power alters the nature of the reasons one might give therein. Compare a discussion about the corporate tax rate that takes place between you and your neighbor, or on a radio talk show, and a similar conversation that takes place in a congressional hearing on tax policy. Because it is only in the latter where the outcome of the exchange of reasons may directly affect decision making, we would expect the reasons offered to be geared specifically toward reaching binding decisions. Parliamentary rules of order are designed precisely to usher deliberations toward decision making, and we expect parliamentarians to approach deliberations in a similar fashion (the criticism that a politician is showboating or performing for the cameras is essentially a claim that the politician isn't living up to the norms of deliberation appropriate for the setting).

In contrast, reason giving in weak publics is closer to "mere talking," where major decisions don't hinge on the nature of the discussion. As a consequence, such discussions will be less bounded than the debates in Congress, in part because there is less at stake. But this is not to say that the conversations one has with a neighbor, and what people talk about on the radio, do not matter. Quite the contrary, both are extremely important, just in different ways. These weak publics create the background chatter, so to speak, against and from which participants in strong publics draw on the reasons that they use when making binding decisions.

Jurgen Habermas (1996, 354–58) describes the way weak publics are connected to strong publics, metaphorically, as "sluices": the ideas, arguments, and values that are hashed out in the public at large "flow" into the halls of representatives and then become the stuff of parliamentary debate and legislation. Because of this, the structure and quality of these sluices are important to the quality of democracy writ large. Decision-making bodies must be able to be informed by what is happening in the public sphere generally, not just about the preferences that people hold but about the reasons that they give. If the sluice is "blocked" as it were, then their deliberations will not be based on what takes place in the public at large. At the same time, we don't want the deliberations of strong publics to simply and unreflectively mirror the loudest voices in the weak public sphere. The goal is for strong publics to reflect, but also to sharpen and clarify, the broader deliberations of weak publics (Fishkin 2011, 15–16).

The distinction between strong and weak publics is abstract and a matter of degree. For example, the exchange of reasons that takes place in some media outlets can be very influential even though participants do not have any formal powers; one can think of the incredible influence that podcasters like Joe Rogan, journalists like Nikole Hannah-Jones, or celebrities like Bono or LeBron James have on the sorts of reasons that affect public debate. Similarly, low-ranking members of a minority party in Congress may be a part of the strong public, but not have much influence or power to speak of. Thus the distinction does not necessarily track "power" or "influence," but it is useful for clarifying the different ways the ideal of deliberation can be implemented, and how such an ideal can be made more practical and realistic.

If we understand democracy in this way—as requiring a more "forum"-like approach to politics, in which deliberations between citizens are culti-vated, and made actionable by connecting weak and strong publics—then we begin to understand the political stakes of marketing. Because marketing aims to affect the way people think about and come to act on their own inter-ests, it is also implicated in the way those interests are converted into the sorts of reasons and public deliberations that democracy requires.

Marketing can affect the democratic quality of deliberations in at least three different ways. First, marketing can affect the degree to which people participate in the public exchange of reasons in the first place, which is to say, whether or not they approach politics in terms of the forum instead of the market. Second, marketing can affect the sorts of reasons people make use of when participating in weak publics. Finally, marketing can affect how people choose their position when attempting to influence strong publics, whether when voting for legislative representatives or in extraordinary circumstances like referenda.

WHETHER TO DELIBERATE AT ALL:
CONSUMERS VERSUS CITIZENS

We begin to examine the possible effects of marketing on public deliberations at the very beginning of the process: whether or not to engage in a discussion over public issues in the first place. The focus here is not on any particular piece of advertising but on the cumulative effect of the industry. How can the practice of marketing, as a whole, affect citizens' orientation toward politics in the first place?

It is sometimes argued that the omnipresence of advertising creates a con-sumer culture that pressures people to keep buying in order to "keep up with the Joneses." This generates a rat race that leads people to focus on work and consumption, leaving little time and mental energy to care about or engage in things like politics. To be sure, this is a very broad generalization. But it tracks the point that people's attention to and knowledge of civic issues is often puny compared to their interest in consumer products. Because of the incentives involved, people are generally less likely to want to learn the intri-cacies of some matter of public importance than they are to wait in line on

Black Friday. Learning about the details of tax policy as an individual will have only a minimal effect on a legislative outcome, while waiting in line will have a very large effect on whether or not an individual can get the sneakers they want.

But, if this is the case, why is it a problem? Why should we care whether people are actually involved or interested in politics, as long as they have the opportunity to be so? If people have the opportunity to inform themselves about politics and get involved in it, then their choice not to do so may indicate that they are satisfied with the status quo. This is sometimes called "rational ignorance": citizens recognize that the cost involved in staying knowledgeable about civic and political issues outweighs the potential benefits of doing so (Caplan 2007). The lack of democratic interest is just a reflection of facts about the demos, not an impediment to its ability to govern.

The problem with this view is that it equates ignorance with passivity (Elliott 2023, chap. 1). The fact that some people are ignorant or apathetic about politics doesn't mean they aren't affecting politics. Christina Lafont (2020, 86) illustrates this with a discussion of racial hierarchies. When White people ignore the existence of racism, even without animus or bigotry, they allow the system of racial exclusion to perpetuate. Being apathetic about politics doesn't equate to being apolitical. On the contrary, one's apathy and ignorance facilitate and enable certain politics to continue at the expense of other alternatives. Political elites rarely act without pressure from the public sphere at large, and even when they do, the success of any political initiative depends on it being accepted by the people. For example, well-intended antidiscrimination laws may prove ineffective if people engage in other social practices that circumvent their effects; laws protecting free speech will increase the diversity of viewpoints only if people avoid socially ostracizing those stating views with which they disagree. Or, as Lafont puts it (2020, 87), "Since citizens' beliefs, attitudes, interests, values, and actions (even as private subjects, consumers, etc.) decisively determine the shape of the polity, the chances that most laws, policies, and political programs will succeed cannot be improved without also improving the attitudes, interests, and values of the citizenry." Lack of engagement or interest in politics, then, affects democracy by entrenching the status quo, throwing up roadblocks to other potential democratic alternatives.

By creating or abetting a culture of consumerism, marketing encourages citizens to approach and prioritize politics in a consumer-like manner. When a particular policy, or politics in general, doesn't seem to affect citizens' particular interests, this consumer mind-set can easily descend into complacency, disincentivizing people from engaging in the sorts of reason

giving that weak publics thrive on, and which feed the legislative and regulatory strong publics. Yet this disengagement is not necessarily a reflection of
rational or autonomous interest but may be an artifact of whether people
are approaching politics as citizens or as consumers—whether they are being
presented politics as if it were a market or as if it were a forum.

All of which is to say that how our social practices encourage either apathy
or engagement in politics is important. People's habits and unreflective beliefs
affect the ways by which the terms of social cooperation are reproduced and
transformed. The role of democratic processes is not just to register preferences, but also to instill a particular orientation toward politics in the first
place, a sentiment captured well by Chapman (2019, 109): "Without a sense of
the value of their own political agency, citizens have little reason to become
politically informed and engaged." When citizens are encouraged to engage
in the public sphere *as citizens*, they are prompted to reflect and try to justify
their beliefs and habitual practices. This opens up the possibility for an exchange of reasons that may lead them to reaffirm their beliefs or change them.
To be sure, this is a highly stylized and linear account of a more complex and
nuanced process. But the main point still stands: unengaged citizens are not
passive citizens. Thus, to the extent to which the totality of the advertising
world creates a culture that encourages people to think of themselves mainly
as consumers and crowds out engagement in politics, the cumulative effect of
this industry can be detrimental to democracy.

Affecting Strong Publics: Political Advertising

Let us now turn to examine the potential effects of advertising "downstream,"
closer to the moment where people make a more explicit political choice,
that is when they are voting. This is perhaps one of the crucial points when
deliberations in the weak public sphere can shape the more action-oriented
decision-making bodies of strong publics.

The quintessential profit-seeking enterprise that "lobbies" citizens regarding their voting decisions is *political* advertising, the use of advertising
techniques to affect political decision making. Since firms that specialize
in political advertising are part of a niche industry, subject to specific market dynamics and regulations, we will not discuss their ethical obligations.
Rather, here, we focus on two more general practices one or two steps "upstream" from the moment of voting that are common to marketing practices
generally: when firms publicly endorse a specific public policy or advertise
their positions on public policy; and when firms associate their product with
a particular political value.

TAKING POSITIONS ON POLICY

Something that has become increasingly common over the past decade is the practice of businesses using their economic power to support or oppose a particular political or policy issue like a proposed environmental regulation or a new tax. Following the murder of Goerge Floyd, and the "racial reckoning" that followed, many companies sought to make public their commitment to racial justice, and their support of the Black Lives Matter movement. Similarly, in the year following the Russian invasion of Ukraine, many businesses gave public support to Ukrainians. Businesses may decide to advertise their position for a variety of reasons, ranging from completely cynical to perfectly earnest. More cynically or instrumentally, the policy in question may directly affect their bottom line; less cynically, the business's leadership may feel pressured to show support for some position by public opinion; or business executives may feel strongly about the policy issue in earnest for some other reason, including a sincere belief in the rightness of the cause.

Critics often view corporate social responsibility generally as being cynically motivated by profit. However, from the perspective of democracy, the intentions or sincerity of business when taking positions on public policy is somewhat beside the point. The question isn't what a business leader truly believes or feels when making a decision. What matters more is that, whether earnestly or cynically, the business is using its economic resources and standing to advertise its position with the effect of "lobbying" public opinion, to put pressure on either decision makers or those who elect them. This should immediately raise alarm bells to those concerned with democracy since it represents the use of outsized financial influence to affect crucial political decisions (Saunders-Hastings 2022). Even when businesses endorse positions in earnest, and even when we agree with their positions, such actions should be met with caution.

At the same time, just like in the case of lobbying, there may be situations in which it is important or unavoidable for businesses to share their position. There are instances when businesses have particular expertise on a topic, or when a policy can affect them or their employees in significant, unexpected, or opaque ways. One can think of tech companies who truly know more about the intricacies of modern internet platforms, and the consequences of potential regulation, as an example of a time when it would be good for public deliberation, or even for voters at the moment they cast their ballot, to have the company's position known.

Sometimes, there may simply not be an option to refrain from such political engagement since any choice the business makes implies taking a position on a contentious political issue. For example, in March 2016 North Carolina signed into law the Public Facilities Privacy and Security Act (also known as the "bathroom bill") mandating that, in government buildings, individuals should use only the bathroom designated to the gender that appears on their birth certificate (this portion of the bill was rescinded in March 2017). In response, a number of businesses issued public statements or took actions to protest the bill. PayPal, for instance, reversed its decision to expand its operation center in Charlotte, North Carolina. In its press release, it suggested that the bill "invalidates protections of the rights of lesbian, gay, bisexual, and transgender citizens and denies these members of our community equal rights under the law" (Rothacker, Portillo, and Peralta 2016). The NCAA moved the semifinals from North Carolina citing the "values of inclusion and gender equity, along with the membership's expectation that we as the Board of Governors protect those values for all" (NCAA 2016). The justification for such explicitly political statements was that failing to make them would have been a political statement in itself; holding the semifinals or expanding operations in North Carolina at that time would have unavoidably had a political effect.

Given the resources available for businesses to air their views and thus influence democratic decision making, when is it right for them to do so? The cases discussed in the previous paragraphs show that this is a complicated question. While there must be democratic worries about such powerful organizations disproportionately influencing debate on an issue, it also seems like overkill to say that all such instances of businesses expressing a view on a political or policy issue are categorically illegitimate. This is especially so given the fact that oftentimes silence can be interpreted as acceptance, and thus skew public deliberations in its own ways—maintaining "business as usual" serves to bias things in favor of the status quo in a way that is not obviously consistent with democratic deliberation either.

What is fairer to say is that recourse to advertising on political issues should be an exceptional practice. Businesses should not use advertising to affect public opinion as part of their normal operation. When businesses marshal their economic resources to underwrite a campaign on any particular issue, they have the power to change public opinion. Put differently, while they may be part of the weak public and thus contribute only their opinions, their economic resources give them a capacity for influence that members of the strong public sometimes lack. As we explained in chapter 3, there is no particular reason to think businesses have the legitimate standing, or the capacity to get such policies right or assess such positions holistically, so as to warrant their outsized influence on public deliberation. Consequently, since doing so undermines democratic qualities of deliberation, businesses should generally limit their advertising activity in this "downstream" zone. Insofar as they do or must engage in such activity, they must do so with heightened concern.

In addition to the due consideration about the appropriateness of the topic, businesses are obliged to advertise their position in a way that opens the door to further conversation and that allows, or perhaps even invites, disagreement. They should try to "sell" the policy in question based on its merits, not by, say, associating it with positive images. Participating in public deliberation requires a fair and transparent presentation of reasons and acknowledgment of the business's partiality in the matter. This enables, rather than short-circuits, the public's ability to assess and evaluate such claims.

[BLANK]-WASHING

One step upstream is the advertising strategy of "washing": cleaning the image of a brand by associating it with trendy political or social causes, or by commandeering the language of social movements. Unlike political advertising, this kind of advertising does not try to "lobby" people to vote in a particular way. Its concern is with the product or the brand. Here one can think of various companies trying to associate their business with, say, LGBTQ+ pride efforts (so-called pinkwashing), or with environmental sustainability (greenwashing).

Such "woke-washing" efforts have been criticized by activists for a variety of reasons. One is that such tactics are cynical, deploying the tropes of a political movement for profit. Another, is that they are hypocritical, trying to associate their brand with some value, while not actually altering their operations to substantially achieve it. For example, many have criticized the NFL's attempt to associate their brand with racial justice despite its dearth of Black coaches (Sheinin et al. 2022). We agree. But a focus on democratic deliberation brings out two other concerns.

First, "washing" can make certain political or social views more salient not because of their merits but because of their ubiquity. By associating their product with a value in advertisements, a business can make such a value appear trendy, potentially enticing citizens to endorse it in order to be part of an in-group. Put differently, such business efforts get citizens to endorse or promote some value, and thus to approach politics, in an unreflective way. Of course insofar as we share the values, that may not seem so bad. After all, in real-world politics, most people don't support positions purely on the merits or based on reasoned argument. If I support environmental sustainability or trans rights, why shouldn't we use such means to gain support, given the fact that the other opposing sides do so as well?

Again, there is something to this, which is why we don't want to say associating one's product with a value is categorically out of bounds. However,
the second concern with woke-washing helps explain why caution should be
the default. While woke-washing may help make some value or idea appear
more in vogue, it also makes it appear to be tied to profit in a way that may
dilute it. Here, the concern isn't that the motives of businesspeople may be
impure or cynical. Rather, the concern is that it can get citizens generally
to view the cause with which the business is trying to align themselves as
cynical or superficial. Critics (on both the left and the right) sometimes refer
to businesses publicly endorsing progressive causes as "woke capitalism": for
right-wing critics, the corporate endorsement of such causes shows just how
thin and cynical the causes were in the first place; left-wing critics claim that
such endorsements reduce such causes to mere jingles or slogans. Either way,
the point is not just that woke-washing may make some political value more
ubiquitous, but that in doing so the business may dilute the message, under-
cutting the social and political movements who are doing work on its behalf.

We talk more about social movements and their significance to democracy in the next chapter. For now we can simply say that while there may be
instances in which associating one's brand with some value or cause is justifiable, it generally raises more problems for democracy than it solves. Instead of
trying to wash one's company with the veneer of racial justice or environmen-
talism in advertising, it is better for businesses to simply focus their energies
on their own carbon footprint or hiring practices in pursuit of such causes.

Marketing and the Norms of the Public Sphere

Most advertising activities do not deal directly or even indirectly with issues
that are on the public agenda. These are the ads and promotional activities for
things like peanut butter, a car, or a dream vacation. Nonetheless, even when
the topic of an ad campaign is not related to politics, such activities can still
affect the democratic quality of public deliberations by altering how people reason with one another in the weak publics of everyday life and informal interaction. There are two "channels" through which this can happen: (1) the choice of
where to place advertisements, and (2) the content of the advertisement.

AD PLACEMENT

One might think that most advertisements are placed in politically "neutral"
locations such as billboards, demographically targeted YouTube channels, bus
stops, or TikTok videos that are determined by market research, not political

aims. Yet even if the bases for such placement decisions are not political, this does not mean they are without political effect. Many advertisements are placed in the same media outlets through which citizens get their information about politics around the world and in their own communities. Media outlets depend on the revenue from advertising, even when they are not-for-profit entities. The need to attract ads is therefore a central consideration for those who live off selling them. Some of the ads underwrite traditional media outlets, such as newspapers or TV networks. Others, perhaps most, appear on our various social media feeds. It is hard to overestimate the significance of the financial support of the marketing industry to the media industry, and of the latter to the quality of our democracy.

There are questions about the ethical obligations of media organizations and any other entities that sell advertising space. The need to attract advertising revenue creates incentives to design algorithms that feed users with content that will keep them engaged with the social media platform. For some users, this means that the algorithm keeps sending them videos of cats doing funny things. But for others, the algorithms create de facto echo chambers that send users content that other similar users engage with. The content that the algorithms pick for them—without assessing its truth value—ends up reaffirming their beliefs, since they are rarely exposed to different positions. These echo chambers are generally detrimental with regard to democracy because they create silos, making it more difficult or impossible for people with competing views to deliberate effectively. When the information that people receive about the world ends up making them live in different realities, meaningful exchange of reasons in both the strong and the weak public spheres becomes more difficult (see Forestal 2022).

However, our focus here is not on the ethical obligations that are unique to the entities that sell advertising spaces, but on the ethical obligations of those who place the ads. In general, there are two broad ways in which ad placement can affect democracy. First, ad placement can feed into and reinforce divisions and cleavages along various demographic lines. Suppose that a brand presents itself as a luxury good and targets its ads to venues that it considers respectable and not "shady." In many societies, this distinction between "respectable" and "shady" will overlap with dominant ethnic or racial divisions. Targeting certain communities or demographics with particular products can have large political effects, even if that's not the business's aim. Here we can think of how minority communities are often targeted for payday loan advertisements, or women-oriented media with particular care-oriented products. In making these kinds of decisions, marketing can affect the ability of community-oriented media to represent their communities or can alter the type of forum they are.

Second, advertising may be placed in (and thus advertising revenue may contribute to) venues that are more or less explicitly antidemocratic. Businesses sometimes use intermediaries to distribute their ads to different venues based on marketing analysis. Some of these ads may end up appearing in venues that are, say, explicitly racist or call for the abolition of democracy. We believe businesses would be justified in choosing not to allocate their advertising money to these venues. Again, these decisions require due reflection and must be public. Businesses should not secretly leverage their advertising money to steer media outlets, and by extension the public conversation, in directions that they find favorable.

THE MOBILIZATION OF STEREOTYPES

Beyond placement, advertising can also affect democratic deliberation by virtue of its content. Advertising is often effective because it associates the product with common and indirect meanings. Advertisers might use a photo that places the product against a background of a forest or use a green font in the ad to make the product appear environmentally friendly. In the same way, advertisers often associate products in a way that produces and reproduces social stereotypes, for example about gender, race, social status, and the like. The social images conveyed by these advertisements can affect the way that the voice of certain groups is perceived. When Black men are portrayed as tough or sexually exotic, or women are portrayed as emotive or domestic, these representations affect the way such groups of people are considered in public deliberations, and the sorts of reasons with which they are associated.

This is hardly a novel claim; many companies are deeply sensitive to such concerns. Indeed as comedians like Dave Chappelle have pointed out, sometimes the efforts to be as politically correct as possible can be obvious to the point of absurdity. The point here is to recognize that whatever other reasons there are for being anxious about perpetuating stereotypes, there are important democratic reasons as well. Affecting the standing of groups, and how they are perceived by others, has the effect of undermining the inclusiveness and quality of public debate. Importantly, this may mean that deploying stereotypes that the advertisers themselves find less politically attractive (e.g., secular advertisers in urban US settings depicting rural southerners as backward or religious people as irrational) is just as democratically harmful as using stereotypes about sexual or racial minorities.

That said, it is not possible to expect marketers to avoid stereotypes altogether. Stereotypes are pervasive and complex, so what they mean can be different for different people. There is no dictionary of stereotypes that advertisers can consult. Most images, symbols, tones, accents, and the like that advertisers use are likely to have some stereotypical connotations. Sometimes these connotations are obvious. Other times they are more fluid and harder to predict. Furthermore, the effects of stereotypes can be complex and are not only negative, particularly when we consider how communities' relationships to stereotypes evolve and change. Larry David's persona is, in many ways, a play on old Jewish stereotypes and archetypes, yet his being a spokesperson for various products isn't undemocratic in and of itself. Indeed, stereotypes can be used as a way to democratically empower groups by strengthening their voice, what is sometimes called "empowerment advertising" (e.g., Tsai, Shata, and Tian 2021). There are, for instance, a large number of advertisements that mobilize tropes about women for the purposes of inspiring and empowering them (see ONEUPWEB 2019 for an example).

Thus we can say it is obviously a good idea for businesses to avoid some stereotypes. But for others, there may be stereotypes that groups don't find problematic (and perhaps even find empowering), and there are other things that may not seem like stereotypes but are perceived as such. Thus, above all else, advertisers are obliged to reflect on the way their advertising can reproduce or transform stereotypes. Businesses have a particular obligation to consider the way their advertising may affect the ability of certain groups to participate in the democratic process by virtue of how they are portrayed and construed in popular media, and to act in such a way as to minimize obstruction or disruption.

PRODUCT PLACEMENT

Finally, sometimes the placement and the content of the advertisement are intertwined. One of the ways marketers bring their products to the attention of potential consumers is indirectly by various forms of product placement: the lead actor in a movie is seen drinking Diet Coke, or key scenes in a TV show are set in a Subway sandwich shop ("Subway" 2022; see also Haigney 2022). What makes these strategies distinct and significant is that they don't immediately appear to be advertising at all but, on first look, just seem like something that happened by chance. In the chapter on lobbying, we have already discussed why duplicity erodes basic trust in the functioning of democracy, by undermining our confidence in the genuineness and adequacy of the everyday things and basic terms by which we understand what is going on. Deceit, at a general level, undermines this second-order trust (Warren 2006a).

Product placement, by being deceptive in its purpose and function, contributes to this. We come to be skeptical of that which is presented to us, suspecting that machinations and cynical power are behind everything. By contributing to the erosion of second-order trust, product placement can breed mistrust in the entire realm of appearances. Of course, as with everything, there are important gradations. Let's consider four cases:

1. A business pays a TV show to use their product and feature it prominently, say, with an actor wearing a particular necklace. The product placement agreement commits the TV show to make sure that there is at least a certain amount of time in which the necklace is in focus, and a line of dialogue that includes a compliment on this necklace. The product placement affects the plot, and viewers may be justified in asking how much of the plot is artistically inspired and how much of it is dictated by commercial concerns.

2. The business can pay for a celebrity to casually and positively mention the product in an interview. Again, this will likely raise questions about the authenticity of the entire interview, and perhaps by extension the authenticity of the genre.

3. A business pays an expert to endorse a program that is in his or her area of expertise: a personal trainer to talk about the benefits of a particular exercise machine, or a doctor to speak about the benefits of a particular prescription drug (or, similarly, to have an actor dressed like a doctor endorsing the prescription drug). The danger here is not just for a particular genre but for the very idea of expertise: one wonders whether scientific expertise can be trusted as a source of valid claims, or whether that too is the product of power and moneyed interests.

4. A business pays for an advertisement that appears to be a genuine news report. It may be an ad that looks very similar to a news report, and the fact that it is a paid advertisement is mentioned only in the tiniest print, or it could be a "story" on a news program about the excitement for a new product. This blurring of the boundaries between advertising and news pollutes the entire news reporting landscape and leads to mistrust in reporting generally.

In each of these cases, product placement sows distrust in consumers, but the democratic danger of such distrust is different. In the first instance, savvy viewers will come to question the artistic integrity of the show they are watching. In the second, the same viewers might come to doubt the integrity of the entire genre if not the whole entertainment industry. In the third, the distrust is at a higher level of expertise. In the fourth, the distrust is aimed at basic communication of facts and events. While the first and second may be bad for art and entertainment, it is less directly deleterious in democracy. The third and fourth, in undermining the ability for expertise to be shared and facts to be presented, distorts public deliberations in dangerous ways by undermining the validity of entire classes of vital reasons.

To be clear, skepticism and distrust are not inherently bad for democracy. The empowered inclusion of individuals in deliberation and decision making is also undermined when those in power are treated too credulously. But distrust that is borne of a skepticism about the motives of those in power is different from one borne of a skepticism about the existence of facts in general. Duplicitous forms of engagement like advertisements that are designed to not appear as such, contribute to the latter and are thus harmful for democratic deliberation. Of course, for such practices, it takes two to tango: product placement requires collaboration between the advertisers and those who provide the outlet for placement. The latter also have ethical obligations in this regard. Nonetheless, advertisers should be aware of their power to undermine the foundational trust that is needed for a reasoned exchange of ideas in the public sphere, and how their otherwise mundane practices might contribute to such problems.

Conclusion

In this chapter we have drawn an analogy between lobbying and advertising. Just as lobbyists try to affect deliberations in the strong publics of government, advertisers try to lobby our internal deliberations about the choices we make as consumers. We have argued that though less explicitly political, such efforts affect democracy by affecting how we exchange reasons and engage in public deliberations with our fellow citizens, itself a crucial part of the equal inclusion that defines democracy. As a consequence, advertisers need to be cautious and reflexive with regards to when and how they affect citizens' willingness to engage in such deliberation, the degree to which they promote particular public positions and values, and the manner in which their advertisements might affect the quality and salience of reason giving.

In the case of lobbying, we argued that lobbyists should avoid engaging in processes that are corrupt in that they duplicitously exclude certain groups from democratic participation. The potential danger of lobbying is not just that it leads to wrong decisions (in the sense that they are not in the public interest), but also that it corrupts the democratic process itself. We have argued here that advertising poses a similar problem, just further upstream, in terms of how citizens relate to and deliberate with one another in weak publics. Advertisers affect political discourse not only by manipulating our consumption decisions but also by shaping the terms under which groups in society interact with each other. Advertisers have the obligation to be particularly mindful of the way their messages can shape these terms.

A skeptical reader may come to a conclusion different from what we have presented here, namely that we should just abolish marketing entirely! If advertising, even its most everyday forms, poses such a threat to democracy, why not just do away with it? Why even have advertising at all? In the same way that we distinguished the question of whether lobbying is ethical from questions about the ethics of lobbying, we need to make a distinction between the question of whether advertising is ethical and the ethics of advertising. Our focus here is on the latter for the same reason we focus only on the ethics of lobbying: the former question about the existence and degree of advertising must be the subject of democratic deliberations. We have thus limited our discussion to the question of how marketing, given its existence, can negatively affect such deliberations.

The Bottom Line and the Picket Line

In the previous chapter, we examined ways in which businesses affect broader and informal democratic processes, either by associating with a particular position, or by affecting how citizens deliberate over such positions. In this chapter, we look at situations of "business-targeted activism," where informal collective political action is directed at businesses, either by consumers or by employees. That is, instead of looking at how businesses engage with politics, we are looking at how politics is directed at the business itself. Such activism can take a variety of forms. In this chapter we focus on two of the most familiar and prototypical forms: consumer boycotts—where would-be consumers refuse to patronize the company unless they change something about how they do business—and labor activism—where employees (through their union or otherwise) alter or withdraw their labor to pressure the company to alter some set of practices or decisions. Our main argument is that businesses must recognize the political importance of such tactics and political expressions, and respond in a way that reflects this significance.

Consider, for example, the pressure on US retailers such as Walmart and DICK's Sporting Goods to stop selling certain kinds of ammunition. After two shooting events in Walmart stores in August 2019, in one of which twenty-two people were murdered, more than 160,000 Walmart employees signed a petition to cease the sale of firearms and ammunition (Walmart Walkout 2019). Employees in different Walmart locations engaged in various protest activities, including a walkout by forty employees in a California location (Bhattarai and Bensinger 2019).

While this case is not strictly one of either consumer activism or a labor dispute, it illustrates pressure on the business to change the way it is doing business for reasons other than the bottom line. Two features of this case are

worth noting. First, regardless of one's position on gun control, it is very clear
that Walmart was not violating any law when it was selling guns and ammunition. Second, while employees expressed concern for their personal safety,
the concern was not that the particular items sold in their Walmart location
would be used against them particularly, but about the availability of firearms in general. Which is to say, the protest was aimed at getting DICK's and
Walmart to use the discretionary power they legally have over their operations
in light of a moral and political value that can't be reduced to economic concerns or self-interest. How should retailers respond to these kinds of actions?

Let's distinguish between three possible perspectives that businesses can
use to frame a response to political action against them. First, they can view
such political action mainly as an illegitimate form of economic competition,
a bunch of righteous branding that people cultivate in order to get what they
would otherwise have to compete for and earn. Since, following the distinctions we introduced in the previous chapter, markets are not forums for reasoned debate but sites of strategic action, businesses shouldn't engage with
the grievances that motivate such political action. Instead, according to this
view, businesses have the obligation to their shareholders to crush this rival
and make it disappear. From a public relations perspective perhaps the best
way to do this is by appearing to be listening or by making token concessions.
But this is for the sake of appearance only. Even when done with a soft touch,
the motivation and justification is strategic and bottom-line oriented.

The second perspective through which to view political action is as an
expression of concern by a stakeholder. As we discussed in chapter 1, at the
core of the stakeholder approach is the view that management has obligations
not only to shareholders but to all the firm's stakeholders, including its suppliers, employees, consumers, and community. While his letter to associates
does not mention the protest, Walmart's CEO clearly presents the company's
decision to discontinue the sale of certain guns and ammunition using this
perspective: "We've also been listening to a lot of people inside and outside
our company as we think about the role we can play in helping to make the
country safer." That is, the company presents the decision not as a market-
type reaction to pressures that may affect profitability, but as a result of reflection that follows extended conversation with stakeholders (Walmart 2019).

While more capacious and civically inclined, this perspective is still business centric: it assumes that the business's core values and purpose are the correct terms on which such stakeholder claims ought to be adjudicated, and that
the business is the proper party to adjudicate. As we show in this chapter, such
a view misses an important element of business-oriented activism. Political
activism has both a normative and a strategic element. The choice to carry a

campaign against a particular business, or a choice of employees to agitate or strike at a particular time, is almost always part of a broader project of transforming society that social activists understand themselves to be carrying out. The particular act of protest that they are taking against a particular business is part of this project of social transformation but not necessarily its center. While specifically targeting Walmart and DICK's, then, these efforts are part of a larger movement to change political practices and social mores surrounding guns. Because of this broader context, we argue, democracy demands a less business-centric manner of responding to business-oriented activists.

We therefore propose a third perspective for thinking about such activism, one more appropriate for a democratic society. In this perspective, businesses should neither approach social activism as another market competitor nor manage such activism as if it were like other stakeholder interests to be filtered into the corporate objective. As we have argued in previous chapters, businesses ought not put themselves in a position of trying to assess the validity of some group's social criticism or their account of a socially beneficial outcome. Such activity is not what businesses are designed to do, and, as a society, we should have little trust in their capacity or motivation to do so effectively.

In this chapter we highlight the high stakes involved in the existence of social activism—its importance for a democratic society. Given this, businesses should respond to social movements in a way that preserves the democratic function of protest activity, without unduly short-circuiting or handicapping it. This doesn't require that businesses agree with such activism, or concede to demands uncritically or without resistance. Activists can be wrong, or overly ambitious, in their demands (often by design); furthermore, even when social movements pursue legitimate aims, these may conflict with a business's legitimate aims. This means that businesses need not ignore the adversarial nature of such movement, and can, to some degree, respond in kind. Yet, it is not the place of businesses to decide if such protest is justified or unjustified. This is for fellow citizens to decide. Consequently, businesses must treat protestors, and particularly the message that protestors are trying to make, according to basic principles of democratic respect. This entails an ethical obligation to avoid responding to such contest with strategies and tactics that take advantage of power differentials in order to neutralize the activists and their ability to act in concert.

Social Inequality and Democracy

In this section, we examine the relationship between democracy and social activism from two perspectives. From the perspective of the activists, we look at why they may view their particular efforts as part of a broader movement on behalf of democracy. From a more holistic perspective, we look at theoretical perspectives that see social activism as an essential part of a functioning democracy.[1]

As we saw in the last chapter when we discussed democratic deliberation, it is never enough to examine only the formal democratic procedures. We must see how democratic procedures operate in a broader social context. Democratic procedures and rules, such as competitive elections or one-person-one-vote, are important because they establish relationships of political equality among citizens. But these political relationships stand side by side with other types of social relationships that may be unequal: competitive elections may have competitors only from particular economic or racial backgrounds, for instance; and while every citizen may have the same vote, wealthier and better-connected citizens may have greater power in deciding what is being voted on in the first place. People who think social movements and activism are crucial parts of democracy focus on the bigger picture, and the political and social dynamics that are created by the interactions between political equality and social inequalities.

DEMOCRACY AND SOCIAL INEQUALITY

To understand the normative status of activism within a democracy, then, we need to examine whether democracy is compatible with significant social or economic inequalities. To begin the discussion, let us review the three democratic commitments that we discussed in chapter 2. First, we suggested that democracy requires formal procedures like competitive elections, inclusive enfranchisement, and accountable representatives. These procedures set a way to address disagreements in a way that respects basic equality. Second, we suggested that democracy requires the open expression and exchange of ideas, and that, third, democracy requires the ability to register social concerns in sometimes nondeliberative fashion through actions like protests, boycotts, strikes, and other familiar mechanisms for voicing discontent. In this section, we want to look more closely at the relationship between these commitments.

To understand the connection it is useful to differentiate between formal and explicit forms of exclusion, on the one hand, and informal and implicit forms of exclusion, on the other. Some exclusions are formal and clear: until 1920 only men could vote in American elections; in most democracies in the world today, noncitizens are not allowed to vote. Other exclusions are more subtle. Religious minorities may not be formally excluded from a town hall meeting but will be de facto excluded if the meeting is held on their religious holiday. Or, as we saw in previous chapters, the interests of some can be duplicitously excluded without their being aware of it if their participation is discounted in favor of the interests of others. This may happen, for example, when a democratic process is corrupted by elected officials influenced by bribery. The point of all this is to say that formal political equality can exist but have its value undermined when social inequalities lead to informal, subtle, and de facto exclusions.

To put the same point in a different way: even if the rules of the game treat people equally, the democratic playing field may still be tilted, which invites us to reassess and readjust our thinking about democracy. If a basketball game takes place on a sloped court with uneven nets, or if a race takes place while one runner's lane is muddy, it would not be fair to use the same criteria of winning that were developed for ordinary games or races and then pretend as if all players engage on an equal field. Similarly, to assess the quality of a democracy based on the formal equality achieved by a political procedure in the face of other widespread inequalities misses how the latter can undermine the validity of the former. Background inequalities constitute a form of implicit exclusion when some are placed in unequal positions, with unequal influence, in a game where they are meant to have equal standing.

In what ways can the playing field of democracy be tilted? How does the voice of some come to count more than others? For our purposes, we can distinguish between two basic forms of exclusion in democratic societies. The first is when some participants have more access to the decision-making process than others. Call this "access exclusion." The second is when the voice of some speakers is heard more than that of others. Call this "impact exclusion." In each instance, otherwise formally equal citizens are excluded from equal positioning by virtue of some other form of inequality.

ACCESS EXCLUSION

The time and attention of those who make political and administrative decisions is a scarce resource. When legislators say that they listen to their constituency, or when administrators say that they consider the views of stakeholders, what they actually do is consider some cross section of these groups. To the extent that access to belonging to this cross section is systematically biased, the democratic playing field is tilted.

The most familiar and basic source of such bias is money. Those with more economic resources have an easier time getting (or buying) access to decision makers, through various forms of campaign finance and, as we discussed in chapter 4, lobbying. To the extent that the rules of the game allow the wealthier to use their money to shape political outcomes, and to the extent that politicians depend on money for reelection, there is a vicious circle in which politicians anticipate the need to recruit the support of rich donors and thus formulate positions that can get their support. Simply put, economic inequality leads to inequality in political access, even when parties are equal in formal political standing, whether because of inequalities in wealth (Solt 2008) or inequalities in organizational resources (Winters 2011; Hacker and Pierson 2010).

Another form of access bias is more subtle and involves sharing, or not sharing, a social network. When those who have positions of power come from a similar social background, attend similar schools or religious congregations, or have a similar professional background, those who are already part of these same circles have easier access to their "buddies." Fraternities often boast of how their networks open up professional and political opportunities after graduation; to the extent that this is true, the flipside is that those who aren't members of these fraternities don't have the same sort of access. At a more general level, such networks form the basis for broader generalizations and stigmas (attaching to race, gender, regional accent, or class) by which competency or social value are assessed (Lopez 2000, 1761–69; Loury 2002), leading to a more pervasive form of access exclusion. On an even broader terrain, economic inequality or gender inequality may prevent some people from fully participating because they work too many hours or have pressing care duties. Nothing formally or explicitly prevents these people from participating, and many do. But their cost of participating, so to speak, is higher than it is for those who have more leisure time on their hands.

IMPACT EXCLUSION

But even when people participate in democratic deliberations, some voices are often heard more loudly than others. People who are marginalized often do not have the education or the communication tools to articulate what may be substantively valid positions in effective ways. Those in positions of social power often ignore or quickly dismiss what people from marginalized groups have to say, in part because what are considered "acceptable reasons" are themselves biased toward the interests of some groups. For example, those who benefit from the existing social order will likely prioritize safety and peace because things are good for them as they are; this makes arguments based on other values (like equal opportunity) seem dismissible, especially when they are delivered in a more antagonistic or less orderly manner.

Perhaps the most pervasive example in the United State is the label of "social-ism," which has been used to dull the impact of claims for, say, single-payer health insurance (which need not have anything to do with socialism).

Another form of impact exclusion emanates from how positions or views are presented (regardless of what the position or view is). Dominant groups sometimes have implicit biases that make them disregard or diminish the ar-guments that are made by women, racial or ethnic minorities, or people who don't speak the local language or speak it with a different accent. Participants in civic deliberation may present themselves or their argument in ways that seem, for example, untoward, crude, or overly emotional, leading others to rationalize their being discounted. Srinivasan (2018, 128) has captured this well in her discussion of anger and its uses in the context of political delib-erations: "The misogynist dismisses a woman's anger by calling her shrill or strident; the racist dismisses the Black person's anger by calling him a thug or an animal. These are not mere insults. These are rhetorical strategies that shift the explanatory context for the subject's anger from the space of reasons to the space of causes. The misogynist or racist explains away the woman's or Black person's anger as a product of inferior character, treating the question 'why is this person angry?' as a request for a causal explanation rather than a justificatory one. And so the bigot says: she is only angry because she's a shrill bitch; he's only angry because he's a thug." In this way, forums that are formally open to everyone and even encourage open and civil dialogue may still reproduce certain forms of social exclusion.

THE CHALLENGES OF UNDOING
DEMOCRATIC EXCLUSIONS

Given these forms of exclusion, what is to be done? Because political sys-tems tend to become tilted toward the elite, and because, as we described above, power inequalities can easily disrupt formal political equality, solving this problem is not easy. One possible democratic answer would be to expect people to use their power as voters to rectify unwanted social inequalities via the political process. But such a solution simply ignores the problem, which is that the formal political processes are set up in a way that de facto exclude or dilute the power of voters who are not part of the elite. A tilted playing field inherently frustrates any attempt at leveling.

Instead, an important way to correct for such imbalances is for the down-trodden to sidestep the formal political process and organize themselves in extra-institutional ways to amplify their voices. As democracies further de-viate from conditions of relative equality, the more these extra-institutional measures of organizing people become central for addressing democratic imbalances (Klein 2022, 44; Vergara 2020). Insistence on using only formal mechanisms to effect political change, against background inequalities that make such mechanisms unequal in access and impact, only serves to entrench such inequalities.

Social Activism as Rebalancing

This is where activism and social movements come in. Different forms of political activism, such as mass demonstrations, may be able to restore the balance of power between elites and the people. In this view, activists may be justified in being rowdy or creating disorder not because these are virtuous activities in themselves but because they are needed to overcome structural or institutional silencing of some voices that is the product of the current order of things. Therefore, a democratic political culture should have tolerance and respect for social activism, even when it does not follow proper decorum, because such actions serve an important democratic function.

HOW SOCIAL MOVEMENTS WORK

Using the language we have developed earlier in this book, we can see social activists as subcontractors of democracy, in the sense that they, in the aggregate, perform work that helps address social problems—namely, the rebalancing of democratic institutions. Of course, in the same way that businesses perform their role as subcontractors even when they pursue their own goals, social activists may do the work of rebalancing democracy indirectly, motivated by other purposes. While sometimes social activism is practiced in the name of democracy, other times activists use different frameworks such as social justice or of human or social rights to justify their actions. Many times activism is framed in terms of group interests, like when workers strike for better wages, or residents of a neighborhood demonstrate in order to keep a power plant away from a river that runs through their town. In fact, sometimes activists do not ground their protest in any fully formed theoretical framework at all. They simply feel that the status quo cannot continue, and they want to change it.

Just as businesses can serve a social purpose even when pursuing their narrower interests, so too can activism perform a democratic function even when individual activists' aims are less high-minded.

There are at least two mechanisms through which social activism may advance democracy. One is through agenda setting: activists grab the attention of decision makers and the public, forcing issues and concerns into the public discussion and, if successful, the legislative agenda. This is in response to access exclusion, discussed above; when people have less formal access to political institutions because of background inequalities, social movements are a way for compensating for this inequity. The Occupy Wall Street protests of 2011, while often derided as not producing any specific legislative change, can also be credited with putting economic inequality and corporate corruption center stage in American political discourse, setting the stage for Bernie Sanders's presidential candidacy, and changes to the Democratic Party platform (Levitin 2021).

The second mechanism by which social activists advance democracy is epistemic, that is, by bringing new or neglected knowledge and unheard perspectives into the discussion. By adding the voice of marginalized groups, public deliberations are enriched through the incorporation of knowledge that they have and by enabling experimentation with social practices that generate new knowledge and new ways of doing things (Zamora 2021; Bohman 1999; Süß 2021). For example, in the 1980s, AIDS activists, speaking on behalf of dying patients, put otherwise-ignored knowledge and experience into the discussion, thereby pressuring scientists to lower the thresholds for statistical validity when approving new experimental drugs (Epstein 1996; Bohman 1999). Sometimes the new knowledge isn't brought to the table by activists but is rather generated by the adversarial conflict itself, as social movements challenge social consensus, instigating new modes of investigation and consideration. When addressing disagreements over the status quo, we need some way of understanding how to proceed under uncertainty, and contentious activism can be a useful method to help us do so. As Ronald Dworkin put it in his influential (1968) essay on civil disobedience, "If the question is whether and to what degree a particular solution would offend principles of justice or fair play deeply respected by the community, it is useful, again, to experiment by testing the community's response. The extent of community indifference to anti-contraception laws, for example, would never have become established had not some organizations deliberately flouted those laws in Connecticut." By challenging the status quo we are able to learn what others think of both the status quo and alternatives to it.

These mechanisms are often combined. Discussing the American civil rights movement, Michelle Moody-Adams (2022, 41) contends that these efforts quite clearly communicated the grave injustice of Jim Crow, forcing it onto the agenda through contentious action. Such activism didn't just communicate the injustice of Jim Crow but also helped Americans figure out how to address it: "the contentious politics of the Civil Rights Movement was a remarkably powerful national experiment in legal interpretation that constructively aided in unfolding the real content of American Law." In challenging extant injustices, and provoking onlookers to be outraged, the movement also created the possibility of figuring out what, for instance, the correct interpretation of the Fourteenth and Fifteenth Amendments is, and what the correct balance of federal authority must be.

In the last section we likened rebalancing the power differential within a democracy to balancing a playing field. However, it is important to emphasize that leveling the democratic playing field is different from leveling a soccer field or race track in two important ways. First, in the case of democracy, there is a question of asymmetry in the political will to repair the broken system. If the tilted democratic playing field benefits some participants at the expense of others, and if those who benefit have more say on the outcome of democratic decision making, then it is difficult to expect the ordinary democratic process to rehabilitate itself. Why would those in power want to repair the system that benefits them? Social activism requires the exercise of political power, not merely a dispassionate academic or bureaucratic discussion of what is wrong.

Second, in democracies, there are often deep disagreements about whether exclusions exist, how they manifest themselves, and the effective ways to repair them. While an unleveled playing field can be objectively proven, the nature of what counts as an undemocratic exclusion is inherently contested. Noncitizens are formally excluded from voting, and the lazy and apathetic are implicitly excluded from civic participation: should such exclusions worry those committed to democratic societies? Some say yes; some say no. Even in the case of economic inequality, where the power inequalities are more apparent and relatively easy to quantify, there are significant disagreements about what would be the right way for amplifying the voice of the less well-off. These questions are even more challenging when it comes to the case of the relative disempowering of historically marginalized groups, where attempts to equalize these forms of access can also be seen as paternalistic and degrading.

Put bluntly, unlike the unlevel playing field, when it comes to democratic exclusions there is no referee to appeal to and no objective leveling device to wield. In democracies there is no obvious or pregiven answer as to what exactly needs to be fixed, how to fix it, or who ought to do it. Activists do the political and epistemic work of identifying, naming, and studying forms of social exclusion, and trying to bring about social change.

FACETS OF SOCIAL ACTIVISM

What exactly is social activism? Such activism is often, though not necessarily, attached to social movements that can be defined as "sustained, organized" endeavors in "extra-institutional 'contentious politics'" that seek to address an "unaddressed need," bring attention to an "insufficiently acknowledged interest," or claim the respect and worth of "a marginalized or excluded group" with the aim of "changing relevant institutions, policies, and practices" (Moody-Adams 2022, 24). Based on this definition, we can identify some features that almost all forms of activism share. We have already seen why activism often involves extra-institutional and adversarial politics. But when engaging in such forms of action, activism generally entails two additional components. First, whether explicitly stated or not, social activists work with some sort of *social theory*, which explains how and why the playing field is tilted in a particular way and not others. To claim a need is unaddressed, an interest is wrongly unacknowledged, or some group is excluded or disrespected, there must be some account of how such needs, interests, or groups ought to be treated, and why they currently aren't. The diagnostic story is what we mean by social theory. Some theories focus on the importance of economic inequality and the way wealth shapes democratic outcomes. Others focus on the way wealth intersects with gender and ethnic biases to create a complex system of marginalization and silencing. Others look at the way secular cultural elites and liberal intelligentsia marginalize and delegitimize religious, traditional, or nationalist voices. This list is not exhaustive but is meant to illustrate the point: different forms of social activism share the view that the playing field is systematically skewed but disagree on how it is skewed. They all have a social theory of inequality, if only implicitly and perhaps not fully worked out.

The second component of social activism is a *strategy for social change*. Even if people roughly agree on the same social theory, they may disagree on how best to address the problems. Disagreements can be over what sort of laws, policies, or practices need to change in order for the inequality to be addressed; but there can also be disagreements over what sorts of strategies will best bring about a change to some set of laws or practices. Radicals, like chiropractors, usually prefer swift and forceful realignments, both in outcome and in method: changing one small policy will not address economic inequality, which requires more structural change to the economy; bringing this about requires radical forms of disruption and contention. Moderates, on the other hand, prefer slower incremental change that allows for reflection and potential modification of strategy in case of unintended consequences. Some believe that we ought to work within the system; others think we ought to remove ourselves from the system. While different in orientation, these are both strategies that are grounded in some understanding of what the problem is and how best to go about addressing it.

Of course, this distinction—between a social theory that diagnoses systemic biases, on one hand, and a strategy for how to address those biases, on the other—does not fully capture the complexity of social change. Still, the distinction between means and ends is important. Social activists generally see their actions as responding to an unfair status quo where the odds are systematically stacked against them, and they are therefore forced to make tough choices. It is easy to see social movements' actions—a boycott, a blocked highway, a boisterous march at city hall—as isolated events, which will often seem odd on their own. For example, sometimes social activists are asked why they protest against a particular cause while there are others that are worse, or why they are callously imposing costs on third parties when they, say, picket a business or shut down traffic in a particular place. The answer is that such activities are viewed as part of a broader strategy, a "game plan" of a sort, and that the target of such activities is part of a broader problem, which they are trying to address.

This is a very general and abstract understanding of social movements. In what follows, we turn to discuss two common forms of democratic social activism that are directed against businesses by two groups of stakeholders: consumer boycotts and labor strikes. Even though these forms of activism are sometimes directed at a particular business, it is important to keep the larger picture in mind. Such activities, whatever their direct target and more immediate effects, are better understood as part of a broader strategy based on a more general understanding of social ills. When looked at in this way, businesses have a different sort of ethical obligation from what is usually thought of, when it comes to responding to such activities.

Consumer Boycotts

We begin with consumer boycotts. What constitutes a boycott is sometimes complicated. At its most simple, a boycott means withholding patronage from a business or organization. But it's not merely the avoidance of an organization that constitutes a boycott. If I prefer Coca-Cola I generally don't say I am "boycotting" Pepsi despite not purchasing their products. A boycott has the wider purpose of either calling attention to, or forcing the change of, an organization's socially or morally problematic practice. That is, boycotts are collective efforts that intend to harm an organization (or threaten to do so; see Friedman 2001) in response to a harm the organization is seen as committing.

CONSUMERS AND THE SOCIAL SUBCONTRACT

As we argued in chapter 2, viewing commerce as part of a social subcontract leads us to deny the idea that markets are an extension of our natural liberty or a by-product of inviolable property rights. Instead, markets are best seen as but one social institution, within a large and complex society, that is designed to perform a particular social function, namely, an efficient allocation of social resources using competitively determined prices. We suggested that when people enter the business world they take on a social role that comes with certain obligations and standards—this is what business ethics is.

But if businesses should be viewed as taking a role in an institutionalized scheme of social cooperation, then consumers can be viewed the same way: as occupying a social role that comes, itself, with certain constraints and obligations. This latter idea may not track with our intuitions about consumption. Aren't people allowed to buy whatever they want? What does it mean to suggest that people are acting in a particular "consumer" role? Waheed Hussain, in a very influential argument that we draw on in this chapter, focuses on one category of consumer behavior, which he calls "social change ethical consumerism." He defines this behavior as "the practice of choosing to buy certain goods and services at least partly on the grounds that doing so will create an economic incentive for other agents to act in ways that will advance some moral, social, environmental, or other nonmarket agenda" (2012, 112). Viewing "the consumer" as a role with certain social ethics attached raises the question as to whether such ethical consumerism is in fact ethical—does it comport with the role of consumer. If so, are there constraints on when and how it may be done?

We usually find such action laudable because we tend to associate it with worthy social causes: boycotting Coors because of discriminatory practices, or Nestlé over deforestation. But, as Hussain notes (2012, 117–18), some forms of ethical consumerism can be deeply problematic. In the 1930s, for instance, "don't buy Jewish" campaigns were common in Europe, the United States, and elsewhere. Today, some religious organizations call for consumer boycotts against what they view as progay businesses because of their supposed effect on the institution of marriage. Despite having the word "ethical" in it, then, it is not obvious that such "ethical consumerism" is in fact always laudable or good, or something we should wish to encourage.

To get some traction on this topic, we can ask: what role does "the consumer" play in our society? Hussein argues that markets perform the tasks that society asks them to do, that is, allocate resources efficiently, when consumers choose products based on the relationship between their price and their quality. The notion of quality is a wide one. People can deem one product better based on a wide range of considerations, including their agreement with the political or social values of the manufacturer. These are part of what constitutes a brand. Brands appeal to various things, including people's normative values and beliefs. To be moved by such concerns in one's purchasing decisions is not outside the social role of a consumer.

The qualitative line is crossed not when consumers rely on their normative values to assess the market value, but when they use their purchasing power *strategically* in order to advance immediate political goals. Thus, for example, if some consumers buy vegetarian food because they believe that it is an ethical choice, this would be part of ordinary consumer choice. However, if they plan to switch to a vegetarian diet as leverage to pressure meat producers to treat their poultry stocks better, this would be a case of "social change ethical consumerism." Such forms of consumerism can be unjust—that is, a misuse of the power people have as consumers—and thus constitute a form of vigilantism when used in ways that subvert core democratic political values. When consumer boycotts are used to undermine others' basic political liberties, when they effect greater political power for some than for others, or when they result in the removal of some issues or considerations from deliberation, such movements can be hostile to democracy.

However, this does not mean that all forms of "social change ethical consumerism" are forms of unjust vigilantism. Using the market to leverage social change is a necessary strategy for those shut out of, or marginalized in, more formal political processes. Hussain argues that ethical consumerism can be legitimated not by the ends it seeks, or the means it uses, but by the manner through which its participants decide on such ends and means. This form of ethical consumerism is a practice of informal democratic self-governance, which Hussain (2012, 132) characterizes as "the 'waiting rooms' of democracy" where citizens can "address issues that need attention but do not get on the formal agenda." Those who engage in ethical consumerism must think of themselves as standing in for the legislature and therefore "shift gears and approach these choices as part of the legislative process: they must focus on the common good, deliberate with their fellow citizens, and make their reasons public" (138). Or, put differently, those who engage in ethical consumerism take on various forms of civic obligation to ensure their activities are in line with overarching values of democratic citizenship.

Now, our focus is different from Hussein's. We are not looking at the obligations of the consumers who organize campaigns of social change ethical consumerism, but at the businesses who respond to them. Still, Hussain's argument is instructive. While we do not believe that businesses have the standing to decide on whether such consumer activism is legitimate or not, businesses *are* in a position to affect the overarching process of deliberation through which that legitimacy is sought. Businesses can harm or hinder the potential legitimacy of such activity in their role as powerful interlocutors, and they have the obligation not to do so. We will return to this discussion at the final section of this chapter.

THE STRATEGIC DIMENSION OF
CONSUMER ACTIVISM

Hussain's argument is helpful in explaining how boycotts can be viewed as a form of democratic activism, which takes place against a background of representative institutions that do not fully do the work of democracy. However, what the comparison to legislature might not capture well is the strategic dimension of boycotting. While legislation has a strategic dimension, legislators are also constrained by what is feasible given institutional and budgetary constraints and the political objectives of reelection. Given their freedom from the burdens of governing, the strategic (as opposed to the pragmatic or prudential) dimension of pursuing ideological objectives is particularly significant for understanding social activism.

When businesses are faced with pressure from boycott movements, one of their most common responses is to claim that they are being unfairly targeted for behaviors that are actually common in the industry. In 2023, the food company Mondelez International was the subject of boycotts in Scandinavia (by other companies) over its continued business in Russia during Putin's invasion of Ukraine. The president of Mondelez's European division responded with incredulity in a memo circulated internally: "It is hard for all of us to see our company singled out and treated differently from other peers despite the realities of the situation. . . . If you look in most kitchen cupboards, you will see many products from food and beverage companies that have not exited Russia. . . . If there were boycotts on all brands that have parent companies with activity in Russia, there would be a food supply issue" (Reuters 2023). Given that they are hardly the only internal company doing business with Russia, isn't it unfair for Mondelez to be singled out in this fashion? There is something to Mondelez's complaint, though the fact that "everyone else is doing it" is generally not a good justification of unethical behavior (Heath 2018a); furthermore, given that Mondelez was being boycotted by other corporations, such boycotts may indeed be an unjust use of disproportionate consumer power, notwithstanding the focus on Mondelez. But it is important to understand that campaigns launched by social activists against a particular firm are often also part of a broader strategy. What they are trying to change is not solely, or even mainly, the actions of a particular firm or even a particular industry. Instead, the offensive behavior is generally seen as a manifestation of a broader problem, and the aim is to use boycotts as a step to bring about a wider social change. The choices of particulars—the firm, the specific cause, the timing of the protest, and so forth—are, in part, strategic choices to advance the boycotters' broader goals. Mondelez, while being singled out for its particular actions, is also part of a broader commercial practice of doing business with Russia (or, more broadly still, with rogue states in general). The focus on Mondelez cannot be assessed without this broader picture in mind.

It may appear problematic that activists are using some particular business as a tool to advance their own ends. Indeed, insofar as a business is totally blameless, targeting it in such a way would be morally troubling. However, the case is often more complicated. Generally, boycotts do target businesses that are seen to be, at least in part, morally culpable for the wrong boycotters are protesting. Mondelez was, in fact, doing business in Russia. The strategic element comes into play in that this particular business, in engaging in this particular wrong, is contextualized against a broader narrative about social injustice and—to our point—failures of democracy to properly regulate the business or provide avenues for others to affect such policies. Boycotts, in other words, are generally an attempt to take the wrong done by a particular business as an opportunity to engage in a broader social conversation.

Labor Activism

We now turn to labor activism. A common way of looking at labor activism, especially in the business community, is as a particular form of rent seeking. From the perspective of mainstream economics, wages—the price of labor—will be determined in relation to labor's marginal product. When laborers organize and use the threat of stopping work to extract higher wages, they politicize market processes and in doing so create inefficiencies in the allocation of economic resources.[2] Put simply, in this view, when engaging in activism, workers simply use their power to stop production in order to allocate to themselves more resources, thereby extracting rents.

Labor organizations of course can and do engage in such practices. To the extent they do, such activism arguably constitutes a worrisome exploitation of a market failure; to the extent such actions enable forms of political influence that subvert core democratic values, we may worry that the political change effected is, like that of vigilante consumers, unjust. However, seeing labor activism solely in such rent-seeking terms is overly reductive. In contrast, such activities are better understood as potential forms of democratic activism in much the same way that consumer boycotts are.

THE EMPLOYER-EMPLOYEE RELATIONSHIP

To explain this position, we need to get a better grasp on the nature of authority in the workplace, to better understand the relationship of workers to the social subcontract. A prominent view, associated with the Chicago school of law and economics, is that firms are nothing more than a nexus of contracts (Alchian and Demsetz 1972), which are privately entered into for instrumental reasons, and thus mutually agreed on by all parties involved. According to this view, employees of the firm voluntarily accept the conditions of employment and are free to resign if they want. Since the relationship is voluntary, the employer cannot be understood as exercising any authority let alone an arbitrary one, over them. The employer can be understood as telling the employee something like the following: "here is what I am asking you to do for this duration of time. For your work, I will pay this level of compensation; if you agree, you are hired."

Hence the rent-seeking critique of labor activism: employer-employee relationships are determined by voluntary agreement to a market-driven contract; to try to leverage collective power is to welch on the agreement and manipulate the market. But this "take it or leave it" view of wage relations misses something fundamental about the labor market, namely the presence of power.

We can identify a number of ways in which power affects labor conditions, which a purely market-based approach elides. There are structural sources of such power. While employees can leave their current employers, for the most part they still need to find employment elsewhere. They can quit their jobs, but they can't quit working, and working generally entails working for those who hold capital. This leads to a social theory underlying labor activism, which sees the economic playing field as tilted in favor of those who hold capital and against wage earners, the latter of whom are forced to work for the former. While, contrary to Marxist formulations, a perfectly competitive market may lead to equal sorts of power between such groups, and thus a constancy in wage rates (Samuelson 1957), in reality markets are far from perfectly competitive; employers often exercise monopsonistic power because of the greater competition among would-be employees than there is among would-be employers, which is aided by various costs and geographical impediments that keep workers from being able to explore all possible work alternatives (Ransom 2022; Ashenfelter et al. 2022). The result is that firms are not simply price takers when it comes to labor, but have significant power to set wages (Sokolova and Sorensen 2021).

The second source of power is interpersonal. As Gourevitch (2018, 908) notes, "Workers are forced to join workplaces typically characterized by large swathes of uncontrolled managerial power and authority." Workplaces are not just contractual affairs, though we do generally agree to terms on being hired. Once hired, however, the day-to-day and moment-to-moment interactions that happen at work are determined not by contractual clauses, but by social norms and power structures (Singer 2018). The employer is called the boss because, well, they get to tell workers what to do. While it can be constrained to higher or lower degrees by contract and statute, the power that bosses wield is still in large part a matter of discretion, meaning that workers are subject to the will of another when on the job. Importantly, while wages are to some extent a reflection of scarcity in the labor market, they are often reflecting the way workers are valued by the firm specifically (Moriarty 2020), a result of both the power that firms have to set wages and also the discretionary power firms have over the relative valuation of employees.

The economist Albert Hirschman's (1970) famously distinguished "exit" from "voice" (which we discuss in chapter 8) to explain different ways people can affect organizations and institutions: either by threatening to leave (or actually doing so) or by staying and expressing their opinion. What others have pointed out (e.g., Malleson 2013) is that often the ability to threaten exit increases the salience of one's voice. So, when employees have a realistic option to leave their job, they can use this actual or implied threat of walking away ("exit") as leverage to have their views heard and be taken seriously ("voice"). This is often the case for employees who possess specialized skills that are in high demand.

Of course for most employees the exit option is less viable, since for them leaving one bad job would mean that they would have to find another bad job. While LeBron James can use his threat of exiting to get the Los Angeles Lakers to take his opinions seriously, the Crypto.com Arena concession-stand worker will have less luck using such a tactic. Consequently, there is no real incentive for the employers to allow them any voice in decisions about the workplace, including decisions about their compensation or health and safety.

The point of which is to say that workers' wages reflect the relative scarcity of their skills only in part; in addition, pay and work conditions are structured by various power imbalances—in the market and within the firm. Given this, labor activism rests on a social theory that understands labor relations as similar to the unlevel playing field: employees appear to have exit options but in reality are caught up in a set of economic employment relations that are oppressive or at the very least not in their favor. Strikes and other labor actions can therefore be viewed as a way to level the playing field. While in-dividually, most employees are in a weak bargaining position vis-à-vis their employer, collectively they are far more powerful. While employers can eas-ily replace any individual employee, they would have a much harder time replacing their entire workforce. Therefore, union activism can be viewed as a means of giving employees more voice in regard to the conditions of their work as a way to rebalance the tilted negotiations table (Dawkins 2019).

LABOR ACTIVISM AND DEMOCRATIC GOALS

Of course, to say that labor activism empowers workers doesn't mean that such activism is always a *democratic* form of empowerment. Not all empow-erment is necessarily good for democracy. After all, cartels empower business owners, and gangs can empower criminals. For our purposes we must note that history is replete with cases of unions using their power in myriad ways that wouldn't be obviously democratic. Indeed, unions can also not be great at empowering workers, when they are corrupted in the ways all institutions can be. So what distinguishes democratic labor activism from mere labor ac-tivism? There are two ways, which are not mutually exclusive, to think about what constitutes democratic labor empowerment.

The first way to understand labor activism as a form of democratic activ-ism is in terms of the goals it pursues. Labor actions like strikes can contrib-ute to the democratization of the workplace by counterbalancing inequalities of voice. Strikes are a way to force management to allow workers access to the decision-making table. From a business perspective it is always easy to see such action as inefficient and disruptive means for some parties to take advantage of others. But according to this view, even if in some particular instance it may be inconvenient, the capacity and ability to stage labor stop-pages is crucial for affecting a more equal standing between labor and capital. That is, such actions are democratic insofar as they are equalizing power rela-tions among parties who are otherwise asymmetrically situated in ways that stunt democratic governance.

The other ways that strikes and labor activism can be viewed as demo-cratic is in terms of the way they are organized. According to this view, labor actions are democratic insofar as they are "autonomy-seeking exercises of collective power" (Medearis 2020, 246). What makes strikes and labor activ-ism generally distinct from an individual act of quitting a job or challenging a company is that they have to be done by groups of people in concert. In order to cultivate this, labor organizing requires working with employees to determine, collectively, the goals they are seeking and the strategies they are willing to use. Simply put, in order for strikes to be effective they have to be done in a way that is democratic in organization. This is embodied informally in intraunion deliberations, but also in the formal procedures of strike authorization votes and election of representatives.

Of course, unions don't always live up to such lofty standards. But when they don't, this fact becomes a point of contention among union members, as evidenced in the effort to democratize the governance structure of the United Auto Workers by the "Unite All Workers for Democracy" campaign (UAWD 2023). As we have suggested earlier, one of the contributions of activism to democracy is in experimenting in new ways of gaining knowledge, articulating interests, and organizing. Aside from the degree to which they help achieve democratic aims, union activism is also important for democracy because it creates contexts that incentivize workers to think about both the need for and the means of collaboration across workplaces, industries, and national borders.

How Should Businesses Respond to Activism?

So far, we have suggested that certain forms of social activism can be viewed as a part of democracy. However, just like there is disagreement about which sorts of procedures and rules are good or bad for democracy, there is also disagreement about which forms of social activism promote democracy, and which can damage it. Protest, after all, is neither always right nor always democratic. But because protest *can* be a form of democratic activism, businesses still have responsibilities in how they engage with and respond to such actions. Generally speaking, this requires a willingness to recognize protest as an act of citizenship and not an act of economic competition in disguise. What this means is that businesses are obliged to respect the role of protest in a democracy, and to avoid doing things that undermine the ability of protesters to collectively act, even if the business ultimately doesn't fully concede either.

NEITHER DELIBERATIONS NOR MORALIZING

What does treating protest as an act of citizenship entail? There are two intuitive possibilities that we don't think fully work. One is to respond to protest in terms of democratic deliberation, as essentially just a means of proffering an argument or claim that would require businesses to focus on listening to the arguments of the activists and assessing their merit. This is plausible. Activists do make claims and do prompt businesses to respond to them; so as a matter of pragmatic necessity, businesses have to understand activists' grievances. There may also be a general and generic democratic obligation to engage in respectful dialogue that involves real listening (cf. Dobson 2012) as the concept of democratic deliberation would suggest. Another way of conceptualizing managerial response to conflict between activists and businesses is in moral terms. In such a view the protesters are construed as forcefully placing a mirror in front of management to demonstrate how the business's profit focus has led to irresponsible or immoral forms of behavior. Activism, then, is a form of moral correction. In this view, businesses ought to listen to this criticism, and heed its lessons.

The problem with approaching activism in either a deliberative or a moralizing spirit is that doing so ignores how existing power dynamics obstruct its efficacy. Responding to activism as if it is merely proffering an argument that the business is entitled to assess and refute misses the broader context, which we discussed in chapter 3: that businesses are poor participants in such deliberations by virtue of the environments they operate in; their instrumental constitution, which predisposes them toward arguments that are in their interest (Orts 2013, 246); and the power imbalances that exist between them and those making demands on them (Sabadoz and Singer 2017). On the flipside, it seems naive to assume the moral righteousness of activists. The mere fact that protesters are attempting to overcome a power imbalance through confrontational tactics does not mean they are always correct and ought to be catered to automatically. It would not make sense, for instance, to think of racist labor actions or "don't buy Jewish" campaigns in terms of righteous voices correcting corporate malevolence. Once we acknowledge the fallibility of activism, we see the moralizing response cannot work. "Listen to and compromise with protesters when they are advocating the right things, and ignore or resist protesters when they want bad things" sounds nice but isn't terribly helpful. The dilemma, again, is precisely that businesses are not well suited to differentiate between the good protesters and the bad protesters. More to the point, to unilaterally make that judgment is out of step with democratic commitments.

Appeals to deliberative or moral norms cannot instruct businesses on how to respond to such protests. Protests, and the disputes that give rise to them, are, in our view, part of a broader democratic conversation. Neither the business nor the protestors should be viewed as democratic vanguards or as the arbiters with the final say. Activists have their own particular social theories and strategic aims, which are important for society generally but may not be correct in and of themselves. Similarly, businesses are not designed to address such complex social problems in a dispassionate manner. Either businesses require an external standard they can use to judge which forms of activism are in support of good causes in ways that cohere with democratic commit‑ ments, or they need a process that would produce something similar to such judgments in a democratic manner. In fact, they need both.

EQUAL INCLUSION AS A STANDARD

As we have seen, a commitment to democracy isn't just requiring a series of majority-rules votes on every collective project. Democratic processes rest on, and produce, certain types of principles and commitments that restrict the domain of majoritarian decision making. For instance, the equal rights of racial, ethnic, or sexual minorities are not (from the perspective of democ‑ racy) open for discussion and thus cannot be democratically restricted. This is both because such rights have emerged through a long history of demo‑ cratic processes and contests, and also because without such rights, collective decisions informed by equal inclusion—which is to say, democracy—can not be said to exist in the first place.

In principle, then, this democratic commitment could inform a standard for businesses to use when assessing protests. Call it the "equal inclusion" principle: protests that have as part of their aim to exclude fellow citizens, or otherwise render them unequal, for arbitrary reasons can be ignored by a business. So, when confronted with the equivalent of a "don't buy Russian" consumer boycott (that seeks to marginalize ethnic and racial groups) or a sex‑ ist labor campaign aimed at barring women from employment in a male- dominated occupation, a business can more confidently appeal to the "equal inclusion" principle and decide: "this protest is out of democratic bounds. At a level of ethical obligation, our business owes it no regard, and we are not doing anything undemocratic in the process."

Of course, the difficulty is that most issues aren't so clear-cut or with‑ out controversy. Is a religious consumer group protesting a television studio that makes queer-friendly shows attempting to exclude sexual minorities, or are they resisting their own marginalization on religious grounds? Do la‑ bor unions that target the hiring of irregular migrants attempt to undemo‑ cratically exclude a certain population, or is the preference for citizens over noncitizens legitimate in a democracy? This is to say nothing of the variety of issues that the "equal inclusion principle" would be relatively silent on— environmental practices, wage disputes, or gun sales. All of which is to say, most cases of business-oriented protest will be either difficult or impossible to adjudicate simply by appeal to an external standard like the equal inclusion principle.

ETHICAL BARGAINING AS A PROCESS

And so, in most instances, there is no standard (like equal inclusion) or process (like deliberation) from outside the power imbalance to adjudicate the dispute. In such instances, the most responsible way for businesses to respond is to recognize their power in the situation. Furthermore, they must understand how this power disparity prevents them from legitimately resolving the dispute unilaterally.

When no external standards are available, businesses should view the process as akin to a bargaining situation, but one wherein they have particular sorts of ethical obligations. This may seem a rather flip or dismissive way of conceptualizing protest. When we think of bargaining we think of self-interested parties whose professed convictions are gambits in a game to maximize their returns. Aren't protesters generally more sincere and less self-interested than all that? The point of the analogy is not to dismiss the intentions of activists, but rather to cue behavioral shifts on the part of the business. Bargaining is distinct from competition, in that in the former parties are trying to settle on terms so that they may cooperate with one another whether in the short term (like a single sale) or in the long term (like in a partnership of some sort). Bargaining, furthermore, is shaped by certain rules informed by the aim of mutual cooperation. Consequently, though quite different from democratic deliberation, the haggling involved in bargaining processes need not be understood in total opposition to such democratic commitments (Mansbridge et al. 2010); within proper constraints, bargaining procedures may be an alternative means to arrive at decisions in a manner that secures democratic equality (Schwartzberg and Knight 2024). Businesses should approach protesters in terms of bargaining in the sense that, despite their adversarial positioning and combative orientation, protests should *not* be approached like rivals in a no-holds-barred competition. Instead, because of the democratic importance of protest and activism, businesses have an obligation to treat protests in cooperative terms, and to avoid acting in ways that undermine activists' ability to be activists, or that preclude the ability for ongoing cooperation.

In other words, businesses should treat themselves and activists as "cooperative antagonists" in a nondeliberative negotiation: "antagonists" because they use threats and other forms of combative and coercive behavior to get what they want, and "cooperative" because these are being used ultimately to facilitate cooperation among the parties (Mansbridge et al. 2010, 90). As cooperative antagonists, parties must choose to restrain the ways they use their power based on democratic norms. Given this, how should businesses restrain their use of power against protests and activism?

1. Abiding by Norms of Democratic Respect

First, at the most basic, treating protests as an exercise of democracy implies certain norms of democratic respect. Businesses, or the individuals who respond on their behalf, do not have to agree with protesters on the meaning of democracy, the way to promote it, or the alleged complicity of the business in wrongdoing. But businesses should avoid making the protest itself appear illegitimate or targeting the organizers of the protest in ways that are not related to the protest. So, ad hominem attacks against organizers, muckraking, or other public relations strategies using extrabargaining means to demote the protesters to a lower position would be offensive to democratic commitments. So too would tactics of intimidation, like unnecessarily calling in security or police presence, or having activists surveilled or contacted at their homes.

This may seem obvious, but often businesses feel empowered to engage in such activities because the protesters are doing something similar (like engaging in character assassination of a CEO or protesting outside one's home). However, whatever the ethical license or restrictions of activists are, businesses are not entitled to respond in kind. The leader of a business enjoys a certain kind of power and occupies an institutional position, which raises the democratic stakes of their behavior. By extending democratic respect, leaders of business demonstrate that they understand that the playing field is not level and that they hold certain powers that activists do not. In general, negotiations with labor activists can be intense and can easily be viewed as existential struggle rather than nondeliberative negotiations among cooperative antagonists. Extending democratic respect is a way of recognizing and reaffirming that both businesses and activists are subcontractors in a democratically authorized differentiated system.

2. Submission to Madisonian Institutions

The second way power can be restrained is through what Mansbridge et al. (2010) describe as Madisonian institutions, which regulate and limit the use of power. In fact, most democracies create some mechanisms for regulating and managing labor disputes (e.g., the National Labor Relations Board [NLRB] in the United States). These institutions don't only limit the way the negotiating sides can use their power, though they do this too. Significantly, such institutions also bring in some kind of third-party arbitration to adjudicate claims. This third party is meant to function both as a dispassionate umpire and as a stand-in for the public interest. Furthermore, these institutions create an environment in which both sides have an expectation to engage in continued moderated bargaining.

Businesses have an obligation to respect such processes. First and foremost this means availing oneself of such institutions when they are voluntary and not impeding the ability of compulsory institutions to do their work. Second, this requires respecting the procedural rules of bodies like, in the US, the NLRB when dealing with labor disputes. But this also means respecting the spirit of such rules as well. Oftentimes mediating institutions will set out rules to prevent certain forms of handicapping behavior or intimidation, but which are vague or outdated. This creates the opportunity to bend or game the rules in advantageous ways. Businesses have an obligation to avoid doing this in ways that undermine the spirit of the rules: even if a particular action that would intimidate workers from forming a union isn't against the rules as written, businesses should still avoid doing so. That would violate the general thrust and purpose of the rules, even if it doesn't violate the letter.

Respecting institutions also means that businesses must avoid using their power to unfairly tilt the institutional processes in their favor. Influencing the selection of arbitrators or mediators in a way that benefits the business, or attempts to rewrite procedural rules in a way that weakens labor, is to disrespect the institutions, which are meant to address this sort of power imbalance, not provide another forum in which it may play out.[3]

More subtly, businesses can use the resources at their disposal to game existing rules in their favor. In response to a large unionization drive in its cafés, Starbucks was accused of numerous forms of union busting, including closing down cafés with strong organization efforts. However, arguably the most effective thing Starbucks did was stall: arriving late to (or abruptly leaving) meetings, not answering emails, and generally being as slow as possible in participating in bargaining. As Megan K. Stack (2023) describes in an opinion piece for the *New York Times*: "The company dedicated to caffeinating the world turns out to be very good at moving slowly, and the inaction is devastating for the workers, many of whom are economically vulnerable. Starbucks, on the other hand, faces little risk. Even if the company eventually ends up losing cases on the final appeal—a stage that could take years—the N.L.R.B. is barred from imposing monetary penalties. The board can only order employers to 'make whole' anyone who lost money and warn them to do better." Even though formally submitting to such Madisonian institutions, Starbucks, according to this account, is doing so in a manner that presses the company's advantage—in terms of financial resources and longer time horizons—and thereby undermines the democratic spirit of such institutions.

3. Avoiding Undermining Activists' Capacity for Collective Action

The third way that businesses should restrict their use of power is to avoid interfering with the ability of protestors to engage in collective action. In the same way that businesses often start with an entrepreneur who has to persuade others to join the venture, protest and labor activism are initiated by a small group of organizers who have to get others on board for the venture to be successful. However, there are at least two important differences between activists and businesses in terms of the challenges of organizing collective action.

First, organizers of protests depend much more heavily on recruiting and sustaining a large coalition of supporters, who often must sacrifice a lot to participate. Businesses, in contrast, may depend more heavily on the continued support of a smaller number of key stakeholders to sustain their business, most of whom share a common interest (namely, profit) and sacrifice less to participate (Hansmann 1996). Put differently, businesses require less in terms of organizing and coordinating collective action than protesters do. While this makes businesses comparatively more efficient than their social movement counterparts, from the perspective of democracy such costs are arbitrary—the fact that businesses require less in terms of coordinating collective action does not mean they or their interests are comparatively more democratic.

Second, the system of incentives is different. Businesses are organized with the promise of pecuniary benefit. While labor activism can bring about better wages and working conditions, we have suggested that oftentimes they are organizing for a broader cause. Consumer activism in particular is generally not based on a promise of economic benefit. For these reasons, the protest activities are heavily dependent on solidarity among its participants. Furthermore, businesses have many institutional means at their disposal that help them achieve collective action, the most obvious being the ability to incorporate, which greatly assists in coordinating and pooling resources. Of course, technically, workers and protesters can incorporate and avail themselves of that instrument (Gindis and Singer 2023), but businesses also have securities markets, commercial banks, and other financial institutions that assist in incentivizing collective action.

At its most basic, businesses tend to have more money, which is a very useful tool in soliciting collective action. The fact that businesses can use money to induce such collaborations may mean something in terms of their market valuation or economic efficiency. But the right of protestors to freely associate has comparable democratic values. That protesters cannot offer monetary incentives to foster cooperation to the same degree as businesses is arbitrary from the perspective of democracy.

Engaging activists in the spirit of democratic ethical bargaining requires that businesses not impede the difficult task of collective action on the part of activists. This will mean different things in different contexts. With boycott movements, this may mean, for instance, not trying to enlist social media sites in silencing or marginalizing content that tries to galvanize collective action. In terms of labor organizing, it means avoiding union-busting tactics, or otherwise trying to prevent the formation of a union or a bargaining unit. To treat activists in the spirit of ethical bargaining requires allowing them access to the bargaining table in the first place, which is impossible if they are not able to use all the means at their disposal to organize and collaborate.

Conclusion

A central contention of this book is that we practice democracy not only when we fill in a ballot at the voting booth or visit the halls of government buildings. Rather, democracy takes place in multiple places where people make important, but often informal, decisions that affect the overall terms of social cooperation. In the last chapter, we began an examination of the informal sites of democracy by considering social deliberation, and the way marketing may affect it. In this chapter, we have considered a more combative, perhaps antagonistic, site of democracy in the form of social activism. While such activism often flouts the deliberative norms discussed in the last chapter, we have argued that such practices are crucial for democracy because of their ability to reveal and correct social and political inequalities.

We have developed the claim that businesses should approach dealing with protestors as a process of ethical bargaining among parties who understand themselves as cooperative antagonists. While both sides may have their own interests, and they engage in a direct confrontation in which only one side can be a winner, they must pursue these interests and approach each other within the limits of democratic norms and procedures. Ethically, we argued, this requires businesses to restrain themselves in various ways that reflect a civic respect for the activity of protest and to the Madisonian institutions that manage it. In the next chapter, we continue with this theme by considering the relationships that exist within the workplace, and how different approaches to workplace governance and personnel management can help or hamper the sorts of relationships that democratic societies require.

7

Democratic Relations and the Workplace

In previous chapters, we focused on businesses as unified actors and discussed how they should interact with their social and political context when they do things such as lobbying, responding to protests, and advertising. In this chapter, we look inward. We ask how the way businesses are internally organized and structured—particularly with regard to their engagement with current and potential employees—may affect democracy.

This topic is one of those areas where there is large divergence between political theorists and business scholars and practitioners. Most in business (including business scholars) take the manager's power to tell workers what to do as a given. The employer-employee relationship, in this view, is entered into freely and is therefore just a private relationship justified by the choices of those who enter into them. This, of course, doesn't mean that bosses ought to have unlimited power. The way workers are treated—in terms of working conditions, wages, the work environment, and other aspects of their work—is constrained both by the terms of the employment contract and, more importantly, by labor law. Still, within such constraints, most in business assume that businesses are entitled to assign work to their employees as they see fit. To be sure, enlightened managers will care for their workforce in order to enhance productivity and secure long-term commitments. In management scholarship, this sometimes entails likening the organization of corporations to governments, to better understand how the use of managerial power can misincentivize subordinates to be overly obsequious or risk avoidant or both (Drucker 1946; Jackall 1988). But this is for instrumental reasons (for a broader perspective, see Aytac, 2023). The justification for such power, and the ends toward which it is wielded, is often taken for granted.

In contrast, many political theorists focus on the power wielded by employers over employees and ask whether this power is legitimate in the first place. In this vein it is common to analogize firms and corporations to states and governments, with managers compared to presidents or, when viewed negatively, dictators (Dahl 1985; Landemore and Ferreras 2016). This makes some intuitive sense. After all, businesses are central to society and often have a significant and immediate influence on the daily lives of most people. While bosses generally don't have a police force to enforce their orders, nor the threat of prison cells to quell disobedience, their so-called requests do come with potential material punishments and rewards and may be followed more diligently than the rules set by government officials (Anderson 2017).

Our goal in this chapter is not to decide which view is right (elsewhere we have defended a third view—that managerial power ought to be assessed in terms of political legitimacy, though this legitimacy rests on different moral consideration from those of states and polities; see Singer 2018; Singer 2019; Singer and Ron 2018; Singer and Ron 2023). In this chapter we want to highlight a different point: the structure of authority in businesses can be an important component of a democratic society and a democratic culture, given its centrality and omnipresence. Thus, regardless of how we might be approaching the firm conceptually—as an outgrowth of private contracting or as the replication of state power writ small—these relationships can have implications for the democratic quality of a society.

To explore this, we first introduce and discuss the meaning of a "democratic culture" in a democratic society. For those who emphasize culture, democracy isn't just a collection of procedures and policies (like majoritarian elections), informal practices (like deliberation and protest), or even socioeconomic commitments (like material or social equality). Democracy also requires that citizens adopt certain informal egalitarian norms when engaging with one another. The American philosopher John Dewey put it poetically when he described democracy as a "way of life" ([1939] 1988, 228) that, according to Forestal, "requires thoughtful consideration and active participation on the part of both individuals and the communities to which they belong" that cannot be reduced to a set of prized procedures (Forestal 2017, 151). When we take the importance of democratic culture seriously, it has implications for how businesses are organized and govern themselves, given the large role that work plays in our lives and its potential to help or hinder our connection to communities (Winkelman 2016). In particular, it points toward ways that managers must be reflexive of the authority they wield over their employees and how it may undermine the basic relations of equality that are at the core of the way of life of democratic societies.

We have already encountered components of the idea of a democratic culture in previous chapters. In chapter 5, we saw that democracy "happens" not only through elections, legislative lawmaking, and executive action, but also through deliberations that take place in the "weak publics" of everyday life: podcasts, newspaper op-eds, and even everyday casual political discussions between neighbors or on subreddits. In chapter 6, we looked at ways in which social movements serve to "rebalance" the economic and social inequalities that "tilt" democratic outcomes in favor of the powerful. What those chapters showed was that businesses can affect democracy not just by influencing formal decision-making procedures and practices, but also by influencing informal behavior among and between citizens. Here we take this a step further, by focusing on the more general norms and orientations that citizens should adopt when interacting with one another. While this may be an intuitive idea, we aim to show there are different ways of understanding what a democratic culture consists of, and how it relates to democratic government more generally. Such views become more complicated when applied to commercial relationships, given the uniqueness of businesses as institutions and social settings.

Top-Down versus Bottom-Up Views of Democratic Culture

The arguments about the importance of social movements and the weak public sphere for democracy illustrate one way of thinking about democratic culture, which we may think of as "top-down." This way of thinking begins with a certain understanding of large-scale, national-level democratic institutions and processes—for instance, representative legislatures, competitive elections, full franchise for adults, engaged parties, and a vibrant civil society—and asks what social conditions and behavioral orientations are necessary for these institutions and processes to function in a legitimate way. Thus, according to such views, inclusive and reflexive deliberation is democratically valuable because it helps legitimate and improve the quality of legislation; social movements are important for democracy because they help secure the social equality needed for interests to be properly represented. A democratic culture, then, is one that supports healthy and vibrant large-scale democratic institutions, which embody and advance the goal of democratic equality (e.g., Christiano 2008; Walzer 2023, chap. 2).

But there is a second—"bottom-up"—way of thinking about the relationship between a democratic culture and democratic institutions. In this approach, democracy is primarily a characteristic of social relations where people are treated, and treat others, as equals (Anderson 1999). This is in contrast to societies in which people are born into hierarchical categories such as nobility status, race, or caste. According to this approach, the culture justifies the institutions; institutions are democratic by virtue of their fitness to govern societies with such a democratic culture. In a culture where people treat one another as equals, the only acceptable governing institutions would be ones where everyone has the ability to participate in and contribute to decision making.

This bottom-up approach is a much wider understanding of the meaning of democracy in terms of what spheres of society are sites of democracy (Frega 2019, 376–77). If democracy lives, first and foremost, in the way we relate to one another, then it is relevant not just for elections or conversations oriented toward policy making, but also in terms of how we organize other aspects of our lives: churches, schools, families, and—as we discuss in this chapter—workplaces. As Forestal (2022, 6–7) puts it, "Democratic politics is the process through which community members are directly involved in making the decisions that affect their communities—communities that range from the small and intimate, like families, all the way up to larger and more impersonal associations like the state." The bottom-up view sees the democratic quality of such organizations as important independently of whether they affect the quality of democracy in our broader political institutions. The democratic culture fostered by such organizational norms is inherently valuable because it contributes to a type of community-oriented problem solving at all levels of society

This bottom-up understanding of democratic culture is useful for thinking through the ways in which the internal organization of firms and the relations of authority within them can affect democracy in society at large. As we see in the following discussion, how workers are treated in their workplace is important for democracy not mainly because it may affect how these workers engage in political institutions (whether they vote more often, or are more inclined to engage in other political activities). Instead, the importance of what happens within the firms is much more basic—affecting how employees come to think about their place in society and the ways they stand in relation to their fellow citizens. Because of this, and because we think the "correct" institutional makeup of democracy is not fixed in stone and must be itself subject to democratic reflection and revision, in this chapter we explore the bottom-up view and its implications for workplaces.[1]

What Is a Democratic Culture?

What does a bottom-up conception of democratic culture consist in? There are a number of approaches. Roberto Frega (2019, 382) offers a particularly nuanced understanding of a democratic culture, made up of social interactions with six key features. We briefly describe these features here, as they help make more concrete this idea of relating to one another as equals.

1. A GENERAL PREFERENCE FOR HORIZONTAL AND SYMMETRICAL PATTERNS OF INTERACTION

Generally speaking, when we engage in ongoing interactions with others, there are different ways of doing so. We might decide collectively, or we might have one person who leads or is otherwise in charge. In a democratic culture, the default and the most common pattern of social engagement is one where the relevant parties have relatively similar standing and power with regards to how decisions are made. A social/political culture in which one group of people perceive themselves to be superior to other people, or one in which some people are mostly in positions of being subordinate to the will of others, cannot be democratic. Nonetheless, a democratic culture does not require that we do away completely with hierarchical forms of decision making. Rather, it requires that hierarchies and power asymmetries be viewed as departures from the default of equality, which must be justified in a manner that conserves respect for others, particularly to those at the bottoms of such hierarchies, and not simply defaulted to (Motchoulski 2021).

2. THE PROMOTION OF COOPERATIVE RELATIONS THAT ACKNOWLEDGE THE REALITY OF INTERDEPENDENCE

Particularly in places where markets and commerce play a large role in our lives, it is easy to think of society as merely a collection of individuals and to romanticize our independence. It is of course important for us to respect people's individuality and enable everyone to decide how to live their lives independently from the burdening influence of others. That said, an over-emphasis on the individual can obscure the ways in which we live in cooperation with others and constantly oscillate between greater and lesser degrees of dependence. As Martha Nussbaum (2002, 136) put it in an influential essay on the continuum between the healthy bodied and the disabled: "As the life span increases, the relative independence many of us enjoy looks more and more like a temporary condition, a phase of life that we move into gradually, and which we all too quickly begin to leave. Even in our prime, many of us encounter shorter or longer periods of extreme dependency on others—after surgery or a severe injury, or during a period of depression or acute mental stress." A democratic culture is one where independence is not fetishized and used as a way of short-circuiting collective problem solving. Instead, the ways in which we live with, and depend on, one another are made central to considerations of how we ought to work together.

3. EQUAL PARTICIPATION IN PRACTICES OF INQUIRY AND DECISION MAKING

Similarly to (1) above, when we are trying to find out facts and make decisions as groups, there are numerous ways of doing so. A democratic culture encourages equal and inclusive participation in such endeavors, to the greatest extent possible (Pateman 2012). It is worth noting that this implies two different things: The first is that those who might otherwise have a privileged place in inquiry and decision making avoid putting up barriers that prevent others from participating. But it also implies, second, that those who might otherwise be inclined to let others make decisions for them actively try to participate and avoid the option of passivity. Again, this isn't to say that such practices always hold sway in every instance, but rather that this is the baseline expectation and that departures from this be done consciously and with reason.

4. DELIBERATION IS PRIVILEGED OVER OTHER METHODS OF MAKING DECISIONS

As a consequence of (2) and (3), a democratic culture tends to privilege deliberation (which we described in chapter 5 as the giving and taking of reasons) over other methods of decision making, like secret voting, mere preference statement, or bargaining. Deliberation attempts to build in respect for the equal standing of others participating and acknowledges the mutual dependence of all participating, by pushing everyone to address each other as equals.

5. PARTICIPANTS ARE EFFECTIVELY INTEGRATED INTO SOCIAL PRACTICES

While the significance of being included in formal decision-making processes is a fairly intuitive feature of democracy, a democratic culture also consists in something more informal. A group or organization is never just a series of formal processes and procedures but involves more informal social engagements and processes. While formal school board meetings may be where official decisions get made, often the parents kibbitzing among themselves after morning drop-off deeply influences who votes on what in those meetings. A democratic culture is one in which all group members are integrated into these more informal social processes as well. This is for two reasons. First, because these processes often shape the *nature* of formal decision making, decision making is affected by these more *in*formal interactions. But second, it is because inclusion in such processes encourages individuals to identify with the group and to internalize the group's collective goals, further enabling the recognition and embracing of interdependence (see [2] above).

6. "THE FUNCTIONAL DIMENSION OF PROBLEM-SOLVING IS INTEGRATED WITH THE EXPRESSIVE DIMENSION OF SELF-REALIZATION"

This is a bit more complicated of an idea, but also a very important one. People cooperate with one another—whether in formal organizations or in more informal ways—for a variety of reasons. Some are instrumental—I go to work to make money; I work with a charity to effect some good in the world; and so on. But, being social creatures, we also work with others because of the intrinsic value in engaging and cooperating with others (Fligstein and McAdam 2012). A democratic culture is one where the instrumental and functional aspects of problem solving—that is, to achieve some end we all want to achieve—is connected to the intrinsic value we get in being part of a group. That is, we get personal value from participating in the processes of solving problems for the group, and the group solves problems in a way that respects and nurtures the good that individuals get from the process.

Of course, none of these will ever be fully or finally realized. A democratic culture is one where these goals are sought and animate the ways in which we engage with one another.

Democratic Culture within Institutions

We are interested in this idea of a bottom-up understanding of democratic culture because it helps us think through the democratic stakes of workplaces—when, and to what extent, hierarchies in the workplace are compatible with democratic relations generally. Yet the application of this broad concern with democratic culture is complicated by the fact of institutional distinctiveness or functional differentiation (as discussed in chapter 1), which reminds us that different institutions will function according to different norms in order to help achieve social objectives. As we saw, markets and firms function according to norms of competition and hierarchy, which are in tension with the way we go about our lives in most other instances. Figuring out how democratic norms and relations apply to specific sorts of contexts like these requires thinking about the specific nature of the context and its broader social significance. We then can consider how these more general norms may be refracted through such distinctions so their applications are appropriate and not undermining.

To get a better grasp of this, it might be helpful to look at other social institutions. Think about families or schools in democratic societies. Most families and schools are organized hierarchically: parents or teachers make decisions for (and, at least ideally, in the interest of) children and students. However, there is a significant variation in the way these hierarchies are played out. Some families and schools are organized more like a dictatorship where students or children cannot reason about the rules they are required to follow. In others, parents and teachers are more open to explaining their decisions, listening to the children or students, and making changes accordingly. Others build democratic practices into the way they run themselves, for instance by taking votes on the curriculum or by seeking consensus on important family decisions.

Intuitively, it is quite clear that families or schools that run as violent dictatorships are not compatible with democracy. But are there any sorts of hierarchies in these settings that can be compatible with a democratic way of life? How deep must democratic culture extend (Brighouse 2006; Brighouse and Swift 2014)? Surely raising safe and thriving children is important for a democratic society, and, as most parents can attest, keeping children safe and healthy sometimes involves making executive decisions against the wishes of your child or resorting to the classic "because I said so." Even the most enlightened and democratically minded teachers often will find a need to develop a curriculum and assignments based on their expertise and experience, even if their pupils don't agree with them.

Furthermore, democratic practices take time and effort that might otherwise be allocated to other educational goals. There may be a good argument for why a math class should spend its time learning algebra and not cocreating the curriculum. Surely the existence of these more "authoritarian" practices—teachers prioritizing trigonometry and parents prioritizing bathtime over voting—doesn't inherently undermine a democratic culture, especially given their instrumental role in achieving goals—the raising of children, the education of citizens—that are democratically valuable. To what extent can we tolerate these more local deviations from democratic culture for instrumental reasons before we start to corrode that democratic culture?

Ultimately the answer will depend on the specific institutions and organizations. Here we are thinking about workplaces: to what extent can a democratic culture tolerate or accommodate departures from democratic norms within the workplace? In answering the question it is important to note that businesses differ from schools and families in at least two important ways. First, at least in their aspirational or ideal forms, there is no built-in conflict of interest between teachers and students or parents and children. Parents generally have an intrinsic desire to do right by their children; teachers generally, both by professional socialization and by selection effect, tend to be concerned with their students' interests for their own sake. Of course, this isn't to deny that parents and teachers sometimes cut corners for personal reasons (as both teachers and parents, we can assure you that they do). Still, parents and teachers don't generally approach their children or students in purely instrumental terms. As a consequence, even when they are excluded from democratic participation, there is at least some reason to think that their interests and good are being considered.

The case is categorically different for businesses, where stakeholders compete over the allocation of the proceeds from the shared enterprise and there is no presumption of shared interests among all stakeholders, which indeed often conflict (Orts and Strudler 2002, 219). Human resources rhetoric aside, managers do not see themselves as primarily being in the business of promoting the welfare of their employees; concern for employees is instrumental to the primary goal of the business, namely profit. Similarly, while employees may express loyalty to a business, this is generally contingent on and secondary to their primary concern of getting a good wage. Given this, there is good reason to have less faith that authority will spontaneously be used in a way that is in the interest of those being governed; managers will tend to govern workers with an eye toward the good of the business and concern themselves with workers' well-being only insofar as it is helpful in that purpose. Thus the exclusion of workers from democratic participation is less likely to be compensated for by a deep concern for their good.

Second, and on the other hand, businesses are more voluntary associations than families or schools. While it is certainly possible for a student to leave school, and in some extreme cases for children to leave their families, it is generally both extremely difficult and costly to do. In contrast, as we have seen in previous chapters, "exit" is the bread and butter of market activity. In theory, employees who are not satisfied with their particular boss or the governance structure of their workplace are free to leave. Perhaps more important than the ability to "exit," however, is the condition of entry: contracts and legal protections. Precisely because stakeholder interests are not aligned with that of management, there are other instruments used to protect and advance different stakeholders' interests. As Boatright (2006, 118) put it: "management decision making is a weaker form of protection than legally enforceable contracts or legal rules. When such contracts and rules are available, they are more likely to be preferred." While a democratic culture prefers participation, horizontal relationships, and the like, departure from them may be easier to justify when parties' standing can be secured through either ease of exit or legal-contractual protection. Given this, democratic considerations may be less important in the workplace than in families or schools.

However, as we have already seen in chapter 6 when discussing labor activism, the power of workers to exit has some significant limits, which are tied to democratic culture of society at large. While employees may leave a particular workplace, they are still bound to an entire economic structure in which their collective power is restricted. Telling people who live in a city ruled by an undemocratic machine government that they are free to move to the suburbs doesn't justify the city' undemocratic quality, especially if neighboring cities and towns are governed similarly (or are influenced by the larger city). While some employees can have choices like working in a co-op or starting their own business, for many workers, their only choice may be under which hierarchy to work. Therefore, while the voluntary nature of working at a particular business is important to consider, it is also important not to overstate it: insofar as workers are tied up in larger institutions where they are subject to the authority of managers, contractual protections or the ability to exit may not really address the concerns of democratic culture.

Given all this, the question of whether hierarchical workplaces can be compatible with a democratic culture is complicated. On the one hand, the fact that some other sorts of institutions are less democratic does not mean workplaces are similarly entitled to be, given the instrumental sort of thing a business is. On the other hand, given the nature of the economy in which a workplace is situated, there are overarching concerns that either compensate for or justify the attenuation of democratic norms in these more local settings. In the remainder of the chapter, we consider two ways of thinking through the question. First, we consider whether hierarchies in business are generally justified, and why there may be strong reasons to make businesses more aligned with the norms of democratic culture. Second, accepting the existence of hierarchical businesses, we consider the ways in which authority must be wielded to be compatible with a general respect for the broader democratic culture of a society.

Why Workplace Hierarchies?

Most workplaces are organized hierarchically. When employees enter the office, they do not decide what they want to do. They follow directives from supervisors or managers. These directions may be very specific (finish this project by the end of the day) or quite general (when working on projects, follow these guidelines). Even when employees have some discretion on how to discharge their duties, this discretion is limited. They simply cannot do whatever they like, because they work for a business that pays them for their time, not for the outputs; whereas subcontractors are paid to complete some task in the manner they choose, employment contracts are open-ended by design, such that employees are paid to be at work and follow organizational direction. Furthermore, even the bosses are limited in their discretion. They have to follow mandates from owners or investors, depending on the particular organizational form of the business, as well as abide by legal and contractual constraint. They, too, cannot do whatever they like.

This is often taken for granted. But it should be asked: Why do we have these hierarchies? Given our democratic commitments to liberty and democracy, why is our economy dominated by what Elizabeth Anderson (2017, 37) described as these "communist dictatorships in our midst"? There are, generally speaking, two arguments for hierarchies in the workplace, both of which center on the efficiency advantages. The first is what we may call the argument from decision making: that hierarchies enable businesses to determine their goals more efficiently than alternatives. The second is what we may call the argument from competency: that hierarchies enable businesses to meet their goals more efficiently. On both accounts hierarchies in workplaces are justified on instrumental terms—by virtue of being hierarchically organized, businesses are able to more efficiently benefit all those involved, as well as contribute to the economy.

THE ARGUMENT FROM DECISION MAKING

The argument from decision making contends that excluding certain groups from governance decisions enables a more efficient organization. Businesses involve the cooperative interactions of a number of stakeholder groups— capital providers, employees, raw goods suppliers, and customers—in principle because such cooperation benefits all these groups. When a business makes a decision it will tend to affect these different groups of stakeholders in different ways. As we saw above, a democratic culture generally privileges organizations where such stakeholders would be able to participate in the formal and informal life of decision making on equal and symmetrical terms. Yet, as Henry Hansmann (1996) famously argued, giving all stakeholders a voice in making business decisions increases the cost of doing business by increasing disagreements; this can lead to suboptimal management decisions by foregoing time-sensitive options in service of squelching disagreements. Deliberating about the purpose of an organization is difficult regardless of the particular purpose. Anyone who has attended a meeting where the purpose of an organization is discussed—be it a meeting at a church, among members of a social movement, or at a faculty meeting—can attest to that. The purpose of the business can be continually negotiated by the different stakeholders, or businesses can choose to pursue a predefined purpose. The latter alternative tends to be much more efficient in terms of the costs of deliberation.

As a consequence, businesses tend to assign ownership to one stakeholder group. Each stakeholder group in the business has a more limited range of interests (e.g., shareholders want to maximize share value or dividends; workers want higher wages or better conditions, etc.). Therefore giving decision-making rights to only one group tends to reduce the amount of conflict and thus the cost of managing such conflict. Put differently, the more clarity there is in defining the purpose of businesses—that is, clarity over whose interests management ought to prioritize—the more efficiently that purpose can be pursued.

However, giving decision-making rights to any particular stakeholder group is by definition exclusive. It prioritizes the welfare or interest of some groups over others. If the purpose of the business is to get a return to investors, as is the case for most businesses, the voice and interests of other stakeholders are excluded from such considerations, left to be protected by laws and contracts. We can think of the hierarchy created by focusing on the interest of one group of stakeholders as creating a hierarchy of reasons: by giving one group of stakeholders the right to participate in decision-making processes, we prioritize the sorts of reasons they bring to the table, allowing the organization to be more efficiently governed and, as a consequence, according to this line of argument, to benefit all involved in the long run— including those from other stakeholder groups who instead contract with this more efficiently governed firm (Boatright 2006).

In this view, whatever the merits of a democratic culture, it would seem radically unfit for the workplace. Businesses exist to help secure the mutual benefit for all those contracting with them. One of the ways they ensure the maximal benefit for all involved is precisely by *limiting* who can participate in governing the firm. It is worth noting of course that efficiency is not the only thing that matters. The same arguments for limiting participants in order to

reduce decision-making costs can be applied to urban and national governments! Excluding particular class, gender, or racial groups from democratic
citizenship may increase the speed with which governments make decisions,
but we rightly don't see that as a bargain worth taking. Businesses are arguably different because their stakeholders voluntarily submit themselves to
them and because their purpose isn't to establish law but to benefit those involved. Thus, though not the only thing to be considered, the efficient governance of the firm does seem to be something that must be taken into account.

The other justification for hierarchies is their competency in helping the organization achieve its purpose. While the decision-making argument is about
the efficiency of a hierarchical structure for the way business organizations
set their goals, the competence argument refers to the efficiency of meeting
these goals. The late Nobel-winning economist Ronald Coase famously argued (1937) that firms are organized as they are because they help reduce
transaction costs—that is, the costs associated with doing business. The basic
idea is that instead of bickering over prices for this or that task, or haggling
over specific terms of a specific contract, the employment contract with the
firm is left open-ended: in return for pay, workers agree to be directed by a
manager.

As organizations, businesses have hierarchical structures in which some
groups of employees—managers or supervisors—have the authority to instruct others on what to do, and this is because it is seen as the most efficient
way to facilitate these tasks: first, because of the cost-reducing nature of hierarchical decision making; and second, because of the supervisor's experience,
credentials, or proven track record that makes him or her competent to command such authority. For this reason, implicit in any management scheme is
an empirical argument about what works best in a particular context—that
this scheme of authority is justified because it enables the business enterprise
to achieve its goals. Again, this will depend on the details of each business.
In some settings, or for some business purposes, it might be better to have a
supervisor that assigns tasks and monitors performance; in others, it might
be better to give employees autonomy to work individually or make decisions in teams. The empirical question is which one turns out to work better
for the business purpose. It is worth noting that such an argument does not
justify *any* sort of managerial authority: that some particular person is justified on efficiency grounds for managing others does not mean he or she gets
to be cruel, reckless, harmful, or demeaning when doing so. The competency

argument presents a justification for why workplace hierarchy could be acceptable and justified, not why that authority is always to be accepted.

Increasing Democracy in the Workplace

We have seen two different ways of thinking about the justification of hierarchy in businesses: some stakeholder groups are given rights to govern over others so that decision making can be done more efficiently; and managers are given authority over workers in order to more efficiently accomplish a set of tasks or goals. While important, neither of these arguments fully rules out the plausibility of democratic relationship in the workplace. As we wish to show, even taking efficiency concerns seriously, there is good reason to try to inject more democracy into the governance of the firm (as we discuss in this section), and to consider the democratic effects of how managerial authority is wielded (in the next section).

THE EFFICIENCY OF WORKPLACE DEMOCRACY

In most capitalist countries, shareholders and capital providers are the group of stakeholders that tend to govern business enterprises. But, there are also models of business that place the interest of employees as the main purpose of the business and accordingly have a governance structure that allows employees to have a voice in board decisions, either directly or through elected representatives. This form of business is generally referred to as a worker cooperative or an employee-owned firm (Dow 1993; Hansmann 1996).

In addition, there are businesses that structure their board in a way that gives voice to different stakeholders, for example by having some number of board seats elected by employees (Frega, Herzog, and Neuhäuser 2019). The argument for the mixed structure is that the benefit of making decisions that take into account the needs of the different stakeholders outweighs the added cost of negotiation. The sociologist and political philosopher Isabelle Ferreras (2017), for instance, has contended that businesses are best understood as an amalgam of two different sorts of reasons—the instrumental reasons that capital providers emphasize, and the expressive reasons (that emphasize intrinsic personal meaning, as discussed above) that labor brings to the table. As a consequence, in order to capture both of these necessary aspects of the firm, businesses ought to be governed by two chambers—not unlike the US Congress—with one board representing labor and one board representing shareholders.

There is a similar argument to be made regarding the authority practiced among managers and workers. While there may be efficiency reasons for a

hierarchical structure of the workplace, there are also efficiency arguments
for creating workplaces governed by norms of cooperation, collaboration, and
employee empowerment. Though gulag-like workplaces may run smoothly in
managing simple tasks, they tend not to be very competent in complex, dynamic
tasks that require flexibility and adaptability. Hence the development of flattened
hierarchies and formless organizations in modern management technique to
harness diversity in experience and values (Stark 2009). Giving employees more
autonomy in how they do their job and creating a collaborative and cooperative
work environment can encourage internal motivation, job satisfaction, responsibility, accountability, and creative problem solving (Krüger 2023).

All of which is to say, while one might justify hierarchical, nondemocratic
firms on efficiency grounds, such grounds do not fully answer the question,
as there can be efficiencies found in other forms of governance and organization. There is voluminous literature and there are heated debates on the merits of different models of governing businesses, and covering it is beyond the
scope of this present discussion. We don't pretend to present the case for one
particular organizational form as *the one* most able to balance concerns for
efficiency and democracy; we have neither the space for such an argument—
which would take a book in itself—nor the desire, since we generally think
different sorts of organizations will be needed to address different sorts of
problems in different contexts. That said, we do think that, at the very least,
firms in which workers are involved in governance are a viable form of business (Malleson 2014), and could be made more competitive through different
institutions that make capital more available, enable workers to diversify their
investments, and so forth (see Dow 2003; Singer 2019).

WORKPLACE DEMOCRACY AND DEMOCRATIC CULTURE

But efficiency advantages aside, worker-managed firms are preferable from
the perspective of democracy. While businesses may not have an ethical obligation to democracy to be governed as worker cooperatives, such cooperatives would appear to benefit a democratic culture. Why would worker cooperatives be preferable from the perspective of a democratic culture? After
all, traditional shareholder businesses have boards that are elected and which
then deliberate. Why shouldn't we see shareholder democracy as contributing to a democratic culture in the same way as worker democracy? There are
a number of reasons.

The workplace is central to workers' everyday lives. One of the key differences
between labor and capital is the way they relate to the firm. While some firms

are managed by the owners, most owners don't take a day-to-day interest in the company. Indeed, in publicly traded corporations this separation of ownership and control is institutionally enshrined (Hansmann and Kraakman 2004). In contrast, workers have much more of their time and lives tied up in the business—many hours of their day, their ambitions, and their relationships happen at work. We have discussed earlier in the chapter the importance of integrating the functional dimension of problem solving with the expressive dimension of self-realization for democratic culture. Empowering workers to make decisions about the workplace may be an example of such an integration (Ferreras 2017). If workers can participate in business decisions, especially ones that have to do with day-to-day operations, the workplace becomes an integral site of exercising democratic citizenship—by its members treating each other as equals and by their engaging in deliberative problem solving. While it would not erase the functional differentiation between work and other spheres of life, giving employees a voice in the workplace creates more of a democratic continuum between the spheres. To put it a bit crudely, when employees are treated as equals in their workplace, they are less likely to "boss around" people in other spheres of their lives.

Employees are the majority in most workplaces and in the economy at large. Generally speaking, within the firm, workers usually outnumber management.[2] Given the importance for a democratic culture of cultivating symmetrical relationships and encouraging participation of group members, empowering employees to participate in the governance of the firm seems to be a powerful way of doing this.

Workplace democracy encourages employees to become more engaged generally. Many of us compartmentalize parts of our lives—no more so than with work. By empowering workers to govern the places at which they work, workplace democracy encourages a more general spirit of inquiry into and participation in the various aspects of people's lives (Pateman 1970). This isn't just in a general sense, but in more concrete ways: people get more experience in formal meetings, learning how to read through official budgets and documents, and so on. Such experience can give citizens not just the inclination but the practice and skills of democratic participation and problem solving in other activities (schools, families, neighborhood associations, and the like).

People are not shares. Crucially, whatever efficiencies are to be gained by shareholder governance, it is less clear that such governance contributes to a democratic culture (Rodrigues 2006). This is because shareholders' votes are proportional to the size of investment; large shareholders have more voting power (and clout) than small ones. Consequently, shareholder governance does not facilitate the symmetrical relationships and equal participation of a democratic culture, nor does shareholders' instrumental relationship with the firm cultivate the acknowledgment of mutual interdependence.

Given this, there are various reasons to think that worker control of firms is better suited for fostering a democratic culture not only in the firm itself but also in society at large.

Mitigating the Effects of Workplace Hierarchy

While the above is meant to help us see why it is both feasible and desirable to inject more democratic governance into the firm, it is not an argument against workplace hierarchy completely. In some industries it might still make more sense to have a less democratic enterprise; in other instances, workers may prefer not to govern the firm, opting instead to channel their time and energy in other directions; in other instances, still, there may be both the ability to achieve and the interest in having, but difficulty in getting the capital for, such arrangements. The point is, even if we think workplace democracy is a good goal, there are still generally going to be hierarchically governed workplaces. The question is what does democratic culture demand of them? Can hierarchy be practiced in a way that does the least amount of damage to democratic culture?

To answer this we need to consider not just the democratic culture within a workplace, but also how practices within the workplace can have broader effects on relationships within society more generally. Here we briefly review some of the sorts of effects that must be considered when making management and personnel decisions with an eye toward increasing the quality of democratic culture more broadly.

COGS NOT CITIZENS

As Adam Smith famously observed in the opening pages of *The Wealth of Nations* ([1776] 1981 [WN I.i.6–24], the division of labor is a crucial way that organizations achieve gains in productivity. By having some workers focus on just one small part of larger tasks, we enable specialization and quality enhancement as well as greater speed and efficiency. And yet, this division of labor can also have negative consequences. For each individual, just a narrow focus of specialization can turn work into drudgery, monotonously doing the same things over and over again. It can also produce what Karl Marx once referred to as alienation, the separation of a worker from the productive power of his or her work. If labor is so divided and specialized, work is transformed into a series of mindless, endless tasks.

There are obviously potential problems with this from the perspective, say, of the worker's well-being, leading some business ethicists to call for a right to meaningful work (e.g., Michaelson et al. 2014). For our purposes here, it is worth noting there is something disquieting from the perspective of democratic culture to such a state of affairs. The democratic culture of participation and deliberation in inquiry and decision making seems to require that the citizen have the ability to examine problems from different perspectives and be able to see things from different points of view. Such skills require exercise.

People who are conditioned to act like cogs in a machine are not being trained to act as citizens. To the extent that they can do so, businesses ought to try to allow people to develop these skills in the workplace. At the very least they ought to avoid contributing to their deterioration through overly rote and mindless tasks.

WHO LEADS, AND WHY?

As we saw, hierarchy generally can be defended on the grounds that it helps facilitate mutually beneficial cooperation in a more efficient manner. Any particular instance of someone being placed in hierarchical relations over another may be defended on grounds of merit or competence: this person ought to be the manager because he or she has training in leadership skills, has proven him- or herself in previous years, has seniority or some other such supposed qualification, and so forth. Be that as it may, in many instances, hierarchies don't wind up with the most competent or qualified person in charge. Instead, people end up in charge because they are good at pleasing the right people, skilled at avoiding blame (as was famously described by Jackall 1988), or just fortunate enough to share common backgrounds with the people making promotion decisions. In fact, sometimes people end up in managerial positions because they are "good" at things like controlling and manipulating others or being cutthroat and unempathic toward their colleagues.

There is often something problematic with this in itself, if not morally then at least vis-à-vis the goals of the business (Bazerman and Tenbrunsel 2011). However, it also raises some important issues in terms of democracy. Most notably, it incentivizes precisely the opposite sorts of habits and approaches to relationships than those that democratic culture prizes. Instead of approaching one's coworkers in terms of mutual interdependence, collective problem solving, and symmetry, rewarding such climbing behavior

encourages aspirants to pander to their superiors and to approach group situations on deeply individualistic and instrumentalist terms.

If we are concerned with reconciling our hierarchies with a broader commitment to democratic culture, then being mindful of the types of people we
put on top of hierarchies, and the organizational pathologies that empower
them, must matter. Even if one views the democratization of the workplace
as overly utopian or idealistic, it seems very important to subject such hierarchies to standards of competence that are sensible and understood by all, and
are actually put into practice.

CLASS BOUNDARIES

In most cases, hierarchies in the workplace are tied to unequal compensation.
Those who hold management positions—that is, those who tell others what
to do—also bring home a larger paycheck. Compensation is an important
tool for businesses to have in order to hire people who have needed skills and
to encourage people to put the effort into developing these skills. In the previous chapter (chapter 6), we have already discussed how economic inequalities
may undermine democratic practices and procedures. But it is important to
notice that these inequalities in the workplace may further undermine democratic culture beyond their effects on the distribution of wealth.

To see why, consider the case of feudal societies. One of the main features
of feudal societies is that inequality is built into the whole system. There is a
class of people—the knightly and princely classes—who are better off in every
way and who give the orders. Now, one important difference between a feudal village governed by a prince and modern workplaces is that the former is
based on ascribed status. Princes are born into nobility, and their aristocratic
upbringing is what allowed them to become skillful knights. In the modern
workplace, everyone is supposed to have a chance to become the manager, so
the prospect of ending up living in the castle (or getting the corner office) is
an important incentive.

But in many ways our society is closer to medieval society than we like to
imagine: as a society, our meritocracy is far from perfect (Markovits 2019).
There are persistent structural inequalities that affect people's chances to get
into upper positions in our social hierarchy based purely on their talents or
skills. Now, unlike medieval societies (or, for that matter, the United State until quite recently), there is generally no formal law that prohibits people from
holding certain positions because they are not part of the nobility, or because
of their race or gender (though we note that there are laws that make it harder
for noncitizens to obtain certain positions). But there are other mechanisms,

that are more subtle and informal yet very powerful, that keep our society stratified. While many of these dynamics are big-ticket social issues, some of them relate to HR policy. Here we consider two such dynamics.

First, there are HR policies that use proxies for merit, which often end up reproducing social stratification. The most obvious is the use of qualifications. One of the biggest barriers to social opportunity is the value employers place on prestigious formal education. Given the various advantages that wealthy and well-connected children have in attending elite schools, prestigious university attendance often tracks a person's social status as much as it tracks their aptitude or merit (Rivera 2016; Kraus, Park, and Tan 2017). Both of us are college professors and obviously think there is value to be found in college education; surely, there are professions and jobs where the ability to complete a rigorous formal education is a good indicator of ability. Yet, an overreliance on such qualifications has the effect of handicapping those who didn't have the opportunity or means to attain such qualifications. Both being more open to different educational and training backgrounds, and creating opportunities for training and certification among those who otherwise wouldn't have access, are powerful tools for challenging these entrenched social inequalities.

Second, social hierarchies are the cause of inequalities in skills as much as they are their effect. The comedian Laurie Kilmartin (2017) illustrates this well in her discussion of how creepy and sexually inappropriate men affect female comedians. As she notes, the effect is far reaching:

> All new comics need the same thing: huge amounts of stage time. There are no shortcuts in standup comedy. The quest to become a good comedian is brutal. It takes at least 10 years of performing, almost every night. You get that performing time in at open mics, where you have to line up during the day for a spot that night, at open mics that run until 1 or 2 a.m., at shows where you have to talk two, or 10, friends into coming just so that you can have a chance to perform. Both male and female comics have to do these things. But if you also have to maneuver around a problematic guy, you'll miss some opportunities. If you perform 10 times a week and your male counterpart performs 12 times a week, he will get better faster. And because you won't get paid work until you're good, your quest will take longer.

Often we think of people's fame and monetary reward as reflecting some combination of innate talent, work ethic, and a certain amount of luck in having others take notice of those talents and ethics. But what Kilmartin shows us is that circumstance doesn't affect just whether talents are noticed, but whether they are cultivated in the first place. If a woman is made to feel uncomfortable in particular clubs, then she is being deprived of the chance not just to showcase her comedy but to develop her craft. Even if we think wealth and opportunity tracks merit, the ability to develop merit is not distributed equally. One can think of HR policies surrounding, say, sexual harassment in the workplace as important not just because people are entitled to safe and secure workplaces, but also because not addressing such things affects the degree to which all people are able to develop the skills necessary to succeed in a workplace.

This applies more generally. Informal barriers can take different forms. Important meetings can take place at a time of day when parents need to pick up their children; holiday displays can make people who are not Christian feel like they do not belong; and so forth. Making sure informal barriers to the development of merit are being actively torn down is a crucial way that employers can contribute to an equal and inclusive democratic culture.

REINFORCING INEQUALITY

Workplace hierarchies are not just a series of formal org-chart relationships between superiors and subordinates. Just as important as these formal relationships are the informal social norms that enable people to work together. There are norms surrounding how to participate in a meeting, how to address one's colleagues, how to dress appropriately, how to speak politely and respectfully, and so on. These aren't written down anywhere but rather are things that people learn and habituate themselves to follow in order to get along with others.

One of the big problems for a democratic culture is that oftentimes these social norms can be deeply inegalitarian (O'Connor 2019, 101–6): particular racial or ethnic groups may be discouraged from participating in certain activities; women are expected to be emotionally supportive and less assertive in social settings; certain modes of speech are seen as intelligent while others are seen as crude and vulgar; and so on. These are obviously bad for a democratic society that is trying to cultivate relations of equality and mutual participation and are made even worse because social norms are so hard to change. Social norms work precisely because we often aren't aware of how much we are following them, and when we are, they seem too entrenched to be successfully challenge.

A very subtle but crucial way that workplaces can undermine democratic norms is by being governed by such unequal social norms. After all, when persistent inequalities exist, taking them into account may be efficient (Singer 2019, 136). It makes economic sense for high-tech companies to focus their recruitment efforts in highly selective colleges and to target demographics that tend to have been encouraged to go into STEM fields. Even though the recruitment effort is being made solely for economic reasons, the result is to reinforce and entrench these unequal social norms. Similarly, certain management positions may require putting in many hours of work and being constantly on call. This gender-neutral job description may exclude parents who have childcare duties, a role that is more likely to be taken on by women.

More subtly still, workplaces often function by allowing gendered social norms to determine tasks. Consider the office birthday party. Who ends up making the arrangements, or cleaning up the cake when the party's over? It is almost always women doing this, and not because they are ordered to do so or because it is their job. Rather it is because men generally understand such duties as falling on women. An important way that workplaces can contribute to a democratic culture is by using the formal power of the workplace to actively challenge these unequal social norms. Indeed, to the extent that they will exist in a democratic society, challenging such social norms may be something that hierarchical firms are relatively competent in doing compared to more formally democratic firms. Resistance to formal hierarchies and power structures in the name of challenging elites can sometimes serve to empower informal elites and to allow extant norms of power to continue (a thesis famously advanced by Jo Freeman 1972). Structured hierarchies like traditional firms, in contrast, precisely because they impose rules and roles on their members, can challenge these norms by prohibiting them in ways that more participatory organizations have difficulty in doing.

Conclusion

To sum up, certain hierarchies may be needed for businesses to operate efficiently, but it is possible that in many contexts more egalitarian and collaborative modes of organization are equally or even more efficient. Furthermore, the inequalities that are created by the hierarchical organization of businesses may undermine the broader sort of equality and mutuality that are central for robust democratic culture. In our view, all these considerations imply that businesses have to strive to organize themselves as much as possible in ways that are consistent with or promote democratic culture. Again, we keep in mind that what is possible is in part an empirical question that is highly dependent on the context.

We do not suggest that more egalitarian forms of organization are always necessarily better. But in most cases the needle leans too far in the other direction: many business organizations are highly hierarchical and stratified organizations with significant pay inequalities and narrowly defined job descriptions that leave little room for autonomy or collaboration. Moreover, such states of affairs are often not based on considered justification or merit but rather exist because this is how things have been done. A commitment to democracy requires that we actively avoid falling back on such reasoning unreflectively. We should always be asking *why* we do things a certain way, and whether it is possible to structure our social settings in ways that facilitate more democratic modes of problem solving.

8

Exit, Voice, and Business Investment Decisions

In May 2023, the Walt Disney Company announced its decision not to proceed with a $1 billion plan to relocate some of its workforce to Florida (Zurcher and Debusmann 2023). The decision was made amid and in light of a public feud with the governor of Florida, Ron DeSantis, who, the month before, was described by Disney's CEO as "anti-business" and "anti-Florida" (Barnes 2023). Most commentators understood Disney's decision as a political statement and a direct attempt to use its economic power to exert political influence. But decisions about relocation can have a significant impact even if they are not intended as a political statement. In the same month, Snider Fleet Solutions, a transportation firm, decided to move its headquarters from North Carolina to South Carolina, planning, as its executive manager stated, to become "an active member in our community, Lancaster County and the state." The decision was made based on what one would think of as purely business reasons—particularly, the logistical operations of the business (South Carolina Office of the Governor 2023). Whether for explicitly political reasons or for mundane economic reasons, businesses shift different kinds of resources across jurisdictional boundaries—both local and international—all the time. In doing so, they move these resources and the benefits that may come from them—employment, tax income, prestige, and so on—from the purview of one community to that of another.

In previous chapters, we have implicitly assumed that democracy is basically a single-locale affair. We asked what the ethical responsibilities of business are given the fact that they operate in some specific democratic society. Yet, one of the questions that often arises with regard to democracy and business ethics is about the place of multinational corporations. When businesses operate in multiple jurisdictions and across different national boundaries, which democracy must they respect? If we understand market activity as licensed by a social contract, who is licensing them? The stakes becomes even higher when the democratic status of some jurisdiction is in question. When social media companies operate in China, should they be beholden to broader democratic norms, or those specific to the Chinese regime (which, in its mandates of censorship, may be antithetical to such norms)? How can we account for the many market and business activities that by their very design cut across different societies, each with different sorts of norms and principles governing cooperation? In this final chapter, we try to think through this topic.

Philosophically speaking, the answer is fairly simple. At the outset, we claimed that business is best understood as a social subcontract, a relatively autonomous domain of activity that is meant to serve a social purpose. The social subcontract is an abstraction meant to convey the claim that markets are not a natural phenomenon but a social creation. Therefore, markets are part of a system of social cooperation that is subject to critical reflection. But we must remember that the social contract (or subcontract) is a conceptual device: there is no actual contract that underwrites commercial activity. As a consequence, the social subcontract does not rely on a commitment to a kind of methodological nationalism, where we start with some particular country and ask what its specific system of social cooperation is and what it demands of market actors (the way integrated social contracts theory does). Instead, just like multinational corporations, our systems of cooperation are not housed or contained solely within national boundaries. Similarly, the democratic demands we may make on such systems also transcend national borders. Philosophically speaking, the differences in various national jurisdictions, and the fact that businesses operate in these various jurisdictions, should not shake us from taking seriously the general democratic norms we have been discussing in this book.

But this philosophical answer does not really address the practical problems that multinational companies present. Even if we think democracy should be understood in more global and less parochial terms, we must surely acknowledge that democracy *as practiced and understood by most* is still largely a national affair. Put differently, even if democracy as an idea need not be constrained by political borders, such units are in fact the primary way that democracy is practiced today, given the contemporary significance of the nation-state and the importance of securing its democratic legitimacy (Bagg 2024, 16–17; El Amine 2016). If businesses have ethical obligations to democracy, the question of which bounded domain of democracy multinational corporations are obligated to is, in practice, an important one. Indeed, even those who think that democracy applies to institutions that transcend national boundaries often insist on the significance of a bounded community for democratic governance. Forestal (2022, 8), for instance, asserts that communities are necessary for the existence of democracy, since the latter necessitates collective problem solving, and that "clearly bounded spaces" are crucial for enabling such communities to form, facilitating the recognition of what people share in common. Even if democracy cannot be contained within the boundaries of some particular national community, it also seems like democracy cannot do without boundaries, full stop.

What does this fact of boundedness imply for a business's democratic responsibilities? This is a difficult problem because it places a crucial discretionary power of business—the ability for businesses to decide where and how to conduct their operations—in tension with the ability of a community to govern itself, which is a crucial aspect of democracy. More difficult still, the democratic processes of many political communities are quite messy and imperfect—far from approximating any democratic ideal. In such contexts, businesses are forced to pick between respecting a community's collective autonomy (undemocratic though it may be) and what they take to be good for democracy (even against the wishes of some political community), all while taking their business interests into account.

Thus, at a more general level, the question addressed in this chapter is what obligation businesses have toward the communities they operate in. For multinational corporations, the pressing question is the fact that they operate in many different national communities, with different political commitments, at once. But it's similar in kind to a business that operates in different cities or local jurisdictions where the laws are different. Given that communities are an essential part of how people understand their relationships with and obligations toward others, the question of how businesses should navigate communities is crucial for a democratic business ethics. The question of multinational businesses, we maintain, is best understood as a subclass of this broader question of interjurisdictional business activity.

In the first section, we examine the alternative ways a business may interact with, or respond to, the communities within which they operate and with which they interact. We use Albert Hirschman's famous distinction between exit, voice, and loyalty to frame the discussion. Businesses commonly understand *exit* as a right that is expressive of their economic freedom to decide where and with whom they do business. Looked at from this perspective, democratically enacted laws, and especially administrative regulations, generate only a limited sort of moral obligation. If one community democratically sets a tax or an environmental threshold at 5 percent and the other at

5.25 percent, businesses might ask why they can't treat these choices as nothing more than market signals comparable to a feature of a product. As with any other product, it is up to the buyer to decide which "brand" they choose to buy. If the business doesn't like the laws a community enacts, they express their displeasure by not buying it in the first place or, if they are already there, by "selling" it and relocating. This is the logic of exit.

On the other hand, some ways of thinking about corporate social responsibility understand the obligations of businesses to communities in terms of *loyalty*. In such a view, businesses have a responsibility of fidelity and care to the particular community in which they operate. This basic responsibility to the community creates an obligation to respect that community's democratically enacted law, regardless of the costs of such compliance.

In contrast to both approaches, we argue that decisions regarding whether to enter or exit some community have to be assessed in part as political decisions—as a political form of *voice*. Sometimes this use of voice is explicit—like when businesses openly lobby localities to adopt friendly regulations, leveraging the threat of exit or the promise of entrance to get what they want. But even when such decisions are made for purely business reasons—for example, in deciding to open offices in some jurisdiction because it has lower tax rates or more lax labor laws—they still affect the way legislators and the public at large consider decisions and policies in their communities. Put differently, decisions about where and with whom to do business are always decisions about in which communities one should enter or exit; such decisions are political, one's intentions notwithstanding.

But looking at it this way only accentuates the problem of locating the place of business in the basic architecture of democracy: do businesses have a right to exercise influence over local politics with their ability to move locations or not? In contrast to the loyalty framework, which focuses on obligations that businesses owe to a community, our focus is on the obligations of businesses toward the *democratic quality* of the community. Businesses don't have an obligation of fidelity toward a community, per se, but they also don't have unconditional moral entitlements to exit, given the latter's ability to undermine the capacity of a community to democratically govern itself.

We examine two ways to think about the meaning of a democratic community and the relationship of businesses to it. We begin with what might be called the "Westphalian model." In this way of thinking about democracy, the world is divided into separate self-governing units, which can be more or less democratic. In such a model, businesses have a special status because they can move relatively easily between entities, which gives them a rather unique leverage to influence the democratic decision making of particular self-governing entities. We then examine approaches to democracy that imagine ways to think about what democracy would look like on a more transnational or global scale. These approaches often understand democracy through the "all-affected model" in which different governing entities, businesses included, manage their relationship with their stakeholders democratically. We explore ways to think through the obligations of businesses to different communities through the lenses of both models.

Exit and Loyalty

We begin with Albert Hirschman's well-known distinction between exit, voice, and loyalty as the different mechanisms through which people express satisfaction or dissatisfaction with a product, a relationship, or an organization (Hirschman 1970). Democracy is generally associated with "voice"— expressing one's opinion in a way that will be registered by the organization. Voice can be more or less formal: a diner may write a restaurant review on Yelp, which others can read, in the hopes of influencing the menu or service at the restaurant; partners may express their concerns to their spouse in order to change relationship dynamics; or a shareholder may try to elect someone to the board of directors in order to change company policy. But this is not the only mechanism of influence. One can also use the option of exit, or what people sometimes call "voting with your feet"—choosing a different restaurant next time, leaving one's partner, or selling one's shares—which can result in a change in orientation or policy.

EXIT

The exit option is central to the logic of a market economy. To be able to choose how to use one's labor or property implies a comparable ability to choose when and how *not* to do so. This is often defended in terms of people's rights and freedoms, with the right-to-an-exit option—to leave the job, sell your shares, or take your money to another shop—understood as the quintessential market freedom.

Yet, the ability to exit need not be understood solely on such libertarian terms. Exit choices can be viewed as signals that consumers send to producers, telling them that they are not interested in any more of this or that product. The companies then read these signals and, if they are good at their jobs, change the product accordingly. Economists often argue that in a market with well-functioning exit options, voice options are redundant. A student is likely to write an angry complaint about a professor only if the withdrawal deadline has passed and they cannot switch to a different class. Similarly, when employees have exit options and can easily find another employer, employers will go out of their way to figure out how to keep them satisfied so that they don't leave (as we have seen in the previous chapter, that exit option is often not so easy for many employees). Using exit as implicit or explicit leverage—if you don't make us happy, we will go elsewhere—is built into the DNA, we could say, of the way businesses think.

It is not surprising, then, that businesses often think about the choice of locations and communities as "shopping." In the following subsections, we discuss other frameworks for thinking about the choice of location. But, before doing that, we want to review several reasons why the "exit" framework may be appropriate, and what the advantages are of allowing businesses to consider only their economic interest, as they understand it, when choosing where to operate.

First, as noted above, one might plausibly think that the freedom to move and to invest where one pleases is a fundamental right that should not be infringed on by political decisions, democratic or otherwise (Maitland 1989; Tomasi 2012). Restricting one's movement is often seen as a major trespass of one's freedom. Consequently, businesses can approach investment decisions in terms of "exit" simply because it is their right to do so. Furthermore, one might argue that they *should* think in such terms since credibly threatening to exit is the most efficient way to get what they want or to get someone to offer it to them. According to such a view, community rules and regulations are just potential costs of doing business. Businesses weigh the potential costs with the potential benefits and then choose the "product"—that is, the location and community—they most want. The ability to choose such locations requires the comparable ability to leave others.

Second, one can argue in favor of exit on instrumental grounds, that generally markets work better when businesses are allowed to move freely. That is, businesses will end up in locations that work best for all if the ability to pick up and go is made as costless as possible. Furthermore, when businesses "shop," localities are incentivized to offer bundles of public goods that attract the kind of industries that they want to attract, such as an educated workforce, good roads, or tax incentives for movie production. Residents will respond in kind, a dynamic that economists refer to as Tiebout sorting, a model of public goods provision where the consumer-citizen "'shops' among different communities offering varying packages of local public services and selects as a residence the community which offers the tax-expenditure program best suited to his tastes" (Oates 1969, 957–58) (for critical discussion, see Levy 2007). So, on this score, even if businesses do not have any natural or fundamental right to move, a well-crafted system of social cooperation should allow them to do so not only for the interests of the business, but for the social goal of enabling a more efficient system of public goods provision.

Finally, it might be argued that treating the regulatory environment of different localities as mere products, a series of potential costs and benefits, rather than as an expression of popular will or a rational system of law, is actually a more accurate assessment of the political environment. As we discussed in chapter 3, rule making is often a messy process that does not resemble any democratic ideal. If everyone knows that this process is messy, there is no reason to expect businesses to treat its outcome with any great moral regard. There may be a reasonable range of acceptable levels of particular industrial pollution. Choosing a city that offers some tax benefits over another with a lower level of acceptable pollution threshold is like choosing between a healthy snack with some sugar and a less healthy snack with no sugar. Since neither really represents any pure expression of democratic will, it is not like choosing the kingdom of darkness over the shining city on the hill.

Whatever the merits of these arguments, none of these arguments assuage the worry of those concerned with democracy. One might concede the significance of business freedom or the efficient level of public goods, and still worry that such things are not conducive to democratic empowerment. Even the claim that local rule making is often messy does not tell us anything about how or whether a business approaching that community in terms of exit helps address or exacerbates such a democratic deficit.

LOYALTY

In contrast to the exit framework, we must note that customers sometimes choose a brand out of a sense of loyalty and that businesses can foster consumer loyalty. In Hirschman's account, such loyalty serves an important economic purpose, by keeping people from exiting too quickly from organizations or communities, when a long-term commitment may be beneficial to all. A loyalty to a neighborhood may mean that people stick around to help improve it, as opposed to just fleeing at the first sign of trouble. The same can apply to businesses when they choose where to operate; instead of adopting an attitude of exit toward the communities in which they operate, they might develop a sense of loyalty. Morally speaking, we might contend that businesses have an obligation to cultivate such loyalty and the responsibilities it comes with. Again, there are a number of reasons why.

First, investment is a two-way street. While a business may choose to invest in a locale and build operations there, a locale also invests in the business, whether through infrastructure development, land incentives, tax breaks, or loosening regulations. As Etzioni (1988, 684–85) put it: "Communities invest in corporations in the expectation, if not explicit understanding, that they will garner a future return for their investment from the businesses at issue in the form of job creation, tax collection, or other benefits. . . . In addition, communities have an interest in ensuring that the resources they provide will not be used by corporations, directly or indirectly, to act in ways that violate their values, for instance, by damaging the environment through strip mining." Given such investment, we might say that businesses have a duty of loyalty toward these communities, which is manifested in the obligation, to quote the former CEO of Coca-Cola (Carroll 1998, 5), "to give something back to the communities that support them." That is, because communities have done something for the business, the business has an obligation to loyally reciprocate.

A related way of arguing for a duty of loyalty is to view the community in which a business operates as a stakeholder. Many stakeholder theories include the local community as one of the groups to which a company has an obligation (R. E. Freeman 1994; Business Roundtable 2019; Waddock, Bodwell, and Graves 2002). According to this view, local communities are cocreators of value for businesses and, as such, are owed fiduciary duties of loyalty. This means that loyalty is owed by a particular business to the specific community not because the community has helped the business and therefore ought to be helped in turn. Rather, loyalty is owed to the community because communities in general are a constitutive part of the business. Businesses rely on the microcontracts of the communities in which they participate, and therefore owe fidelity to those more local norms (Donaldson and Dunfee 1999).

Finally, a business might choose to be loyal and develop a longer-term relationship with the community for strategic reasons. The "exit" framework views businesses as short-term residents, akin to guests in an Airbnb, who are expected to respect the local rules but also write a bad review and go elsewhere if they are not happy with the accommodation. But this may be shortsighted. Edmund M. Burke (1999, 24) offers the "principle of the neighbor of choice" to describe the relationship between corporations and their communities: "successful companies have to act in ways that make them a supplier of choice, an employer of choice, and for public companies, an investor of choice. I now add to these principles of success the fourth—neighbor of choice. The term *neighbor of choice* refers to the reputation of the company in the community." That is, just as it is in the business's interest to establish a reputation of being a trustworthy producer or honest employer, it is in its interest to be loyal to its community in order to secure ongoing cooperation and good relations.

These sorts of loyalty views see businesses as owing more to the communities than an exit mind-set can accommodate. Yet the loyalty framework is not necessarily more helpful in addressing the question of the relationship of communities to *democratic governance*. Loyalty can be cashed out in terms of fiduciary care, reciprocity, or strategy, but none of these speak to whether or how a business should conceive of its relationship to the manner in which a community is governed or how such governance affects the empowerment or inclusion of community members. While a business's lack of loyalty may disempower communities in undemocratic ways, a conception of loyalty might also lead businesses to be overly involved with the community's politics in ways that undemocratically disempower community members.

Treating Communities Like States?

Another way of putting all the above is that an emphasis on exit or loyalty, while differing on how to interpret the moral status of the community, similarly takes the existence of communities for granted, and treats them as the relevant object of analysis. But communities constantly change and can be more or less democratically empowering of their members—something that business activity affects. So, while the ability for exit and the need for loyalty are important for businesses, there still remains the question of how a concern for democracy ought to affect a business's relationship to communities, when communities are treated as a potential vector for either democratic empowerment or undemocratic disempowerment.

This brings us to the main question of this chapter: in a complex environment of exit and loyalty, in which businesses can choose to simultaneously operate in multiple locations, to which democratic demos are they accountable?

THE WESTPHALIAN MODEL

A very common way of thinking about democratic communities is according to the model of what is known as the "Westphalian state." This refers to the political structure that emerged in Europe after the 1648 Peace of Westphalia that ended the Thirty Years' War. The Westphalian political structure, which is the one we are all familiar with, envisions a world that is divided into different geographically bounded political units that are each sovereign within their own borders. The power of each government ends at the border, where the power of another country begins. Each country decides on its own how to govern itself. Countries can have treaties with other countries, but these treaties do not change the fundamental structure of the system.

This model of sovereignty is often tied to the idea of popular sovereignty, which suggests that the right to decide on how to exercise power belongs to the people of each country.[1] In this Westphalian way of thinking about sovereignty, political communities are the outcome of an explicit or implicit agreement among people to interlink their fates by imposing on themselves a system of rules. From a democratic perspective, the rules are legitimate because, and to the extent that, those who are subjected to them can be considered their authors. They are an expression of the people's collective autonomy. This conception of peoplehood as collective autonomy is, in the Westphalian view, understood in geographic terms. For example, the people who live in the territory of the United States are the demos who have a right to participate in the process by which rules are made.

But this notion of peoplehood need not be geographically defined. If a group of people decides to form a business partnership and make decisions via democratic procedures, these people and only these people are viewed as the demos. We might think of a professional association as a similar sort of Westphalian-like community that is not geographically defined. Still, the assumption is that there is an enclosed, delineated "people" over whom the leadership organization (be that the state, corporate management, or an association) wields legitimately sovereign power.

In Hirschman's terms, the Westphalian model of democracy can be understood as a system of governance based on voice monopoly (Warren 2011). When the world is divided into self-governing units, citizens are understood to be mostly immobile and therefore "stuck," so to speak, in a community. Because of this stuck-ness, and the lack of an exit option, the democratic processes give them a voice and thus make the exercise of power legitimate.

In the next section, we argue that businesses are entities for which exit is relatively easy. But, before we discuss the case of businesses, we need to note that membership in democratic communities is always to some extent more fluid than the Westphalian voice-monopoly view captures. People regularly move in and out of cities and countries. Many times, people move for personal or family reasons. But in other cases, decisions about emigration (or immigration) are expressions of political discontent. That is, the choice people make to move to a different place serves as a signal that implicitly or explicitly affects the decision making of the political unit in question (Kirkpatrick 2017, chap. 4). This can happen when a well-known person chooses to relocate because of some grievance (for instance Elon Musk moving Tesla to Texas) or when a large number of people choose to relocate (e.g., Americans moving to Canada during the Vietnam War).

In general, an emphasis on "exit" poses a problem to this Westphalian understanding of democracy: if people are influencing decisions of a jurisdiction by leaving it, they are seeking to influence it precisely by puncturing the boundaries that constitute the community! The issue becomes more acute when the exit options are not distributed equally—for example when richer people are able to leave a community more easily than others, thus acquiring a lever for influence that others don't have. As we see in the next section, this is the case for businesses.

As we indicated in the previous section, while "exit" is not unique to businesses, businesses are unique in that exit is their primary modus operandi. In the market, players express their dissatisfaction through the mechanism of exit. If consumers are not satisfied with a product, they do not buy it; if employees are not happy with their job, they leave; if investors are not happy with how their investment performs, they sell their shares. Indeed, influencing an organization through exit is sometimes referred to as the "Wall Street rule." In a similar way, businesses generally approach other organizations in a similar manner. When businesses are not satisfied with local rules, they see themselves as free to go elsewhere.

There are two features that make the case of businesses' exit unique in the way it challenges the Westphalian voice-monopoly view of democracy. First, in some cases, it is much easier for businesses to shift the center of operation from one locality to another than it is for other sorts of organizations to do so. It is very easy to move certain types of capital from one location to another in comparison to moving a community organization or a church, both of which are tied more directly to the people and geography of the local community. Some invested capital is, of course, very location specific or difficult to move, and so this ease of exit is especially salient with regard to financial capital, which is particularly mobile. Second, since businesses provide employment and pay taxes, decisions about location and relocation of businesses—about entry and exit—are typically more impactful on the localities of business than are those of individual people. It is one thing for Elon Musk to move to Texas; it is entirely a different thing for Tesla's operations to do so.

Combined, these two features of business exit—its widespread usage and its pervasive effects on others—make it more of a basic challenge to the Westphalian voice-monopoly view of democracy. Earlier, we presented the idea that businesses relate to communities like Airbnb guests who are expected to respect the rules of the house while there. But it might be more accurate to say that as guests, these businesses are able to alter and affect the house rules because there is such great competition among hosts to get guests to come and stay.

Given this, one might ask whether democracy has much of anything to do with such business decisions. Why not just let businesses shop around for the correct mix of regulatory environment, access to human and physical resources, convenience of transportation, and so on, and let communities democratically decide what sort of package they want to offer in a manner similar to the Tiebout model? That is, if communities are the products that businesses are shopping for, then democracy is just the means by which community residents name their price relative to the benefit they think they will receive. In such a view, the threat of business exit raises no particular democratic worry.

The problem with a model that asks democratically governed entities to compete over businesses is that it naturalizes and takes as given circumstances that are not natural or inevitable. Markets—and especially advanced markets aided by regulation, infrastructure, and economic integration—are not a natural phenomenon but political creations. Businesses have the ability to approach local regulatory policy as a set of prices and make exit decisions accordingly only because and to the extent that the terms of social cooperation allow them to do so. To view democracy as only limited to the degree to which a community sets the terms of doing business is to accept the initial position of community relative to business as legitimate or justified. Now, of course, these might be good arrangements that people want. But this can be known only if this overarching political arrangement—the very structure of the current Westphalian system, where moving across borders is difficult for people and easy for businesses—is subject to democratic self-reflection and oversight. This is often not the case, presenting a serious problem for democracy since it limits the collective capacity for self-reflection by placing it under duress. People have some power to change the rules of the game within each territorial unit, but they have less ability to change the rules of the game of the system itself. We have previously distinguished the first- and second-order rules of democracy. The division of the political space along Westphalian logic can itself be viewed as a first-order decision that should be subject to second-order revisions (Abizadeh 2012).

Democracy in the Plural and in the Abstract

Therefore, it is useful to ask the question in a different way. Instead of asking what the obligations of businesses are toward a particular jurisdictionally bounded democratic process, we should ask about their obligations toward democratic processes in the plural or to the democratic process at a larger scale. That is, insofar as a business has power to leverage influence on community decisions with the threat of exit (or the promise of entry), its effect is not limited to one particular community, but to communities in general who respond to such threats and promises. Thus, businesses affect democratic processes in the plural. Similarly, given that the position of these communities relative to business is a political artifact, not a natural brute fact, there is a more general democratic question about whether this positioning is itself justified.

When thinking about the obligation of businesses to democracies in the plural or democracy in the abstract we suggest that the important factor to consider is *the manner in which* businesses shop around between different localities. At the most basic level, we can simply say that businesses should generally refrain from directly and intentionally targeting the democratic process in order to achieve favorable outcomes. The argument that we made in chapter 4, where we discussed lobbying, applies here as well. Thus, even if we concede that businesses may use exit as a bargaining tool (unless prohibited by law), they must do so in ways that are transparent and discernible. They must still avoid participating in practices that are duplicitous, in that they make it appear like people are making the decisions but, in fact, the decision is made behind their backs.

Amazon's famed search for a location for a second headquarters in 2017 can serve as an example. Amazon issued a request for proposals and invited localities to explain why they should be considered. As the request explained, "Amazon is performing a competitive site selection process and is considering metro regions in North America for its second corporate headquarters. We encourage states, provinces and metro areas to coordinate with relevant jurisdictions to submit one (1) RFP [request for proposal] for your MSA [master service agreement]" (Banister 2017). In principle, insofar as these RFPs were constructed in a relatively democratic manner, insofar as they were transparent for other potential localities to see, and insofar as Amazon's criteria and decision making were transparent, one might contend that Amazon did nothing to harm democratic norms of the community. Indeed, doing so may have even contributed to an open process of local deliberation about the benefits and costs of bringing in Amazon. Such a transparent process, for instance, can make it harder for local politicians to rush into some dubious incentive deal based on short-term electoral interests.

Many, however, criticized Amazon's engagement with communities, claiming that it "was a con, not a contest" (Johnson 2018). According to this view, even if we accept the premise that Amazon is entitled to use its threat of exit or promise of entry as bargaining leverage, Amazon still misbehaved, because the terms of the contest were not out in the open. Particularly, to the degree that Amazon worked with only certain members or segments of communities—real estate developers, chambers of commerce, and so on—to secure favorable terms in ways not open to the public, the company corrupted democratic practices within those communities. That is, an RFP was being presented as representative of a community's decision; but some members of the community were excluded from the decision-making process in a duplicitous manner, because the terms were not shared with them; much less were all members of the community allowed to be part of the process of deciding the terms. Thus, we argue that the process being both transparent and participatory in such negotiations is a crucial part of respecting the democratic governance and constitution of communities.

However, businesses can also inflict harms to democratic communities in other ways. More generally, we might argue that Amazon, by pitting communities against one another, created a process that generally precluded the possibility of collective decision making *among* cities, to democratically determine baseline conditions for an HQ2 in whatever city. Instead, cities raced to the bottom, in the form of tax breaks and the like, to outbid others (Florida 2018; Holder 2018). Within each city, not all were included; and as each city as a whole was also a stakeholder in the larger project of democracy, each stakeholder city was also kept in the dark about the other stakeholders and prevented from democratically determining minimal standards for the larger society. Thus, transparency and participation are the minimal responsibilities to democracy that businesses have.

Beyond the Westphalian Model

In this section, we examine an entirely different strand of thinking about the meaning of a democratic community and then look at its implications for the ethical obligations of business in making decisions with regard to location. For this alternative strand, the logic of democracy requires that all those who are affected by a decision should have the opportunity to have a voice in it. Such a principle extends beyond the boundaries of a given community. The claim to have one's voice counted cannot be limited only to the rules one is being subjected to as citizens. People who are significantly affected by decisions that they cannot shape are not free. Therefore, in this view, the real democratic demos must include all those who are affected by a certain decision, extant rules of national citizenship or associational membership notwithstanding.

THE ALL-AFFECTED PRINCIPLE

The idea of allowing all those affected by a decision to have a voice in making it—the so-called all-affected principle—sounds compelling in theory. If we think of democracy as entailing a kind of equality in the way that people relate both to government and to each other, then being subject to decisions that affect you that you've had no say in seems to flout such egalitarian commitments. However, the all-affected principle also runs into significant difficulties when trying to implement it.

For instance, people are generally affected by a decision at different levels and in different ways. A policy about disposing of pollutants in a lake will affect community members generally, but also those who live on the lake will be affected more directly and specifically, as will those who have businesses that would be affected by this policy. Should all those affected have the same amount of influence over a policy, or do those more affected deserve more of a say? If the former, why should such influence be the same? Given that being affected warranted inclusion in the decision making in the first place, it seems plausible to think that those who are more affected ought to have more of a say. Following that line of thought would require some form of weighted voice that is proportional to the extent different people are affected, which is difficult enough. It gets more complicated when considering that people are affected differently not just by magnitude but also by type. For a piece of land conservation policy, should someone who is financially affected be given more say than someone whose sense of identity or tradition is being affected? Should people who have other forms of protection—say, easier ability to exit, contractual entitlements, and so on—be given the same amount of voice as those who don't have such protection, or should political influence be proportional to the degree to which one is vulnerable to the effects of some decision?

Even if we could sort out these principled issues, implementing the all-affected principle also raises empirical challenges. Cause-and-effect relationships are always complicated and hard to predict. To say that anyone affected by a decision ought to have a say in it presumes we know who will be affected by any decision. Yet that is often precisely what we don't know. Consequently, determining the relevant demos for any particular decision will involve either unreliable projection or an overreliance on previous examples, which can lead to the sort of accepted boundaries of decision making that the all-affected principle is meant to challenge.

BEYOND WESTPHALIAN DEMOCRACY

Democratic theorists, therefore, struggle with the question of the practical meaning of this all-affected principle. Some suggest that it simply provides a different foundation for the Westphalian structure of political communities. People who live together and regularly interact with each other are likely to affect each other, and therefore geographic boundaries on the democratic demos are the best proxy for determining the "all" in "all-affected." Others claim the exact opposite. Most notably and radically, Robert Goodin argues that democracy requires all decisions be open to everyone who wants a voice in the decision, regardless of their location (Goodin 2007). Finally, some suggest narrowing the scope of this principle by claiming that the right to have a voice applies only when one's basic or fundamental interests are at stake (e.g., Gould 2006; Pavel 2016, 327–28).

But—generally—the idea points toward a more complex way of thinking about democracy that goes beyond the Westphalian model. Such a complex view of democracy requires acknowledging that there can be different ways to think of, or claim, democratic inclusion. Even if one wants to maintain a Westphalian, member-based approach to democracy, the all-affected principle points to a very different reason for why, rendering membership a much weaker basis for democratic inclusion. On the more radical approach, one dismisses membership as a criterion at all for democratic inclusion.

More interesting for our purposes, the all-affected principle doesn't just challenge the "who" of democracy, but also the "what": it's a question not just of who ought to be able to participate in decision making, but of what decisions trigger such inclusion in the first place. In particular, this principle points to the potential democratic obligations of entities other than legislatures, such as administrative bodies, civic organizations, governments of other societies, and, as we elaborate below, businesses (Fung 2013, 237). According to the Westphalian model, the members of the community are the ones to be included in a democratic process because they are uniquely subject to the dominant authority—the state, but also, say, the board of directors—because they have a voice monopoly. Yet, according to the all-affected view, because people have a say by virtue of being affected, there is no reason to limit its application only to the dominant authority. In this view, different kinds of organizations may have obligations to engage those who are affected by their decisions democratically even if they don't have any formal ties to or membership in the organization.

STAKEHOLDERS AND THE ALL-AFFECTED PRINCIPLE

There are direct parallels between the vision of democracy proposed by the all-affected principle and certain interpretations of stakeholder theory. As we have seen in chapter 1, the core of stakeholder approaches is that the fiduciary duties of business managers are not only to its shareholders but also to a larger group of stakeholders that includes employees, customers, suppliers, and local communities. However, as Ponet and Leib (2011) suggest, the exercise of legal fiduciary duties may require deliberative engagement. Without it, how would managers know what the preferences or interests of the stakeholders are? Expanding this claim, some advocates of stakeholder democracy argue that the exercise of these fiduciary obligations can or should require using democratic practices of allowing the different stakeholders to articulate their interests, express them, and influence the decision (Gould 2002; Moriarty 2014).

As Carol Gould observes (2002, 7), one of the challenges of stakeholder theory is that the notion of stakeholders is quite vague. Therefore, she proposes a distinction between a class of stakeholders who codetermine the operation of the business and thus have a right to participate in its decisions, and a class of stakeholders who are merely affected and therefore have a right only for their interests to be heard and considered (see also McMahon 1995). In either version, the terrain is different from that of the Westphalian model. The relevant feature of businesses in this perspective is that they are entities that have the capacity to exercise power in ways that significantly affect various stakeholders. This feature of the firm then creates an obligation to engage stakeholders democratically.

In Gould's view (2002, 17), the multinational character of many of today's corporations makes the focus on their democratic obligations all the more relevant, since the decisions that they make many times affect distant stakeholders. So, for example, if American consumers are affected by a decision of an American company, they have recourse to the political process to try to change the regulatory environment or to apply other kinds of pressure, a recourse that is not available for consumers in another country. This would require democratic obligations of that company toward these disempowered stakeholders that they may not have to their American customers.

POLITICAL CORPORATE SOCIAL RESPONSIBILITY

Scherer and Palazzo (2007) push one step forward in arguing that the global transnational political reality requires us to blur the distinction between a firm's stakeholders and its broader social environment. They argue that globalization increases the political power of multinational corporations relative to that of nation-states. Therefore, businesses have to consider themselves political actors that have a responsibility—one that goes beyond the fiduciary obligation to stakeholders—to participate in the public exchange of reasons that legitimate their own activities. In their view, a "political understanding of CSR, therefore, no longer builds on the established division of labor between economic and political actors" (1111). Businesses should transform themselves into the site of democratic deliberation among different constituencies—as a seat of democratic legitimacy.

To the degree that PCSR claims businesses have an obligation to govern themselves democratically, it is in some tension with the social subcontract perspective that we propose in this book. The subcontract perspective maintains that businesses should be viewed as subcontractors that are licensed by a social contract to pursue efficiency and that they cannot be expected to be their own governing body. In chapter 7, we suggested that workplace democracy is a viable governance option for businesses and that, to the extent possible, businesses should prefer collaborative forms of management over hierarchical ones. But both suggestions are inward looking, and the justification for preferring democratic practices is that they reinforce a democratic culture in society at large. It is important to recognize that what Scherer and Palazzo are calling for is different. They ask businesses to engage in democratic deliberation as if they were government-like themselves.

In our view, this is in error: businesses must recognize that they can affect people and therefore are subject to democratic obligations like other entities, but that they ought not to see themselves as heirs apparent to the Westphalian state, with similar aspirations to legitimacy. There is nothing that prevents businesses from taking on political tasks and sometimes doing it successfully (or at least not less successfully than other nonbusiness agents). Businesses can promote good social causes, meaningfully listen to different groups, help in negotiating peace, and participate in other political activities. Still, we must be wary of the blurring of the distinction between businesses and other types of social and political actors. Since businesses are at least in part in the business of making profit, there should be deep suspicion when businesses attempt to arbitrate the processes by which groups in society discuss the overall terms of social cooperation.

Conclusion: Democratic Business Ethics
and Undemocratic Communities

A different way of putting all the above is to say that though bounded communities are important facts about democracy as it is commonly practiced, they are not necessarily the core of the democratic project. Democracy is not just or only about a people of some nation or group governing itself; rather, democracy is a commitment to determine the terms of social cooperation in a manner that respects certain values of equality and inclusiveness. This general commitment can be realized in different ways in different contexts. In some of them, like the Westphalian model of the nation-state, democracy is exercised through exclusive control over territory. In others, democratic values are articulated by, for example, the way businesses engage stakeholders or employees. One important way of addressing this plurality of democratic practices is by making sure that businesses engage with these localities in transparent ways that don't undermine the democratic empowerment of community members. This is, we argued, no small task.

Things become more difficult when we recognize not just the fact of bounded communities, but the fact that many of those bounded communities are deeply undemocratic. What should businesses do when operating in nondemocratic environments? In some sense, this question puts in conflict the principles of the Westphalian and all-affected models discussed in this chapter. Take a society where women are legally relegated to second-class status. Do businesses have an obligation to follow such nondemocratic laws given the importance of respecting community autonomy? The Westphalian model assumes that communities have a right to decide how to organize themselves free from the dictates of outside powers. Or should their obligation be to ensure the equality and inclusion of those affected by their decisions, in spite of the laws of the local community?

As we argued in chapter 3, we think businesses generally ought to obey laws, even ones they disagree with. This isn't because the law is sacrosanct or infallible or that governing bodies are immune to moral or practical error. Rather, it is because businesses are generally not constituted to break the law in ethical ways, given both their profit orientation, and the high bar that one needs to clear to engage in civil disobedience. Furthermore, because of businesses' power and influence, their breaking of the law constitutes a power to act unilaterally, which other citizens don't have. Simply put, when businesses break the law they assume the power to judge what laws are legitimate or illegitimate, a power that they have by virtue of their financial and social position. This flies in the face of democratic commitments.

When businesses operate in foreign countries, these concerns are exacerbated in that the power is being assumed by parties who are often transient guests, prone to using their power of exit and willing to pick up and leave if given the profitable opportunity. Given neocolonial relations, where Western and industrial powers wield enormous control over the affairs of the Global South, this sort of power is one that fits into a larger worrisome context and history. While it is not difficult to think of specific horrendous instances where businesses ought to disobey local law and government (as clear-cut violations of what integrated social contract theorists call "hypernorms"), generally speaking, the best thing businesses can do to support democracy abroad is often to avoid undermining the efforts of local movements that are pushing for such reforms, not to try commandeer such movements.

Furthermore, there are other ways to address such democratic deficits. Rather than strengthening democracies within borders, we can think about democratizing relations across borders. One way is for governments to collaborate through international organizations in regulating business activities. Another is to empower agents that operate across borders—for example, nongovernmental organizations or social movements—to take on democratic roles and mobilize and engage different stakeholders who are affected by their actions (Dryzek and Tanasoca 2021; McKean 2020). Businesses can help contribute to democracy by respecting and aiding such processes—by enabling multilateral and collective action, as opposed to trying to do this by unilateral fiat. To be sure, none of these solutions is simple or easy, and we cannot explore here the complexities of each. What we have argued in the previous section is that even though businesses are powerful and engage multiple stakeholders across various borders, they are poor vehicles for the project of democratizing global governance, because of their particular orientations and parochial interests.

This point generalizes. Speaking as Americans, and given our country's own hardly spotless record of democratic inclusivity and empowerment, we might reasonably ask: from where does the US (or its businesses) get the moral authority to judge others as undemocratic? The idea that business ought to support and defer to, as opposed to lead and commandeer, democratic efforts seems like a good maxim across the board whether abroad in "authoritarian" countries or domestically in "democratic" countries. Democracy is not for the faint of heart and requires efforts to keep and maintain. Democracy lasts only so long as those within its purview are capable of and committed to maintaining it. While businesses should not be the vanguards of such efforts, they can often be the spoilers, even without meaning to be. They must actively avoid being so. The quality and legitimacy of our democracies hang in the balance.

Conclusions

In this book we have advanced the claim that business ethics must be informed by a concern for democracy. In doing so we have conceived of business in terms of a social subcontract. A social subcontract model encourages us to see businesses as having distinctive sorts of obligations by virtue of their role in society and, consequently, their unique form of social power. The social subcontract grants businesses a degree of autonomy to pursue the ends they wish. But the social subcontract of business also obligates them to do so in a way that does not undermine other parts of our social system. As a consequence, business ethics isn't just about profit, stakeholders, social responsibility, sustainability, or any of the other buzzwords that often get thrown around. Business ethics also requires *political awareness* in the broad sense of the term—how businesses can disproportionately affect political systems and how businesses occupy positions of political power. This awareness, we claim, should be cashed out in terms of a commitment to democracy.

This is complicated for a number of reasons, first of all because democracy is not as straightforward as we sometimes think it is. We have argued that democracy is not just about competitive elections and rights, but is rather defined at root by the *empowered inclusion* of people in the formal and informal processes of decision making. In terms of institutions and practices, this will look different in different societies given the distinctive problems they face. This means there is no single fixed set of guidelines that businesses can just consult, since such guidelines are always themselves open to democratic revision, and responsive to democratic decision making.

Second, while business practices may be legitimized by these democratic processes, businesses are also always a potential threat to how inclusive such practices are, and the degree to which citizens are empowered. We thus have argued that businesses' ethical obligations toward democracy consist less in pursuing some just or egalitarian policy goal, and more in avoiding undermining democratic processes, both electoral and formal, and deliberative and informal. Throughout the different chapters of this book, we have tried to articulate what this looks like in specific domains of business activity.

When we have told colleagues and friends about this project, there have been questions that we are often asked. It now occurs to us that though we have addressed these questions obliquely, we have not addressed them head on. We imagine that the reader may have similar questions. And so, by way of a conclusion, we want to briefly review and address these questions and the answers our analysis suggests.

Can Businesses Really Be Ethical?

Perhaps the most common question we get is about the usefulness of business ethics. Businesses are under institutional pressure to generate profit in order to attract investors and stay competitive. The ethos that guides businesses often focuses on the need to innovate by disrupting the way things are done, which encourages *breaking* conventional rules rather than following them. Thus, the argument goes, asking businesses to follow ethical guidelines is expecting too much of them in a way that is unrealistic.

As we argued in chapter 1, we think this overstates just how much the competitive marketplace determines business activity, and understates how much discretion businesspeople actually have. Here, we want to offer a different way of thinking about this question. The point isn't just that business ethics is inevitable but that it's necessary. Businesses operate within a competitive market, which is a social institution that permits competitive behavior within certain boundaries; this scheme is justified insofar as this behavior can be socially advantageous in aggregate. But, as we explain throughout the book, the kind of work that society wants markets to do—what sort of advantage society thinks markets can secure—cannot be answered in a fixed way and must be continuously experimented with and negotiated by members of society. Absent a robust democratic system that allows for the reflective experimentation necessary to steer and legitimize markets, the claim that markets are socially beneficial is empty. Since even when they are heavily regulated businesses have a disproportionate capacity to affect these negotiations, some form of principled self-restraint is needed to allow markets to be democratically governed.

To be sure, some critics of markets argue that businesses are incapable of exercising ethical self-constraint, rendering markets incompatible with democracy. We are not naive. We recognize the power of institutional pressures that force businesses to prefer profits over ethical behavior. The vast history of corporate misbehavior and white-collar crime speaks to this. However, the conclusion that markets cannot coexist with democracy is too simplistic. We want to insist that businesses *do* have the capacity to act ethically, even though, just like other individual and collective agents, they often fail to do so. As we explain in chapter 1, businesses are organizations that are governed by norms. Most of these norms are developed to increase the business's capacity to pursue profits efficiently. But these norms are shaped by both a local, more proximate culture and the broader culture of the business community. While business managers do not pull out their ethics manual from the shelf before they make any decision, their decisions and standards are ultimately shaped by the conventional wisdom of which behaviors are acceptable. By challenging and reshaping this conventional wisdom on behalf of these democratic concerns, we can enable more ethical and responsible behavior in business.

What's the Point of Business Ethics?

John Maynard Keynes once famously wrote, "Practical men, who believe themselves to be quite exempt from any intellectual influences, are usually the slaves of some defunct economist. Madmen in authority, who hear voices in the air, are distilling their frenzy from some academic scribbler of a few years back" (1936, 383). His point was that ideas matter; even when people think they are just pursuing profit or power, how they understand profit or what they see as an acceptable or reasonable means to secure power are shaped by ideas and norms in the background. Thus, thinking about and teaching business ethics isn't necessarily about ensuring that people in business act better (though obviously that would be nice too). Instead, business ethics provides businesspeople (and citizens generally) with the ability to identify ethical problems in commerce as such and tools for reflecting on the norms that we otherwise would just accept as given. Consider, by analogy, the field of civics. The mere teaching of civics classes in school is not expected to transform students into good citizens or address all the shortcomings in democratic systems. Rather, it gives students tools to discuss and normatively assess relevant features of the political system. It helps turn students into citizens.

Similarly, we do not think that merely learning business ethics will make business actors more responsible or interested in solving the structural problems our market economies pose. Indeed, the argument we have advanced is animated by skepticism regarding the possibility or desirability of such motivations. The approach that we offer to business ethics invites business-people to view themselves as subcontractors whose responsibility is to allow the democratic process to run its course. Business ethics is not a substitute for the collective action necessary to "fix capitalism," but it is important for helping us to understand what the moral nature of commerce is, what it is not, and what citizenship demands of businesses.

But there is a different version of the same criticism about the viability of a business ethics: even if business ethics can have some effect on the conduct of businesses, the "scholarly energy" invested in articulating the ethical obligations of businesses is not well spent. According to this criticism, the intellectual and political focus of those who want a democracy-friendly business environment should be put toward changing the regulatory environment in which they operate. Put simply, if the goal is to have managers conduct business in ways that do not undermine democracy, there need to be rules that require them to do so and penalties when they do not follow them. All the rest, according to this argument, is mainly a waste of time.

Obviously, we do not agree. Studying business ethics is neither a waste of scholarly energy, nor an impediment to academic and public discussion of regulations. Even under more ideal conditions of more equal distribution of social wealth and a robust regulatory environment, businesses will still have discretionary power in any sort of market economy. They still have to make decisions on issues such as investment, relocation, marketing campaigns, and HR policies that can affect the terms of social cooperation. Even if business lobbying is highly regulated, businesses can still affect government decisions in important ways; thus an ethos that complements regulation is required.

This becomes even more important when we recognize that we do not live under ideal conditions. Businesses are very powerful players and, as we detail in the book, have an outsized influence on any deliberations of political import. Businesses are quite often active participants in the writing of the very rules that regulate their conduct. Ideal conditions or not, there is no escape from the need for a complex and realistic discussion of the expectations of businesses given the power they actually wield.

So You're Saying Business Should Do What's Right, Not What's Profitable?

In a manner of speaking. However, we have to be careful with how we think about the relationship between being moral or doing right on the one hand and pursuing profit on the other. It's not always the case that what is "right" is so distinct from "profitable." Often, when people distinguish between morality and profit, they are distinguishing between being a good person and being a selfish or self-interested person. But this is too quick. Pursuing profit isn't the same as being selfish or self-interested: profit is something that *businesses* accrue, which means that when individuals pursue business profit, they often need to constrain their self-interest in the name of the firm's profit. Furthermore, even if profit were to mean the same thing as self-enrichment, that doesn't necessarily mean one is only thinking of oneself or being selfish. One might make lots of money with the goal of giving it to charities, spending it on local and deserving artists, or some other prosocial activity.

This is of course, a conceptual point: many people do in fact pursue profit for self-interested and selfish reason. Our larger point is that business ethics, in our view, isn't about assessing the motivations or character of people— whether or not they are genuinely moral or selfish or whatever. It's about actions, and the principles that underlie those actions. Given this, the question isn't whether profit speaks to businesspeople's selfishness, but rather whether it tends to encourage activity that leads to problematic behavior or unwanted social outcomes. The pursuit of profit, in and of itself, is not a problem insofar as it leads to socially favorable outcomes. This is what the idea of the social subcontract is meant to capture. Ethics, accordingly, is not antithetical to profit seeking but requires that it be limited and curtailed in principled ways.

The question is who gets to determine what these principles are. Answering this is difficult since we fundamentally disagree on the nature of such things. As we argued in chapters 1 and 2, pluralism with regards to moral judgments is a fact of modern societies that cannot be ignored. When businesses use their economic and social power to make these sorts of moral judgments, they privilege their own narrow view over those of everybody else's. This is why—whatever other obligations businesses have—democracy is crucial to consider for business ethics. Democratic processes and principles are how diverse societies decide on these principles, and therefore businesses are obliged to respect such second-order commitments.

So, Businesses Should Work to Fight for Democracy?

Not exactly. As we argued in chapters 3 and 8, even when business leaders have good civic intentions, they are not well positioned to take the lead in democratic reform for two reasons. First, because of the sorts of incentives and strategic pressures that businesses structurally face, those making business decisions are not positioned to properly deliberate on the civic and public-oriented terms that deliberation requires. Business leaders should be skeptical of their own ability to effectively distinguish what would be good for democracy from what would be good for them under a democratic guise. Second, and perhaps more importantly, by virtue of being powerful and well resourced, businesses are inherently poor vanguards for democratic reform. What democracy means or demands is itself something that we disagree about and therefore must be decided through inclusive processes. When businesses advance some agenda in the name of democracy, even if they do it sincerely and earnestly, they are inevitably advancing their particular, partisan, and controversial vision of democracy, and doing so with the social and economic standing they hold. As a consequence, such efforts are inherently in tension with democracy.

So, You're Saying Businesses Should Just Stay Out of Democracy?

Were it so simple! Unfortunately, there is no nonpolitical place for businesses to retire to! As we have argued, democracy isn't just about elections and legislatures; it is also about the way citizens deliberate among themselves (chapter 5), the way social movements form and are responded to (chapter 6), and the sorts of relations that constitute democratic communities (chapters 7 and 8). That is to say, politics is pervasive, and so businesses cannot choose to be nonpolitical. Even when it comes to formal political engagement like lobbying, there are reasons to think that business should not be completely absent, given their specific sort of knowledge and expertise (chapter 4).

Claiming business have an ethical responsibility toward democracy, then, is not about business staying out of democracy. That is impossible. It is not about abstaining from, but being deferential to, democracy. Businesses have an ethical obligation to make sure their impact on politics is in line with democratic commitments of equality and empowered inclusion.

So What Are Businesses Expected to Do with Respect to Democracy?

We argued that businesses have three basic duties when interacting with the democratic process. First, they must respect the outcomes of established democratic processes. Second, they have a duty of reflection to consider and be aware of how they may be affecting democracy in both direct and indirect ways. Finally, they have a duty of publicity, to make transparent and open the relevant details of such democracy-affecting behavior, and to offer reasons that are scrutable to the public for what they are doing. These duties, we argued, are not merely individualistic. Given the considerable pressure for businesspeople to think in terms of bottom lines and market competition, discharging such duties demands that organizational resources be used to enable such abidance, reflexivity, and publicity. In the different chapters of the book, we have tried to explain the specific forms these three duties take in different contexts.

Lobbying. As we discussed in chapter 4, when it comes to lobbying, businesses have a duty to avoid taking part in practices that corrupt democracy by duplicitously excluding certain groups from participating. This kind of corruption can take various forms:

- what we called "epistemic corruption," when business withholds from the public information to which they have exclusive or advantageous access;
- what we called "representational corruption," when business contributes to the misrepresentation of the interest of another group;
- what we called "access corruption," when business uses its great financial power to lobby the government in ways that are not transparent, thus excluding from decision making those who don't have such resources.

Marketing. In chapter 5, we suggested that the ethics of marketers should be shaped by democratic commitments. These are related to the proximity of marketing activity that we described as the deliberation of "strong publics"— the formal and institutional bodies where deliberation leads to direct decision making. In general, the more marketing activities target the deliberations of strong publics, either directly as in political advertising or indirectly as in various types of "woke-washing," the more businesses have a duty to offer public justification for their decision. If businesses choose to use their economic resources to engage directly in public debate, they have to do so in a manner that is open to deliberative scrutiny.

However, even when businesses engage in ordinary marketing activities that have nothing to do with political or policy issues, the marketing strategies that they adopt have the power to affect the terms of public discussion in significant ways. We have described in the chapter how decisions about where to place ads, the use of stereotypes in advertising, and certain practices of product placement can impact the quality of the democratic deliberations of weak publics. Thus, even when engaging in ordinary marketing practices, businesses have a duty to reflect on the ways that their strategies might impact the quality of democratic deliberations and avoid using strategies that negatively affect these deliberations.

Response to activism. While businesses are inclined to see social activism as a form of market competition, we have suggested in chapter 6 that businesses should view these protest activities as part of the democratic process. This is true even when activists are directing their energies at the business. Businesses need to engage with activists in ethical bargaining, based on norms of democratic respect, with a willingness to submit to the judgment of Madisonian institutions that are based on third-party mediation, and avoid undermining the capacity of protestors to engage in collective action.

"How Can Firms Be Expected to Treat Democracy Like Some Precious Flower When Political Actors Are Busy Trashing It?"

A colleague asked this question on an early draft, and we liked the wording so much that we have quoted it in its entirety. Throughout this book we have contended that businesses ought to be sensitive to, and reflect on, how their actions can be detrimental to democracy, and take steps to avoid this. Yet in doing this, it may seem like we set the bar too high relative to that of other actors. After all, it is not at all obvious that those in political roles—legislators, candidates, public activists, organizers, and the like—are any better on this score. Political campaigns often strive to suppress or depress the turnout of demographic groups who might otherwise vote for the opposition; legislators often treat legal loopholes in cynical and self-serving ways in order to solicit corrupting favors; and political actors generally often strive to exercise power in ways that serve the goals of some to the detriment of democratic equality and inclusion. Because of this, it might seem like we are asking business to abide by standards that nobody else is, least of all those formally engaged in democratic politics.

As we have tried to make clear throughout the book (often with this question in mind), our arguments don't rest on any assumptions about democracy working in some ideal way, or about those engaged in politics being virtuous and civic-minded, in contrast to the venality of the business world. Democratic practices and institutions are deeply imperfect, and those who act within them are often implicated in their imperfection. Insofar as we have any strong assumptions about human nature, we assume that the tendency to act opportunistically and immorally is evenly distributed throughout the population, and well represented across professions, politicians very much included.

However, there are still good reasons to emphasize the democratic obligations of business. There is the most simple point, which is that others' failure to do what's right doesn't justify one's own misbehavior. The fact that Congress is giving democracy a bad name doesn't entitle business to do the same. But, more importantly, even if it were to excuse such behavior on pragmatic

grounds, it wouldn't relieve us of articulating firms' democratic obligations—
even if they're not being met—lest we extol what we should merely excuse.

As noted above, business ethics (and the ethics of social actors generally)
is not just about counseling what people are entitled to do or are forbidden
from doing in given scenarios; it is not only, or primarily, a set of maxims that
businesspeople abide by. It is also, importantly, a set of concepts and ideas
society uses to ground a critical reflection on the practices and institutions
that constitute business activity. The fact that politicians and activists often
fail to live up to the demands of democracy doesn't undermine the necessity of articulating businesses' democratic obligations. To the contrary, such
failure helps us understand why being clear on such obligations is necessary.
The fact is, we already have a shared language for criticizing politicians for
harming democracy—there is no shortage of commentary in editorial col-
umns, cable news, internet missives, or casual conversation among neighbors
that articulates politicians' failure to live up to democratic ideals. The widespread critique of politicians is proof positive that such standards exist.

For businesses, in contrast, there is less consensus and more confusion regarding not just what firms owe to democracy, but whether they have democratic obligations in the first place. Trying to understand the civic obligations
that attach to businesspeople as businesspeople is thus crucial, even if the
obligations are slightly idealistic. This is for three reasons. First of all, we need
to know what sort of conduct we, as a society, would like our institutional actors to conform to, if only aspirationally. Second, even if firms don't or can't
live up to such standards, we need to be able to articulate that; just as we can
lament politicians' civic failures to live up to what we want of them, we need
an understanding of business's democratic responsibilities so we can similarly
scrutinize and criticize their conduct, and avoid simply accepting it as given.

Third, and finally, articulating business's democratic responsibilities is
important because it reminds us just how pervasive politics are in society. It
is easy to succumb to the idea that political actors are subject to democratic
ideals because theirs are public affairs; in contrast, businesses are private actors to whom such ideals don't apply. What thinking through the democratic
obligations of businesses helps us to remember, and what we have tried to
articulate in this book, is that there is no nonpolitical space for firms to retire
to. The institutions that constitute, structure, and orient business activity are
themselves social artifacts, which both reflect and shape political configura-
tions of power. Business, and business ethics, is inevitably political, regardless
of whether anyone acts with particularly political motivations. As such, how
businesses conduct themselves is everyone's business!

Acknowledgments

This book has been in the works, in one form or another, for many years. As a consequence we have accumulated various debts. The authors would collectively like to thank everyone who read a draft of this book, either in whole or in part, at some point and gave us much needed feedback: Samuel Bagg, Kiran Banerjee, Jason Brennan, Matt Caulfield, Cedric Dawkins, Kevin Elliott, Jennifer Forestal, Giunia Gatta, Jennifer Griffin, Jonathan Havercroft, Joseph Heath, Michael Illuzzi, Alisa Kessel, Doron Navot, Victoria Presser, and Carson Young. We would like to give a special thank-you to Elizabeth Joka and Ramzy Wehbi, who not only read drafts but provided crucial research assistance.

Many chapters began as paper drafts, which were presented in various forums where we received useful comments and directions, including presentations at the Zicklin Workshop in Normative Business Ethics at Wharton, the Society for Business Ethics, the Western Political Science Association, and the Association for Political Theory, as well as invited talks at the University of Utrecht, Seattle University, and the Summer School in Political Philosophy and Public Policy at the University of Minho. While those who provided comments at these talks are too numerous to count here, we would like to mention Rutger Claassen, Amy Sepinwall, Rob Hughes, Brian Berkey, Julian Jonker, Gaston De Los Reyes, David Silver, Jeffrey Moriarty, Jeffery Smith, Marc Cohen, Caitlin Carlson, Eric MacGilvray, Kate Jackson, Turku Isiksel, David Watkins, Emma Saunders-Hastings, Daniele Santoro, Antonio Baptiste, Brookes Brown, Lisa Herzog, Alan Thomas, and Gabriel Monette.

We would like to add a special thanks to our University of Chicago Press editor Chad Zimmerman; our copyeditor, Kathleen Kageff; and the entire editorial and production team, for their support, guidance, and patience in seeing this manuscript through, as well as two reviewers who provided fantastic comments to help improve this book.

On the occasion of publishing this book, Amit would like to express continued love and gratitude to his lifelong partner, Ronit, and their daughters, Noa, Shira, and Maya, to whom the book is dedicated; and to his parents, Noah and Ofra, and his sisters, Eti and Yael.

Abe would like to acknowledge and express gratitude to tía Olga, Nannette, and Catalina (Cati), who made writing this book possible during difficult times. For their support he would like to thank Lucas, Matt, Ben, and Dave of JwP; Luke and Noaman of LAN; and, of course, Luisa and Minerva, to whom also the book is dedicated.

This book draws on ideas developed in work that we have published previously. We thank the editors and reviewers of those journals for their contribution in strengthening our work, and the publishers for their permission to reproduce some of the work found in Abraham Singer and Amit Ron, "The Social Subcontract: Business Ethics as Democratic Theory," *Political Research Quarterly* 76 (2) (2023): 654–66; Abraham Singer and Amit Ron, "Prioritizing Democracy: A Commentary on Smith's Presidential Address to the Society for Business Ethics," *Business Ethics Quarterly* 30 (1) (2020): 139–53; Amit Ron and Abraham Singer, "Democracy, Corruption, and the Ethics of Business Lobbying," *Interest Groups and Advocacy* 9 (2020): 38–56. Copyright © 2019, Springer Nature Limited.

Notes

Introduction

1. The character Gordon Gekko, played by Michael Douglas in the 1987 film *Wall Street*, famously says, "greed—for lack of a better word—is good." The entirety of this speech can be found on the website American Rhetoric Movie Speeches, https://www.americanrhetoric.com /MovieSpeeches/moviespeechwallstreet.html (accessed February 19, 2024).

2. We are happy to say that in addressing this question, this book is not alone. The Erb Institute at the University of Michigan, for instance, released its "principles for corporate political responsibility" (Lyon and Doty 2023) while the present book was under review. Its emphasis on legitimacy, accountability, responsibility, and transparency, reflects a burgeoning sea-change in how scholars think about business ethics and corporate social responsibility.

Chapter One

1. This discussion is influenced by von Kriegstein (2019) and Heath (2018b).

2. It is also worth noting that the certifications of incorporation of many corporations list their purpose in a very general way as "engage in any lawful act or activity" (Pollman 2019a, 720).

3. It is worth noting that in his most recent iteration of the MFA, Heath has conceded this point to some extent (2023, 194–95).

Chapter Two

1. In using the philosophical device of hypothetical ideal worlds, we follow the example of Lipsey and Lancaster 1956 and, especially, Heath 2013.

Chapter Three

1. For a more thorough discussion, see Pollman 2019a and 2019b.

2. We note here that what follows is a rather Rawlsian/legalistic reading of King's account of civil disobedience, which has been challenged (e.g., Livingston 2020). We do this without disavowing the more radical readings of King, but rather just to bring out his point that law-respecting lawbreaking requires certain conditions, which corporations are rarely in the position to realize.

Chapter Four

1. This chapter rehearses and expands on arguments and distinctions we made in Ron and Singer 2020.

Chapter Five

1. Of course, this assumes that people really are that easy to manipulate. There is a large literature on the nuances of this sort of question. For our purposes, we need not delve into the matter too deeply. The advertising industry exists, so presumably advertisements are or are believed to be effective at such influence. Given that perceived ability, what are advertisers' responsibilities?

Chapter Six

1. We should note here that there are democratic theorists who focus on the potential negative effects of protest on democracy. According to critics, protests are nondeliberative, and they may subvert the representation of the majority, prompt authoritarian backlash, and sometimes promote repugnant causes (see Stokes 2020).

2. It is important to emphasize that unions engage in many activities to support employees other than strikes and work stoppages. Among other things, they lobby government on behalf of employees, they engage in orderly and institutionalized negotiations, and they represent employees in disputes with employers (for a discussion of the democratic function of such activities, see Klein 2023). We focus here on strikes because, even when they are regulated activities, they tend to be the most confrontational, high-stakes, and often rowdy form of labor activism, and thus less intuitively democratic.

3. It is important to emphasize that many on the left criticize these institutions and see them as tilted toward businesses. However, this is a question for the democratic process to sort out, and it does not affect the obligations of businesses.

Chapter Seven

1. There are, of course, approaches to workplace hierarchy that start with a more top-down understanding of democratic culture, seeing democratizing workplaces as important for strengthening larger-scale democratic institutions (see Singer 2019, 139–47, for an overview).

2. While it is true that in publicly traded corporations, shareholders may outnumber workers, shareholders don't actually interact with the firm in any functional way. Their interests are made present within the firm by management, which is generally outnumbered by workers.

Chapter Eight

1. This Westphalian model captures a common understanding of the international system, and its underlying logic and structure. We should note that the international system, insofar as there is one, is actually far more complicated and nuanced than the simple principle of sovereignty suggests. But this is not our topic of discussion here.

Bibliography

Abizadeh, Arash. 2012. "On the Demos and Its Kin: Nationalism, Democracy, and the Boundary Problem." *American Political Science Review* 106 (4): 867–82.

Achen, Christopher, and Larry Bartels. 2016. *Democracy for Realists: Why Elections Do Not Produce Responsive Government*. Princeton, NJ: Princeton University Press.

Alchian, Armen, and Harold Demsetz. 1972. "Production, Information Costs, and Economic Organization." *American Economic Review* 62:777–95. Reprinted in *The Collected Works of Armen A. Alchian*, vol. 2, *Property Rights and Economic Behavior* (Indianapolis: Liberty Fund, 2006), 151–78.

Alzola, Miguel. 2012. "The Possibility of Virtue." *Business Ethics Quarterly* 22 (2): 377–404.

———. 2018. "Role Duties, Role Virtues and the Practice of Business." In *Cultivating Moral Character and Virtue in Professional Practice*, edited by David Carr, 42–54. New York: Routledge.

Anderson, Elizabeth. 1999. "What Is the Point of Equality?" *Ethics* 109 (2): 287–337.

———. 2012. *The Imperative of Integration*. Princeton, NJ: Princeton University Press.

———. 2017. *Private Government: How Employers Rule Our Lives (and Why We Don't Talk about It)*. Princeton, NJ: Princeton University Press.

Armus, Teo. 2020. "GOP Ohio House Speaker Arrested in Connection to $60 Million Bribery Scheme." *Washington Post*, July 22. https://www.washingtonpost.com/nation/2020/07/22/ohio-house-speaker-arrested-republican/.

Ashenfelter, Orley, David Card, Henry Farber, and Michael R. Ransom. 2022. "Monopsony in the Labor Market: New Empirical Results and New Public Policies." *Journal of Human Resources* 57 (3): 1–10.

Aytac, Ugur. 2023. "In Defense of Shirking in Capitalist Firms: Worker Resistance vs. Managerial Power." *Political Theory*. OnlineFirst. https://doi.org/10.1177/00905917231205624.

Bagg, Samuel Ely. 2024. *The Dispersion of Power: A Critical Realist Theory of Democracy*. Oxford: Oxford University Press.

Bakan, Joel. 2003. *The Corporation: The Pathological Pursuit of Power*. New York: Free Press.

Banister, Jon. 2017. "Amazon HQ2 Could Finally Bring D.C. Region Together, but Divides Run Deep." *Forbes*, September 15. https://www.forbes.com/sites/bisnow/2017/09/15/amazon-hq2-could-finally-bring-d-c-region-together-but-divides-run-deep/?sh=1637e98c6f52.

Barley, Stephen R. 2007. "Corporations, Democracy, and the Public Good." *Journal of Management Inquiry* 16 (3): 201–15.

Barnes, Brooks. "DeSantis and Disney Clash Anew over Florida Theme Park's Authority." *New York Times*, April 3, 2023. https://www.nytimes.com/2023/04/03/business/media/ron-desantis-disney-world-florida.html?searchResultPosition=13.

Bazerman, Max H., and Ann E. Tenbrunsel. 2011 *Blind Spots: Why We Fail to Do What's Right and What to Do about It*. Princeton, NJ: Princeton University Press.

BBC. 2018. "Facebook Scandal 'Hit 87 Million Users,'" April 4. https://www.bbc.com/news/technology-43649018.

Bennett, Michael. 2023. "Managerial Discretion, Market Failure and Democracy." *Journal of Business Ethics* 185 (1): 33–47.

———. 2024. "An Epistemic Argument for an Egalitarian Public Sphere." *Episteme* 21 (1): 1–18.

Bhattarai, Abha, and Greg Bensinger. 2019. "Walmart Employees Stage a Walkout to Protest Gun Sales." *Washington Post*, August 7. https://www.washingtonpost.com/business/2019/08/07/walmart-employees-staging-walkout-protest-gun-sales/.

Bingham, Tom. 2007. "The Rule of Law." *Cambridge Law Journal* 66 (1): 67–85.

———. 2011. *The Rule of Law*. London: Penguin.

Boatright, John R. 2006. "What's Wrong—and What's Right—with Stakeholder Management." *Journal of Private Enterprise* 21 (2): 106–30.

Bohman, James. 1996. *Public Deliberation: Pluralism, Complexity and Democracy*. Cambridge, MA: MIT Press.

———. 1999. "Democracy as Inquiry, Inquiry as Democratic: Pragmatism, Social Science, and the Cognitive Division of Labor." *American Journal of Political Science* 43 (2): 590.

Bowie, Norman E. 2017. *Business Ethics: A Kantian Perspective*. Cambridge: Cambridge University Press.

Bowie, Norman, and Ronald Duska. 1990. *Business Ethics*. 2nd ed. New York: Prentice Hall.

Bradt, George. "Wanamaker Was Wrong—the Vast Majority of Advertising Is Wasted." *Forbes*, September 14, 2016. https://www.forbes.com/sites/georgebradt/2016/09/14/wanamaker-was-wrong-the-vast-majority-of-advertising-is-wasted/?sh=33d0623a483b.

Brenkert, George. 1998. Marketing and the Vulnerable. *Business Ethics Quarterly* 8 (S1): 7–20.

Brennan, Jason. 2016. *Against Democracy*. Princeton, NJ: Princeton University Press.

Brennan, Jason, and Hélène Landemore. 2021. *Debating Democracy: Do We Need More or Less?* Oxford: Oxford University Press.

Brighouse, Harry. 2006. *On Education*. New York: Routledge.

Brighouse, Harry, and Adam Swift. 2014. *Family Values: The Ethics of Parent-Child Relationships*. Princeton, NJ: Princeton University Press.

Brinkmann, Johannes. 2002. "Business and Marketing Ethics as Professional Ethics: Concepts, Approaches and Typologies." *Journal of Business Ethics* 41:159–77.

Buckley, Michael. 2013. "A Constructivist Approach to Business Ethics." *Journal of Business Ethics* 117 (4): 695–706.

Burke, Edmund M. *Corporate Community Relations: The Principle of the Neighbor of Choice*. Westport, CT: Praeger, 1999.

Business Roundtable. 2019. "Statement on the Purpose of the Corporation." https://www.businessroundtable.org/business-roundtable-redefines-the-purpose-of-a-corporation-to-promote-an-economy-that-serves-all-americans.

Caplan, Bryan. 2007. *The Myth of the Rational Voter.* Princeton, NJ: Princeton University Press.

Carr, E. H. 1941. *The Twenty Years' Crisis: 1919–1939.* London: Palgrave Macmillan.

Carroll, Archie B. 1998. "The Four Faces of Corporate Citizenship." *Business and Society Review* 100–101 (1): 1–7.

Carroll, Archie B., and Kareem M. Shabana. 2010. "The Business Case for Corporate Social Responsibility: A Review of Concepts, Research and Practice." *International journal of Management Reviews* 12 (1): 85–105.

Celikates, Robin. 2016a. "Democratizing Civil Disobedience." *Philosophy and Social Criticism* 42 (10): 982–94.

———. 2016b. "Rethinking Civil Disobedience as a Practice of Contestation—beyond the Liberal Paradigm." *Constellations* 23 (1): 37–45.

Chambers, Simone. 1996. *Reasonable Democracy: Jürgen Habermas and the Politics of Discourse.* Ithaca, NY: Cornell University Press.

Chandler, Alfred. 1977. *The Visible Hand: The Managerial Revolution in American Business.* Cambridge, MA: Belknap Press of Harvard University Press.

Chapman, Emilee Booth. 2019 "The Distinctive Value of Elections and the Case for Compulsory Voting." *American Journal of Political Science* 63 (1): 101–12.

———. 2022. *Election Day: How We Vote and What It Means for Democracy.* Princeton, NJ: Princeton University Press.

Christiano, Thomas. 2008. *The Constitution of Equality: Democratic Authority and Its Limits.* Oxford: Oxford University Press.

Clark, Terry Nichols. 2011. "The New Chicago School: Notes toward a Theory." In *The City, Revisited: Urban Theory from Chicago, Los Angeles, and New York,* edited by D. R. Judd and D. W. Simpson, 220–41. Minneapolis: University of Minnesota Press.

Coase, Ronald. 1937. "The Nature of the Firm." *Economica* 4 (16): 386–405.

Cohen, J., and C. Sabel. 1997. "Directly-Deliberative Polyarchy." *European Law Journal* 3 (4): 313–42.

D'Agostino, Fred, Gerald Gaus, and John Thrasher. 2019. "Contemporary Approaches to the Social Contract." In *The Stanford Encyclopedia of Philosophy,* edited by Edward N. Zalta. https://plato.stanford.edu/archives/win2021/entries/contractarianism-contemporary/.

Dahl, Robert. 1971. *Polyarchy.* New Haven, CT: Yale University Press.

———. 1985 *A Preface to Economic Democracy.* Vol. 28. Berkeley: University of California Press.

Dale, Brady. 2017. "Does Travis Kalanick Think Ignoring Regulators Counts as Civil Disobedience?" *Observer,* May 8. https://observer.com/2017/05/uber-travis-kalanick-civil-disobedience/.

Davis, Aaron C., Rick Noack, and Douglas Macmillan. 2022. "Uber Leveraged Violent Attacks against Its Drivers to Pressure Politicians." *Washington Post,* July 10. https://www.washingtonpost.com/business/2022/07/10/uber-taxi-driver-violence/.

Dawkins, Cedric. 2019. "A Normative Argument for Independent Voice and Labor Unions." *Journal of Business Ethics* 155 (4): 1153–65.

Dewey, John. (1939) 1988. "Creative Democracy—the Task before Us." In John Dewey, *The Later Works, 1925–1953,* vol. 14, edited by Jo Ann Boydston, 224–30. Carbondale: Southern Illinois University Press.

Dobson, Andrew. 2012. "Listening: The New Democratic Deficit." *Political Studies* 60 (4): 843–59.

Donaldson, Thomas, and Thomas W. Dunfee. 1999. *Ties That Bind: A Social Contracts Approach to Business Ethics.* Cambridge, MA: Harvard Business School Press.

Dow, Gregory K. 1993. "Why Capital Hires Labor: A Bargaining Perspective." *American Economic Review* 83 (1): 118–34.

———. 2003. *Governing the Firm: Workers' Control in Theory and Practice*. Cambridge: Cambridge University Press.

Drucker, Peter. 1946. *The Concept of the Corporation*. New York: John Day.

Dryzek, John S., and Ana Tanasoca. 2021. *Democratizing Global Justice: Deliberating Global Goals*. Cambridge: Cambridge University Press.

Durkee, Melissa J. 2017. "Astroturf Activism." *Stanford Law Review* 69 (1): 201.

Dwidar, Maraam A. 2022. "Diverse Lobbying Coalitions and Influence in Notice-and-Comment Rulemaking." *Policy Studies Journal* 50 (1): 199–240.

Dworkin, Ronald. 1968. "On Not Prosecuting Civil Disobedience." *New York Review of Books*, June 6. https://www.nybooks.com/articles/1968/06/06/on-not-prosecuting-civil-disobedience/.

———. 1981. "Part 1: Equality of Welfare." *Philosophy and Public Affairs* 10 (3): 185–246.

———. 2010. "The 'Devastating' Decision.'" *New York Review of Books* 57 (3): 39–39.

Easterbrook, Frank H., and Daniel R. Fischel. 1982. "Antitrust Suits by Targets of Tender Offers." *Michigan Law Review* 80:1155–78.

———. 1991. *The Economic Structure of Corporate Law*. Cambridge, MA: Harvard University Press.

El Amine, Loubna. 2016. "Beyond East and West: Reorienting Political Theory through the Prism of Modernity." *Perspectives on Politics* 14 (1): 102–20.

Elliott, Kevin J. 2023. *Democracy for Busy People*. Chicago: University of Chicago Press.

Elster, Jon. 1997. "The Market and the Forum: Three Varieties of Political Theory." In *Deliberative Democracy: Essays on Reason and Politics*, edited by J. Bohman and W. Rehg, 3–34. Cambridge, MA: MIT Press.

Epstein, Stephen. 1996. *Impure Science: AIDS, Activism and the Politics of Knowledge*. Berkeley: University of California Press.

Etzioni, Amitai. 1988. "A Communitarian Note on Stakeholder Theory." *Business Ethics Quarterly* 8 (4) (October): 679–91.

Farrell, Henry, Hugo Mercier, and Melissa Schwartzberg. 2023. "Analytical Democratic Theory: A Microfoundational Approach." *American Political Science Review* 117 (2): 767–72.

Federal Trade Commission. 2019. "For Release: FTC Issues Opinion and Order against Cambridge Analytica for Deceiving Consumers about the Collection of Facebook Data, Compliance with EU-US Privacy Shield." December 6. https://www.ftc.gov/news-events/news/press-releases/2019/12/ftc-issues-opinion-order-against-cambridge-analytica-deceiving-consumers-about-collection-facebook.

Ferreras, Isabelle. 2017. *Firms as Political Entities: Saving Democracy through Economic Bicameralism*. Cambridge: Cambridge University Press.

Fink, Larry. 2022. "Larry Fink's 2022 Letter to CEOs: The Power of Capitalism." BlackRock. https://www.blackrock.com/corporate/investor-relations/larry-fink-ceo-letter.

Fishkin, James S. 2011. *When the People Speak: Deliberative Democracy and Public Consultation*. Oxford: Oxford University Press.

Fligstein, Neil, and Doug McAdam. 2012. *A Theory of Fields*. Oxford: Oxford University Press.

Florida, Richard. 2018. "The Hypocrisy of Amazon's HQ2 Process." *Bloomberg*, May 10. https://www.bloomberg.com/news/articles/2018-05-10/why-the-contest-for-amazon-s-hq2-is-a-race-to-the-bottom.

Forestal, Jennifer. 2017. "The Architecture of Political Spaces: Trolls, Digital Media, and Dew-eyan Democracy." *American Political Science Review* 111 (1): 149–61.

———. 2022. *Designing for Democracy: How to Build Community in Digital Environments*. Oxford: Oxford University Press.

Fraser, Nancy. 1990. "Rethinking the Public Sphere: A Contribution to the Critique of Actually Existing Democracy." *Social Text*, no. 25/26:56–80.

Freeman, Jo. 1972. "The Tyranny of Structurelessness." *Berkeley Journal of Sociology* 17:151–64.

Freeman, R. Edward. 1994. "The Politics of Stakeholder Theory: Some Future Directions." *Business Ethics Quarterly* 4 (4): 409–21.

———. 2017. "The New Story of Business: Towards a More Responsible Capitalism." *Business and Society Review* 122 (3): 449–65.

Freeman, R. Edward, Jeffrey S. Harrison, Andrew C. Wicks, Bidhan L. Parmar, and Simone De Colle. 2010. *Stakeholder Theory: The State of the Art*. Cambridge: Cambridge University Press.

Frega, Roberto. 2019. "The Normativity of Democracy." *European Journal of Political Theory* 18 (3): 371–92.

Frega, Roberto, Lisa Herzog, and Christian Neuhäuser. 2019. "Workplace Democracy—the Recent Debate." *Philosophy Compass* 14 (4): e12574.

Friedman, Milton. 1970. "The Social Responsibility of Business Is to Increase Its Profits." *New York Times*, September 13. Reprinted in *Management of Values: The Ethical Difference in Corporate Policy and Performance*, edited by Charles McCoy, 253–60. Boston: Pitman, 1985.

Friedman, Monroe. 2001. "Ethical Dilemmas Associated with Consumer Boycotts." *Journal of Social Philosophy* 32 (2): 232–40.

Fung, Archon. 2013. "The Principle of Affected Interests and Inclusion in Democratic Governance." In *Representations: Elections and Beyond*, edited by Jack Nagel and Rogers Smith, 236–68. Philadelphia: University of Pennsylvania Press.

Gaus, Gerald. 2016. *The Tyranny of the Ideal: Justice in a Diverse Society*. Princeton, NJ: Princeton University Press.

Gauthier, David. 1982. "No Need for Morality: The Case of the Competitive Market." *Philosophic Exchange* 3 (3): 41–54.

Gilbert, Dirk Ulrich, and Michael Behnam. 2009. "Advancing Integrative Social Contracts Theory: A Habermasian Perspective." *Journal of Business Ethics* 89 (2): 215–34.

Gilbert, Dirk Ulrich, Andreas Rasche, Maximilian J. L. Schormair, and Abraham Singer. 2023. "Guest Editors' Introduction: The Challenges and Prospects of Deliberative Democracy for Corporate Sustainability and Responsibility." *Business Ethics Quarterly* 33 (1): 1–25.

Gindis, David, and Abraham A. Singer. 2023. "The Corporate Baby in the Bathwater: Why Proposals to Abolish Corporate Personhood Are Misguided." *Journal of Business Ethics* 183 (4): 983–97.

Goodin, Robert E. 2007. "Enfranchising All Affected Interests, and Its Alternatives." *Philosophy and Public Affairs* 35 (1) (Winter): 40–68.

Gould, Carol C. 2002. "Does Stakeholder Theory Require Democratic Management?" *Business and Professional Ethics Journal* 21 (1): 3–20.

———. 2006. "Self-Determination beyond Sovereignty: Relating Transnational Democracy to Local Autonomy." *Journal of Social Philosophy* 37 (1): 44–60.

Gourevitch, Alex. 2018. "The Right to Strike: A Radical View." *American Political Science Review* 112 (4): 905–17.

Gowder, Paul. 2013. "The Rule of Law and Equality." *Law and Philosophy* 32 (5): 565–618.

Gustafson, Andrew. 2013. "In Defense of a Utilitarian Business Ethic." *Business and Society Review* 118 (3): 325–60.

Gutmann, Amy, and Dennis F. Thompson. 1996. *Democracy and Disagreement*. Cambridge, MA: Harvard University Press.

Habermas, Jürgen. 1975. *Legitimation Crisis*. Boston: Beacon.

———. 1995. "On the Internal Relation between the Rule of Law and Democracy." *European Journal of Philosophy* 3 (1): 12–20.

———. 1996. *Between Facts and Norms: Contributions to a Discourse Theory of Law and Democracy*. Cambridge, MA: MIT Press.

Hacker, Jacob S., and Paul Pierson. 2010. *Winner-Take-All Politics: How Washington Made the Rich Richer—and Turned Its Back on the Middle Class*. New York: Simon and Schuster.

Haigney, Sophie. 2022. "Anatomy of a Product Placement." *New York Times*, June 24. https://www.nytimes.com/interactive/2022/06/23/arts/product-placement.html?utm_source=pocket-newtab.

Hall, Richard L., and Alan V. Deardorff. 2006. "Lobbying as Legislative Subsidy." *American Political Science Review* 100 (1): 69–84.

Hansmann, Henry. 1996. *The Ownership of Enterprise*. Cambridge, MA: Harvard University Press.

Hansmann, Henry, and Reinier Kraakman. 2004. "What Is Corporate Law?" In *The Anatomy of Corporate Law: A Comparative and Functional Approach*, edited by Reinier Kraakman, 5–15. Oxford: Oxford University Press.

Heath, Joseph. 2008. "Business Ethics and Moral Motivation: A Criminological Perspective." *Journal of Business Ethics* 83 (4): 595–614.

———. 2009. "The Uses and Abuses of Agency Theory." *Business Ethics Quarterly* 19 (4): 497–528.

———. 2013. "Ideal Theory in an Nth-Best World: The Case of Pauper Labor." *Journal of Global Ethics* 9 (2): 159–72.

———. 2014. *Morality, Competition, and the Firm: The Market Failures Approach to Business Ethics*. Oxford: Oxford University Press.

———. 2018a. " 'But Everyone Else Is Doing It': Competition and Business Self-Regulation." *Journal of Social Philosophy* 49 (4): 516–35.

———. 2018b. "The Contribution of Economics to Business Ethics." In *The Routledge Companion to Business Ethics*, edited by E. Heath, B. Kaldis, and A. Marcoux, 290–305. London: Routledge.

———. 2020. *The Machinery of Government: Public Administration and the Liberal State*. Oxford: Oxford University Press.

———. 2023. *Ethics for Capitalists: A Systematic Approach to Business Ethics, Competition, and Market Failure*. Altona: FriesenPress.

Herzog, Lisa. 2018. *Reclaiming the System: Moral Responsibility, Divided Labour, and the Role of Organizations in Society*. New York: Oxford University Press.

Hirschman, Albert O. 1970. *Exit, Voice, and Loyalty: Responses to Decline in Firms, Organizations, and States*. Cambridge, MA: Harvard University Press.

Holder, Sarah. 2018. "California's Lessons for the Amazon HQ2 Bidding War." *Bloomberg*, April 9. https://www.bloomberg.com/news/articles/2018-04-09/california-s-lessons-on-bargaining-to-win-amazon-hq2.

Hussain, Waheed. 2012. "Is Ethical Consumerism an Impermissible Form of Vigilantism?" *Philosophy and Public Affairs* 40:111–43.

Hussain, Waheed, and Jeffrey Moriarty. 2018. "Accountable to Whom? Rethinking the Role of Corporations in Political CSR." *Journal of Business Ethics* 149:519–34.

Jackall, Robert. 1988. *Moral Mazes: The World of Corporate Managers.* Oxford: Oxford University Press.

Jaworski, Peter M. 2014. "Blame the Politicians: A Government Failure Approach to Political Ethics." *Georgetown Journal of Law and Public Policy* 12:521–34.

Johnson, Eric. 2018. "Amazon's HQ2 Was a Con, Not a Contest." *Vox,* November 9. https://www.vox.com/2018/11/9/18077342/amazon-hq2-headquarters-jeff-bezos-dc-ny-virginia-long-island-kara-swisher-scott-galloway.

Jones, Thomas M., and Will Felps. 2013. "Shareholder Wealth Maximization and Social Welfare: A Utilitarian Critique." *Business Ethics Quarterly* 23 (2): 207–38.

Kerr, Dara, and Maddy Varner. 2021 "Uber and Lyft Donated to Community Groups Who Then Pushed the Companies' Agenda." *Markup,* June 17. https://themarkup.org/news/2021/06/17/uber-and-lyft-donated-to-community-groups-who-then-pushed-the-companies-agenda.

Keynes, John Maynard. 1936. *The General Theory of Employment, Interest, and Money.* London: Palgrave Macmillan.

Kilmartin, Laurie. 2017. "Being a Female Comic in Louis C.K.'s World." *New York Times,* November 10. https://www.nytimes.com/2017/11/10/opinion/sunday/louis-ck-harassment.html.

King, Martin Luther, Jr. (1963) 1986. "Letter from Birmingham City Jail." In *A Testament of Hope,* edited by James Melvin Washington, 289–302. New York: Penguin.

Kirkpatrick, Jennet. 2017. *The Virtues of Exit.* Chapel Hill: University of North Carolina Press.

Klein, Steven. 2022. "Democracy Requires Organized Collective Power." *Journal of Political Philosophy* 30 (1): 26–47.

———. 2023. "Towards a Democratic Theory of Labour Unions." *Public Ethics: Expert Analysis of Ethical Issues in the News* (blog). Stockholm Centre for the Ethics of War and Peace, September 28. https://www.publicethics.org/post/towards-a-democratic-theory-of-labour-unions?fbclid=IwAR0NGkjxsDAYgPRkolci4p401_vacLMESobRGSODnJdrvcFTWpPOYnx1-5k.

Knight, Jack. 1992. *Institutions and Social Conflict.* Cambridge: Cambridge University Press.

Knight, Jack, and James Johnson. 2011. *The Priority of Democracy.* Princeton, NJ: Princeton University Press.

Koehn, Daryl. 1995. "A Role for Virtue Ethics in the Analysis of Business Practice." *Business Ethics Quarterly* 5 (3): 533–39.

Kraus, M. W., J. W. Park, and J. J. X. Tan. 2017. "Signs of Social Class: The Experience of Economic Inequality in Everyday Life." *Perspectives on Psychological Science* 12 (3): 422–35.

Krishna, Aradhna. 2012 "An Integrative Review of Sensory Marketing: Engaging the Senses to Affect Perception, Judgment and Behavior." *Journal of Consumer Psychology* 22 (3): 332–51.

Krüger, Alexander. 2023. "Islands of Deliberative Capacity in an Ocean of Authoritarian Control? The Deliberative Potential of Self-Organized Teams in Firms." *Business Ethics Quarterly* 33 (1): 67–101.

Lafont, Christina. 2020. *Democracy without Shortcuts.* New York: Oxford University Press.

Landemore, Hélène, and Isabelle Ferreras. 2016. "In Defense of Workplace Democracy: Towards a Justification of the Firm-State Analogy." *Political Theory* 44 (1): 53–81.

Larson, Zeb. 2022. "Don't Believe a Corporation That Promises to Do Better." *Jacobin*, April 29. https://jacobin.com/2022/04/corporation-promise-greenhouse-gas-emissions-sullivan-principles-south-africa-climate-change.

Levenson, Michael. 2021. "Ohio House Expels Ex-Speaker Charged in $60 Million Corruption Scheme." *New York Times*, June 16. https://www.nytimes.com/2021/06/16/us/larry-householder-expelled-ohio-house.html.

Levitin, Michael. 2021. *Generation Occupy: Reawakening American Democracy*. Berkeley, CA: Counterpoint.

Levy, Jacob T. 2007. "Federalism, Liberalism, and the Separation of Loyalties." *American Political Science Review* 101 (3): 459–77.

Lipsey, Richard, and Kelvin Lancaster. 1956. "The General Theory of Second Best." *Review of Economic Studies* 24 (1): 11–32.

Livingston, Alexander. 2020. "Power for the Powerless: Martin Luther King, Jr.'s Late Theory of Civil Disobedience." *Journal of Politics* 82 (2): 700–713.

Locke, John. (1689) 1980. *Second Treatise on Government*. Edited by C. B. McPherson. Indianapolis: Hackett.

Lopez, Ian F. Haney. 2000. "Institutional Racism: Judicial Conduct and a New Theory of Racial Discrimination." *Yale Law Journal* 109 (8): 1717–884.

Loury, Glenn. 2002. *The Anatomy of Racial Inequality*. Cambridge, MA: Harvard University Press.

Lyon, Thomas P., and Elizabeth Doty. 2023. "The Erb Principles for Corporate Political Responsibility." *Harvard Law School Forum on Corporate Governance*. April 4. https://corpgov.law.harvard.edu/2023/04/04/the-erb-principles-for-corporate-political-responsibility/.

Lyon, Thomas P., and John W. Maxwell. 2004. "Astroturf: Interest Group Lobbying and Corporate Strategy." *Journal of Economics and Management Strategy* 13 (4): 561–97.

Maitland, Ian. 1989. "Rights in the Workplace: A Nozickian Argument." *Journal of Business Ethics* 8 (12): 951–54.

Malleson, Tom. 2013. "Making the Case for Workplace Democracy: Exit and Voice as Mechanisms of Freedom in Social Life." *Polity* 45 (4): 604–29.

———. 2014. *After Occupy: Economic Democracy for the 21st Century*. Oxford: Oxford University Press.

———. 2023. *Against Inequality: The Practical and Ethical Case for Abolishing the Superrich*. Oxford: Oxford University Press.

Mansbridge, Jane, James Bohman, Simone Chambers, David Estlund, Andreas Føllesdal, Archon Fung, Cristina Lafont, Bernard Manin, and José Luis Martí. 2010. "The Place of Self-Interest and the Role of Power in Deliberative Democracy." *Journal of Political Philosophy* 18 (1): 64–100.

Marcoux, Alexei. 2003. "A Fiduciary Argument against Stakeholder Theory." *Business Ethics Quarterly* 13 (1): 1–24.

Marens, Richard. 2012. "Generous in Victory? American Managerial Autonomy, Labor Relations and the Invention of Corporate Social Responsibility." *Socio-economic Review* 10 (1): 59–84.

Markovits, Daniel. 2019. *The Meritocracy Trap*. London: Penguin.

McKean, Benjamin. 2020. *Disorienting Neoliberalism: Global Justice and the Outer Limit of Freedom*. Oxford: Oxford University Press.

McMahon, Christopher. 1995. "The Political Theory of Organizations and Business Ethics." *Philosophy and Public Affairs* 24 (4): 292–31.

Medearis, John. 2020. "On the Strike and Democratic Protest." In *Protest and Dissent: nomos LXII*, edited by Melissa Schwartzberg, 237–68. New York: New York University Press.

Michaelson, Christopher, Michael G. Pratt, Adam M. Grant, and Craig P. Dunn. 2014. "Meaningful Work: Connecting Business Ethics and Organization Studies." *Journal of Business Ethics* 121:77–90.

Monaghan, Jake. 2023. *Just Policing*. Oxford: Oxford University Press.

Monteverde, Danny, and Paul Dudley. 2018. "'Everything's in Question' after Entergy Admits Fake Actors Used to Support New Plant." WWL-TV. May 18. https://www.wwltv.com /article/news/local/everythings-in-question-after-entergy-admits-fake-actors-used-to -support-new-plant/289-554334205.

Moody-Adams, Michele. 2022. *Making Space for Justice: Social Movements, Collective Imagination, and Political Hope*. New York: Columbia University Press.

Moriarty, Jeffrey. 2014. "The Connection between Stakeholder Theory and Stakeholder Democracy: An Excavation and Defense." *Business and Society* 53 (6): 820–52.

———. 2020. "What's in a Wage? A New Approach to the Justification of Pay." *Business Ethics Quarterly* 30 (1): 119–37.

Morreall, John. 1976. "The Justifiability of Violent Civil Disobedience." *Canadian Journal of Philosophy* 6 (1): 35–47.

Motchoulski, Alexander. 2021. "Relational Egalitarianism and Democracy." *Journal of Moral Philosophy* 18 (6): 620–49.

Muldoon, Ryan. 2016. *Social Contract Theory for a Diverse World: Beyond Tolerance*. New York: Routledge / Taylor and Francis.

NCAA. 2016. "NCAA to Relocate Championships from North Carolina for 2016–17." September 12. Media Center, NCAA. https://www.ncaa.org/news/2016/9/12/ncaa-to-relocate -championships-from-north-carolina-for-2016-17.aspx.

Norman, Wayne. 2011. "Business Ethics as Self-Regulation: Why Principles That Ground Regulations Should Be Used to Ground Beyond-Compliance Norms as Well." *Journal of Business Ethics* 102:43–57.

Norman, Wayne, and Ancell, Aaron. 2018. "Democratic Theory for a Market Democracy: The Problem of Merriment and Diversion When Regulators and the Regulated Meet." *Journal of Social Philosophy* 49 (4): 536–63.

Nussbaum, Martha. 2002. "Capabilities and Disabilities: Justice for Mentally Disabled Citizens." *Philosophical Topics* 30 (2): 133–65.

Oates, Wallace E. 1969. "The Effects Of Property Taxes and Local Public Spending on Property Values: An Empirical Study of Tax Capitalization and the Tiebout Hypothesis." *Journal of Political Economy* 77 (6): 957–71.

O'Connor, Cailin. 2019. *The Origins of Unfairness: Social Categories and Cultural Evolution*. Oxford: Oxford University Press.

ONEUPWEB. 2019. "10 Ads Empowering Women and Breaking Stereotypes." February 20. https://www.oneupweb.com/blog/10-ads-inspiring-women/.

Orts, Eric. 2013. *Business Persons*. Oxford: Oxford University Press.

Orts, Eric W., and Alan Strudler. 2002. "The Ethical and Environmental Limits of Stakeholder Theory." *Business Ethics Quarterly* 12 (2): 215–33.

———. 2009. "Putting a Stake in Stakeholder Theory." *Journal of Business Ethics* 88 (4): 605–15.

Ostas, Daniel T. 2007. "The Law and Ethics of K Street: Lobbying, the First Amendment, and the Duty to Create Just Laws." *Business Ethics Quarterly* 17 (1): 33–63.

Pamuk, Zeynep. 2021. *Politics and Expertise: How to Use Science in a Democratic Society*. Princeton, NJ: Princeton University Press.

Pateman, Carole. 1970. *Participation and Democratic Theory*. Cambridge: Cambridge University Press.

———. 2012. "Participatory Democracy Revisited." *Perspectives on Politics* 10 (1): 7–19.

Pavel, Carmen. 2016. "Boundaries, Subjection to Laws, and Affected Interests." In *The Oxford Handbook of Freedom*, edited by David Schmidtz and Carmen Pavel 319–34. Oxford: Oxford University Press.

Philips, Robert, Jay B. Barney, R. Edward Freeman, and Jeffrey S. Harrison. 2019. "Stakeholder Theory." In *The Cambridge Handbook of Stakeholder Theory*, edited by J. S. Harrison, J. B. Barney, R. E. Freeman, and R. A. Phillips, 3–18. Cambridge: Cambridge University Press.

Pineda, Erin R. 2021. "Civil Disobedience, and What Else? Making Space for Uncivil Forms of Resistance." *European Journal of Political Theory* 20 (1): 157–64.

Pollman, Elizabeth. 2019a. "Corporate Disobedience." *Duke Law Journal* 68:709–65.

———. 2019b. "Corporate Oversight and Disobedience." *Vanderbilt Law Review* 72:2013.

Ponet, David L., and Ethan J. Leib. 2011. "Fiduciary's Law's Lessons for Deliberative Democracy." *Buffalo University Law Review* 91:1249.

Ransom, T. 2022. "Labor Market Frictions and Moving Costs of the Employed and Unemployed." *Journal of Human Resources* 57 (S): 137–66.

Rawls, John. (1971) 1999. *A Theory of Justice*. Rev. ed. Cambridge, MA: Harvard University Press.

———. 2005. *Political Liberalism*. Expanded ed. Cambridge, MA: Harvard University Press.

Reuters. 2023. "Mondelez 'Singled Out' in Boycott over Russia Business: Executive." *Reuters*, June 16. https://www.reuters.com/business/retail-consumer/mondelez-singled-out-boycott -over-russia-business-memo-2023-06-16/.

Rivera, Lauren A. 2016. *Pedigree: How Elite Students Get Elite Jobs*. Princeton, NJ: Princeton University Press.

Rodrigues, Usha. 2006. "The Seductive Comparison of Shareholder and Civic Democracy." *Washington and Lee Law Review* 63:1389.

Ron, Amit, and Abraham Singer. 2020. "Democracy, Corruption, and the Ethics of Business Lobbying." *Interest Groups and Advocacy* 9 (2020): 38–56.

Rönnegard, David, and N. Craig Smith. 2024. "A Rawlsian Rule for Corporate Governance." *Journal of Business Ethics* 190:295–308. Published online April 5. https://doi.org/10.1007 /s10551-023-05333-z.

Rothacker, Rick, Ely Portillo, and Katherine Peralta. 2016. "PayPal Withdraws Plans for Charlotte Expansion over HB2." *Charlotte Observer*, April 5. http://www.charlotteobserver.com /news/business/article70001502.html.

Sabadoz, Cameron, and Abraham Singer. 2017. "Talk Ain't Cheap: Political CSR and the Challenges of Corporate Deliberation." *Business Ethics Quarterly* 27 (2): 183–211.

Samuelson, Paul. 1957. "Wages and Interest: A Modern Dissection of Marxian Economic Models." *American Economic Review* 47 (6): 884–912.

Sankaran, Kirun. 2021. "Structural Injustice and the Tyranny of Scales." *Journal of Moral Philosophy* 18 (5): 445–72.

Saunders-Hastings, Emma. 2022. *Private Virtues, Public Vices: Philanthropy and Democratic Equality*. Chicago: University of Chicago Press.

Scharding, Tobey K. 2015. "Imprudence and Immorality: A Kantian Approach to the Ethics of Financial Risk." *Business Ethics Quarterly* 25 (2): 243–65.

Scherer, Andreas, and Guido Palazzo. 2007. "Toward a Political Conception of Corporate Responsibility: Business and Society Seen from a Habermasian Perspective." *Academy of Management Review* 32 (4): 1096–120.

Scheuerman, William E. 2015. "Recent Theories of Civil Disobedience: An Anti-legal Turn?" *Journal of Political Philosophy* 23 (4): 427–49.

Schouten, Gina. 2019. *Liberalism, Neutrality, and the Gendered Division of Labor*. Oxford: Oxford University Press.

Schumpeter, J. A. (1943) 2003. *Capitalism, Socialism and Democracy*. London: Routledge.

Schwartzberg, Melissa, and Jack Knight. 2024. *Democratic Deals: A Defense of Political Bargaining*. Cambridge, MA: Harvard University Press.

Scudder, Mary F. 2020. *Beyond Empathy and Inclusion: The Challenge of Listening in Democratic Deliberation*. Oxford: Oxford University Press.

Serviodo, Luca, and Latia Curry. 2020. "Three Elements of Successful Corporate Social Justice Initiatives." *MIT Sloan Management Review*, December 1. https://sloanreview.mit.edu /article/three-elements-of-successful-corporate-social-justice-initiatives/.

Shane, Peter M. 2013. "The Rule of Law and the Inevitability of Discretion." *Harvard Journal of Law and Public Policy* 36:21–28.

Sheinin, Dave, Michael Lee, Emily Giambalvo, Artur Galocha, and Clara Ence Morse. 2022. "How the NFL Blocks Black Coaches." *Washington Post*, September 21. https://www.wash ingtonpost.com/sports/interactive/2022/nfl-black-head-coaches/.

Silver, David. 2021. "Democratic Governance and the Ethics of Market Compliance." *Journal of Business Ethics* 173:525–37.

Singer, Abraham. 2018. "The Political Nature of the Firm and the Cost of Norms." *Journal of Politics* 80 (3): 831–44.

———. 2019. *The Form of the Firm: A Normative Political Theory of the Corporation*. Oxford: Oxford University Press.

———. 2023. "What Sal Owes Mookie: What *Do The Right Thing* and *Mangrove* Teach Us about Business Ethics." *Journal of Business Ethics* 188 (3): 419–27.

Singer, Abraham, and Amit Ron. 2018. "Models of Shareholder Democracy: A Transnational Approach." *Global Constitutionalism* 7 (3): 422–46.

———. 2020. "Prioritizing Democracy: A Commentary on Smith's Presidential Address to the Society for Business Ethics." *Business Ethics Quarterly* 30 (1): 139–53.

———. 2023. "The Social Subcontract: Business Ethics as Democratic Theory." *Political Research Quarterly* 76 (2): 654–66.

Sison, Alejo G. 2010. *Corporate Governance and Ethics: An Aristotelian Perspective*. Cheltenham: Edward Elgar.

Smith, Adam. (1776) 1981. *The Wealth of Nations*. Indianapolis: Liberty Classics.

Smith, Jeffery. 2019. "Navigating Our Way between Market and State." *Business Ethics Quarterly* 29 (1): 127–41.

Sokolova, Anna, and Todd Sorensen. 2021. "Monopsony in Labor Markets: A Meta-analysis." *ILR Review* 74 (1): 27–55.

Solt, Frederick. (2008). "Economic Inequality and Democratic Political Engagement." *American Journal of Political Science* 52 (1): 48–60.

Somin, Ilya. 2016. *Democracy and Political Ignorance: Why Smaller Government Is Smarter*. Stanford, CA: Stanford University Press.

South Carolina Office of the Governor. 2023. "Snider Fleet Solutions Relocating Headquarters to Lancaster County." May 23. https://governor.sc.gov/news/2023-05/snider-fleet-solutions-relocating-headquarters-lancaster-county.

Srinivasan, Amia. 2018. "The Aptness of Anger." *Journal of Political Philosophy* 26 (2): 123–44.

Stack, Megan K. 2023. "Inside Starbucks' Dirty War against Organized Labor." *New York Times*, July 21. https://www.nytimes.com/2023/07/21/opinion/starbucks-union-strikes-labor-movement.html.

Stark, Andrew. 2009. "Business in Politics: Lobbying and Corporate Campaign Contributions." *The Oxford Handbook of Business Ethics*. Oxford: Oxford University Press. https://doi.org/10.1093/oxfordhb/9780195307955.003.0018.

Stokes, S. 2020. "Are Protests Good or Bad for Democracy." In *Protest and Dissent: nomos LXII*, edited by Melissa Schwartzberg, 151–58. New York: New York University Press.

Stout, Lynn. 2008. "Why We Should Stop Teaching *Dodge v. Ford*." *Virginia Law and Business Review* 3 (1): 163–90.

"Subway." 2022. *Last Week Tonight with John Oliver*. HBO. Season 9, episode 12.

Süß, Rahel. 2021. "Horizontal Experimentalism: Rethinking Democratic Resistance." *Philosophy and Social Criticism* 48 (8): 1123–39.

Thompson, E. P. 1975. *Whigs and Hunters: The Origins of the Black Act*. New York: Pantheon Books.

Tomasi, John. 2012. *Free Market Fairness*. Princeton, NJ: Princeton University Press.

Tsai, Wan-Hsiu Sunny, Aya Shata, and Shiyun Tian. 2021. "En-gendering Power and Empowerment in Advertising: A Content Analysis." *Journal of Current Issues and Research in Advertising* 42 (1): 19–33.

UAWD (Unite All Workers for Democracy). 2023. September 26. https://uawd.org/.

US Attorney's Office. 2023. "Former Ohio House Speaker Sentenced 20 Years Prison Leading Racketeering Conspiracy." June 29. https://www.justice.gov/usao-sdoh/pr/former-ohio-house-speaker-sentenced-20-years-prison-leading-racketeering-conspiracy.

US Department of Justice. 2012. Office of Public Affairs. "Press Release: GlaxoSmithKline to Plead Guilty and Pay $3 Billion to Resolve Fraud Allegations and Failure to Report Safety Data." July 2. https://www.justice.gov/opa/pr/glaxosmithkline-plead-guilty-and-pay-3-billion-resolve-fraud-allegations-and-failure-report.

Vellanki, Bhamini. 2020. "Is Corporate Social Responsibility a Scam?" Kenan Institute for Ethics, May 22. https://kenan.ethics.duke.edu/is-corporate-social-responsibility-a-scam/.

Vergara, Camila. 2020. *Systemic Corruption: Constitutional Ideas for an Anti-oligarchic Republic*. Princeton, NJ: Princeton University Press.

von Kriegstein, Hasko. 2019. "Oxymoron: Taking Business Ethics Denial Seriously." *Journal of Business Ethics Education* 16:103–34.

Waddock, Sandra A., Charles Bodwell, and Samuel B. Graves. 2022. "Responsibility: The New Business Imperative." *Academy of Management Perspectives* 16 (2): 132–48.

Walmart. 2019. "McMillon to Associates: Our Next Steps in Response to the Tragedies in El Paso and Southaven." Walmart Corporation News. September 3. https://corporate.walmart.com/content/corporate/en_us/news/2019/09/03/mcmillon-to-associates-our-next-steps-in-response-to-the-tragedies-in-el-paso-and-southaven.html.

Walmart Walkout. 2019. "Petition: Stop the Sale of Guns at Walmart Stores." Change.org. August
    5. https://www.change.org/p/doug-mcmillon-stop-the-sale-of-guns-at-walmart-stores?utm
    _content=bandit-starter_cl_share_content_en-us%3Av4&recruited_by_id=fc7b5740
    -b810-11e9-be8a-6fbcafd3c27d&recruiter=989859201&utm_source=share_petition
    &utm_medium=copylink&utm_campaign=share_petition.
Walzer, Michael. 2023. *The Struggle for a Decent Politics: On "Liberal" as an Adjective.* New Ha-
    ven, CT: Yale University Press.
Wangrow, David B., Donald J. Schepker, and Vincent L. Barker III. 2015. "Managerial Discretion:
    An Empirical Review and Focus on Future Research Directions." *Journal of Management* 41
    (1): 99–135.
Warren, Mark E. 2006a. "Democracy and Deceit: Regulating Appearances of Corruption."
    American Journal of Political Science 50 (1): 160–74.
———. 2006b. Political Corruption as Duplicitous Exclusion. *PS: Political Science and Politics*
    37 (4): 803–7.
———. 2011. "Voting with Your Feet: Exit-Based Empowerment in Democratic Theory." *Ameri-
    can Political Science Review* 105 (4): 683–701.
———. 2017. A Problem-Based Approach to Democratic Theory. *American Political Science Re-
    view* 111 (1): 39–53.
Whyte, Liz. 2014. "Corporations, Advocacy Groups Spend Big on Ballot Measures." *Time*, Octo-
    ber 26. https://time.com/3532419/ballot-measures-corporations/.
Williams, Cynthia A. 1998. "Corporate Compliance with the Laws in the Era of Efficiency." *North
    Carolina Review* 76:1265–385.
Williamson, Oliver. 1985. *The Economic Institutions of Capitalism.* New York: Free Press.
Winkelman, Joel. 2016. "John Dewey's Theory of Vocation." *American Political Thought* 5 (2):
    303–25.
Winters, Jeffrey A. 2011. *Oligarchy.* Cambridge: Cambridge University Press.
Yackee, Susan Webb. 2015. "Invisible (and Visible) Lobbying: The Case of State Regulatory Poli-
    cymaking." *State Politics and Policy Quarterly* 15 (3): 322–44.
———. 2019. "The Politics of Rulemaking in the United States." *Annual Review of Political Sci-
    ence* 22:37–55.
———. 2020. "Hidden Politics? Assessing Lobbying Success during US Agency Guidance Devel-
    opment." *Journal of Public Administration Research and Theory* 30 (4): 548–62.
Zacka, Bernardo. 2017. *When the State Meets the Street: Public Service and Moral Agency.* Cam-
    bridge, MA: Harvard University Press.
Zamora, Justo Serrano. 2021. *Democratization and Struggles against Injustice: A Pragmatist Ap-
    proach to the Epistemic Practices of Social Movements.* Lanham, MD: Rowman and Littlefield.
Zheng, Lily. 2020. "We're Entering the Age of Corporate Social Justice." *Harvard Business Re-
    view*, June 15. https://hbr.org/2020/06/were-entering-the-age-of-corporate-social-justice.
Zurcher, Anthony, and Bernd Debusmann Jr. 2023. "Disney Scraps $867M Florida Plan amid
    Ron DeSantis Feud." *BBC News*, May 18. https://www.bbc.com/news/world-us-canada
    -65639132.

Index